Literary Li

This classic series, offering fascinating accounts of the literary careers of the most admired and influential English-language authors, has established itself as a major contribution to literary biography. The volumes follow the outline of the writers' working lives, not in the spirit of traditional biography, but aiming to trace the professional, publishing and social contexts that shaped their writing. 'John Barrell has observed acutely... that the so-called literary biography seems now to have become markedly less "literary", subordinating or virtually ignoring the work of the writer concerned, except insofar as it can be made to mirror the ups and downs, pleasures, pains and supposed secrets of his or her personal existence. This observation seems regrettably true, although the balance is... redressed by such excellent studies in the accurately titled Literary Lives series published by Palgrave as Michael O'Neill's Percy Bysshe Shelley (1989) or Caroline Franklin's Byron (2000).' - Anne Barton, London Review of Books Series founded by Richard Dutton.

More information about this series at
http://www.springer.com/series/14010

Linda Wagner-Martin

John Steinbeck

A Literary Life

Linda Wagner-Martin
Chapel Hill, North Carolina, USA

Literary Lives
ISBN 978-1-349-71657-9   ISBN 978-1-137-55382-9 (eBook)
DOI 10.1057/978-1-137-55382-9

Library of Congress Control Number: 2017931315

© The Editor(s) (if applicable) and The Author(s) 2017
Softcover reprint of the hardcover 1st edition 2017 978-1-137-55381-2

The author(s) has/have asserted their right(s) to be identified as the author(s) of this work in accordance with the Copyright, Designs and Patents Act 1988.
This work is subject to copyright. All rights are solely and exclusively licensed by the Publisher, whether the whole or part of the material is concerned, specifically the rights of translation, reprinting, reuse of illustrations, recitation, broadcasting, reproduction on microfilms or in any other physical way, and transmission or information storage and retrieval, electronic adaptation, computer software, or by similar or dissimilar methodology now known or hereafter developed.
The use of general descriptive names, registered names, trademarks, service marks, etc. in this publication does not imply, even in the absence of a specific statement, that such names are exempt from the relevant protective laws and regulations and therefore free for general use.
The publisher, the authors and the editors are safe to assume that the advice and information in this book are believed to be true and accurate at the date of publication. Neither the publisher nor the authors or the editors give a warranty, express or implied, with respect to the material contained herein or for any errors or omissions that may have been made. The publisher remains neutral with regard to jurisdictional claims in published maps and institutional affiliations.

Cover illustration: © Everett Collection Historical / Alamy Stock Photo

Printed on acid-free paper

This Palgrave Macmillan imprint is published by Springer Nature
The registered company is Macmillan Publishers Ltd.
The registered company address is: The Campus, 4 Crinan Street, London, N1 9XW, United Kingdom

For Jackson J. Benson

Preface

I

Nearly every American writer who has won the Nobel Prize for Literature met with a barrage of questioning at the time. Such early award winners as Sinclair Lewis and Pearl S. Buck (1930 and 1938, respectively) began this kind of tradition—Lewis was very young, critics said; Buck was termed *some woman* whose parents had been missionaries to China, as she also was.[1] The outright hostility diminished slightly for dramatist Eugene O'Neill's receiving the award in 1936; in 1948, T. S. Eliot escaped acrimony because he had earlier given up his United States citizenship to become British. (The onus on *Americans* being awarded the most prestigious literary prize in the world seemed to stem from the youngness of this country's literature. After all, England could look back more than four hundred years for its heritage in the great verbal art.)

The cantankerous reactions began anew when in 1949 the Nobel Prize was awarded to William Faulkner, the taciturn Southerner whose greatest novels were then out of print. It calmed somewhat for Ernest Hemingway's receiving the prize in 1954: international acclaim for Hemingway's novella, the 1952 *The Old Man and the Sea*, had transformed that author's macho bullfighting and hunting image, and the world had begun recognizing that Hemingway's prose style had become synonymous with the stylistic modernism that influenced international fiction.

The sense of outrage appeared again in 1962 when John Steinbeck received the Nobel Prize in Literature. As the commentary suggested,

vii

Steinbeck's great works (always in the shadow of questioning whether or not *he* had written any great works) were years in the past. *The Grapes of Wrath* was a 1939 publication, and it had already been honored in 1940 with the Pulitzer Prize for Fiction. *In Dubious Battle*, Steinbeck's earlier "strike" novel, was, like *The Grapes of Wrath*, leaning toward a Communist perspective, siding with Russian—or at least expressing "un-American"—sentiments. No other American writer whose work expressed a proletarian perspective had been so honored. In fact, few authors of American proletarian novels were even remembered.

The award came as a great surprise to Steinbeck and Elaine, his beloved third wife. They heard the television announcement as they prepared breakfast in their modest Sag Harbor home. Even though Steinbeck had been mentioned as a possible winner during the 1940s, and even though his recent books—*The Winter of Our Discontent* in 1961 and *Travels with Charley* in 1962—had been reasonably well received, he knew that this prize was for his writing in the late 1930s. As his biographer Jackson Benson summarized, "about the only periodical to come out in his favor after the prize had been announced was the New York *Herald Tribune*. The rejection cut very, very deep—he would even make reference to it later in his acceptance speech—but he was determined to bear up with dignity [and] play his part with credit to his profession and to his country" (Benson 916). Steinbeck himself wrote to his friends the Beskows about "the attack on the award to me not only by Time Magazine... but also from the cutglass critics, that grey priesthood which defines literature and has little to do with reading." He concluded that the critics "have never liked me and now are really beside themselves with rage. It always surprises me that they care so much..." (*SLL* 754).

With Elaine, Steinbeck traveled to Sweden, where he read his acceptance speech slowly and carefully. He wore a well-tailored tuxedo. And in retrospect, he called the week in Stockholm "a curious medieval dream."

II

Interested in a tangled mass of pursuits, John Steinbeck entered Stanford University at seventeen, and declared himself an English major. He wanted to read everything. In fact, Steinbeck had more formal education than the American modernist writers who were his contemporaries. Born in 1902 (Hemingway was born in 1899, Faulkner in 1897, and Fitzgerald in 1896), Steinbeck had as much education as those three other writers combined—though his erratic attendance at his university classes was reminiscent of Fitzgerald's patterns at Princeton. On the quarter system, Stanford allowed students to drop out regularly to work—to earn their next quarter's tuition. Steinbeck's letters during his Stanford years repeatedly emphasized how long he worked to earn that tuition money (twelve-hour days at the sugar-processing plant, equally long hours in the coastal fisheries, long days sandwiched between stints clerking at department stores or breaking horses on nearby ranches). For Hemingway and Faulkner, reading and studying literature contemporary with them became their university. For Fitzgerald, who early on received top prices for his magazine stories, the arduous years of apprentice writing were almost nonexistent.

Steinbeck early described his aims in writing to a friend, saying "I have the instincts of a minstrel rather than those of a scrivener" (*SLL* 19). The classically British reading lists for traditional university courses included a range of Shakespeare—the comedies, the tragedies, and the sonnets; a great deal of Milton, John Donne, and the work of writers that fed into the study of religion; classic myths—the Grail narratives—and other medieval works like *The Pearl* and Chaucer's *Canterbury Tales*; and English novelists (Jane Austen, George Eliot, Charles Dickens, Thomas Hardy) and such poets as Wordsworth and Coleridge.

Important to the English major as well were courses in world literature in translation: students knew Dostoyevsky's *Crime and Punishment*, but they did not know Melville's *Moby-Dick*. American literature was not yet a subject field; the poetry of Walt Whitman, Emily Dickinson, Henry Wadsworth Longfellow, or John Greenleaf Whittier was seldom studied. Instead, Steinbeck read much of Tolstoy and Flaubert, and—as he bragged—all of Pushkin and Balzac, the latter of whose many novels created a realistic community of the imagination (Benson 23, 33–34).

The liberal arts student studied Western civilization and philosophy and French and music appreciation. "Culture" was seldom radicalized. Despite the Latino workers picking tomatoes and fruit, California farm owners seldom spoke Spanish—nor did they read Lorca. They still studied Latin (Steinbeck knew his Latin; he also studied Spanish). Being *radical* most often meant reading Franz Kafka's "Metamorphosis."

Nowhere in Steinbeck's reading for English courses were to be found contemporary works in either British or American literature. What appeared to be more important to the budding writer that Steinbeck professed to be was his capturing a mythic plot that most readers would recognize. Drawing from long conversations with friends—both at

Stanford and at the places where he often worked—Steinbeck believed that good writing shared universal appeal, and that such universal appeal tended to draw from stories either mythic or folkloric. It could be said that modernism's impact seemed to have missed John Steinbeck. All around him, other American writers were searching for the new—the new style, the new language, the new theme. Yet Steinbeck worked his often ornate prose into yet another reiteration of the Arthurian legend.

Living in the beautiful Salinas Valley, either with his encouraging parents and sisters or with friends from Stanford, or in San Francisco, or at Lake Tahoe where he worked as a caretaker during several winters, Steinbeck was surrounded with mountains and plateaus, lakes and oceans, wildlife and fish—yet to read his fiction, one would think it stemmed from libraries and not this amazing natural world. (He loved to learn about marine biology; he spent hours in the Pacific and along its coasts; and eventually he would write about marine life; but very little of those enthusiasms showed in his early fiction.) As his close friend Nathaniel Benchley remarked after editing Steinbeck's *Paris Review* interview, he was consistently motivated by "a searching interest in anything new" (Benchley 184).

Steinbeck's "early fiction" ran for more than a decade. Few would-be writers who were serious about learning their craft took so long to find a voice and a language appropriate to their stories. At one point, Steinbeck is on record as purposefully not knowing Hemingway—he admitted to reading "The Killers," but nothing else. He saturated himself in nineteenth- and twentieth-century Irish writers, and in the works of Southernist James Branch Cabell. Steinbeck also read his own fiction aloud to anyone who would listen: he seemed intent on monopolizing his friends, or at least in cutting off opportunities for them to share writing they liked with him. Loquacious, aggressive, focused on directions he found for himself, Steinbeck wrote and wrote and wrote versions of the centuries-old legends of Western civilization.

After he stopped attending Stanford, Steinbeck worked his way to New York City, crewing as a "workaway" on a freighter through the Panama Canal. He lived first in Brooklyn and then in a room overlooking Gramercy Park. He finally found a job as a laborer on the construction of Madison Square Garden; then his uncle got him work on the New York *American*, where he covered the Federal Court. He found that his reporting was "lousy," but he learned style: "it became my duty sometimes to send the same story to Graphic, American, Times, Tribune and Brooklyn Eagle, each in its own vernacular" (*SLL* 8–9).

When the *American* fired him, Steinbeck worked his way back to San Francisco on another freighter. The following two years he was grateful to have the overseeing job at the Lake Tahoe lodge; there he met Carol Henning and, several years later, Carol and Steinbeck were married.

In 1929, lucky that a friend of his from Stanford who was now a New York lawyer had found a publisher for *Cup of Gold*, Steinbeck's story of the English pirate Henry Morgan, the author complained that the 1500 copies the novel sold were inadequate. (His next two books, coming from other houses, did not, combined, sell that many copies.) *The Pastures of Heaven*, a story collection, appeared in 1932, despite the Great Depression's driving publisher after publisher into bankruptcy. In 1933 his often-reworked philosophical novel, *To a God Unknown*, was published by yet a third publisher. Difficult as it was for Steinbeck to believe, he was thirty-one years old, writing steadily and hard, and although he had earned little money from his writing, he had three published books to his credit.

NOTE

1. Until 1992, when Toni Morrison was awarded the Nobel Prize, no other American woman had been so honored. The image of the *significant writer* seemed to be etched indelibly as male.

Acknowledgments

Because there are now so many editions of Steinbeck's work in print, I have used the original publication dates and publishers in the bibliography so that readers will have a clear chronology in mind. Within this book, however, and for ease of reference, I have used the Library of America editions of Steinbeck's fiction. These volumes are 1) *Novels and Stories* (1994), 2) *Novels 1942–1952* (2001), and 3) *Travels with Charley and Later Novels, 1947–1962* (2007). All the page references from nearly all Steinbeck's writings will refer to these volumes, except for *Travels with Charley* (in that case I have used the Steinbeck Centennial Edition, published by Penguin in 1969, because the Library of America edition does not include the last chapter as currently published) and one omitted story collection, *The Long Valley*, which was published as a kind of compendium by Viking in 1938. I have used the Penguin edition of *The Long Valley* from 1995.

Contents

1	Steinbeck and the Short Story	1
2	*Tortilla Flat*, the Book of the Others	19
3	Journalism v. Fiction	31
4	*The Grapes of Wrath*	45
5	*The Sea of Cortez*: A Leisurely Journal of Travel and Research	65
6	World War II	75
7	*Cannery Row* and *The Pearl*	87
8	The Ed Ricketts Narratives	99
9	*East of Eden* and the 1950s	113
10	*The Winter of Our Discontent*	127
11	*Travels with Charley*	141

12 The Nobel Prize for Literature	155
Bibliography	163
Index	175

ABBREVIATIONS OF STEINBECK'S WORKS USED WITHIN THIS STUDY

Cup	*Cup of Gold: A Life of Sir Henry Morgan, Buccaneer* NY: Robert M. Mcbride,1929
POH	*The Pastures of Heaven* NY: Brewer, Warren and Putnam, 1932
God	*To a God Unknown* NY: Robert O. Ballou, 1933
Flat	*Tortilla Flat* NY: Covici-Friede, 1935
IDB	*In Dubious Battle* NY: Covici-Friede, 1936
Mice	*Of Mice and Men* NY: Covici-Friede, 1937
Long	*The Long Valley* NY: Viking, 1938
GOW	*The Grapes of Wrath* NY: Viking, 1939
FV	*The Forgotten Village* NY: Viking, 1941
Sea	*Sea of Cortez*, with Edward Ricketts NY: Viking, 1941
BA	*Bombs Away: The Story of a Bomber Team* NY: Viking, 1942
Moon	*The Moon Is Down* NY: Viking, 1942
Cannery	*Cannery Row* NY: Viking, 1945
Pearl	*The Pearl* NY: Viking, 1947
Bus	*The Wayward Bus* NY: Viking, 1948
RJ	*A Russian Journal* NY: Viking, 1948
Bright	*Burning Bright* NY: Viking, 1950
Log	*The Log from the Sea of Cortez* NY: Viking, 1951
East	*East of Eden* NY: Viking, 1952
Sweet	*Sweet Thursday* NY: Viking, 1954
SR	*The Short Reign of Pippen IV* NY: Viking, 1957
Pony	*The Red Pony* NY: Viking 1959 (re-issue of 1945 illustrated edition)
Winter	*The Winter of Our Discontent* NY: Viking, 1961
Travels	*Travels with Charley in Search of America* NY: Viking, 1962
Journal	*Journal of a Novel: The* East of Eden *Letters* NY: Viking, 1969

SLL	*Steinbeck: A Life in Letters.* Ed. Elaine Steinbeck and Robert Wallsten NY: Viking, 1975
ACTS	*The Acts of King Arthur and His Noble Knights.* NY: Viking, 1976
Days	*Working Days: the Journals of* The Grapes of Wrath. Ed. Robert DeMott NY: Viking, 1989
AAA	*America and Americans and Selected Nonfiction.* Ed. Susan Shillinglaw and Jackson J. Benson. NY: Penguin Classics, 2003

CHAPTER 1

Steinbeck and the Short Story

The short story form was a natural expression of the "minstrel" characterization that Steinbeck had chosen. Whether he saw in himself the lusty travelers telling tales in *The Decameron* or the Canterbury stories, Steinbeck enjoyed nothing so much as sharing stories with his friends. Fantastic or macabre, some of his stories emphasized the grotesque. Others, if not particularly exotic, were meant to describe the people who farmed the Salinas Valley, or who worked in the Pacific fisheries and canneries. Still others were based on the even more difficult lives of the people who struggled to survive after being handicapped by birth or accident. Twenty years later, Steinbeck wrote to John O'Hara, "I have been accused so often of writing about abnormal people" (*Paris Review* 193).

Steinbeck did not just write or tell stories. He shaped his letters to friends around stories, as when he corresponded with another would-be writer, Carl Wilhelmson, devoting much of his space to reminding Wilhelmson of a story he had once told about "the machinist who made engines and felt a little omnipotent until his own machine pulled his arm from him" (*SLL* 7). To Ted Miller, in a 1931 letter of reminiscence, Steinbeck asked, "were you at the beach with us the night he [Toby Street] nearly drowned in his soup? I heard a gurgling noise beside me and there was Toby with his nose submerged in his soup snoring it in and gradually drowning" (*SLL* 52). In 1933, to his agent Mavis McIntosh he explained that he wanted to write stories about his night-chemist job, which included being "majordomo of about sixty Mexicans and Yuakis taken from the jails of northern Mexico. There was the Guttierez family that spent its accumulated money for a Ford and started from Mexico never thinking they might need gasoline" (*SLL* 67). In 1957, to William Faulkner, he told the story of being in Greece and hearing this account from the brother of the Queen: the narrator was "walking with the King in the countryside and stopping where a man was tilling a field. They asked him what kind of fertilizer he was using. The man straightened up, looked in the face of his sovereign and said: 'You stick to your kinging and let me stick to my farming'" (*SLL* 565).

Ubiquitous, Steinbeck's stories appeared in everything he wrote. In early 1930 he wrote to fellow novelist George Albee that he was working on two novels and some stories. (*Dissonant Symphony* concerns a paranoid character who will never reach normalcy again; Steinbeck reported that *To an Unknown God* [based on "one of the Vedic Hymns"] and the story later titled "Murder" were both nearly finished.) He was thinking about the stories that would help build *The Pastures of Heaven*, running his ideas for that collection past his parents, who had been supportive of his writing—but who would like to have a good book or two, financially successful books, to show their neighbors. Steinbeck seemed to see his role with Albee as mentoring, giving advice about writing: several years later, he reprimanded him,

> "you should never let any one suggest anything about your story to you. If you don't know more about your character and situation than anyone else could, then you aren't ready to write your story anyway. It is primarily a lonely craft.... If you eliminate that loneliness of approach, you automatically eliminate some of the power of the effect. I don't know why that is." (*SLL* 84)

Impatient that Albee was becoming more and more didactic in his fiction, Steinbeck told him that he felt like setting him an exercise, say about "A Piece of String." Steinbeck wrote,

> I am convinced that a story is not particularly a matter of background at all, but of the ability to see, together with the ability to arrange, together with an inventive strain. I should like to set you the story of the lean boy with the funny name who had money, or of the next door neighbor who bought the piano so she could put the music on it. These are stories. You insist on being a social critic and historian. You will never find a place where social history is

more in the making than in Los Angeles.... There is no reason to believe that Cape Cod is more literary than Universal City. (Benson 263)

Working toward preparing an introduction to a book about writing that Edith Mirrielees was publishing, Steinbeck wrote to his early creative writing teacher, "The basic rule you gave us was simple and heartbreaking. A story to be effective had to convey something from writer to reader." Besides the key emotional charge, considering the question of form, Steinbeck recalled that "no two stories dare be alike." Whether or not Mirrielees echoed Ezra Pound's conviction that the best art needed to "make it new," she recognized that the best story was to be a canvas for the *writer's* individual experience. In Steinbeck's memory, "The formula seems to lie solely in the aching urge of the writer to convey something he feels important to the reader" (*Paris Review* 190–91). He also admitted to Mirrielees that even "after many years, to start a story still scares me to death."

Steinbeck's tentativeness showed through much of his correspondence. He called the process of writing "mystical," "a clumsy attempt to find symbols for the wordlessness. In utter loneliness a writer tries to explain the inexplicable." He still abhorred beginnings:

> I suffer as always from the fear of putting down the first line. It is amazing the terrors, the magic, the prayers, the straitening shyness that assails me. It is as though the words were...spread out like dye in the water and color everything around them. A strange and mystic business, writing. Almost no progress has taken place since it was invented. The Book of the Dead is as good and as highly developed as anything in the twentieth century and much better than most. (*Paris Review* 197)

Much of the above discussion comes from Steinbeck's 1949 letter to John O'Hara, and as he segues there into the fact that he needs to begin his real work for the day, which is writing *East of Eden*, he noted once more how amorphous the process of writing is: "Now I had better get into today's work. It is full of strange and secret things, things which should strike deep into the unconscious like those experimental stories I wrote so long ago..." (ibid.).

Not all the fiction Steinbeck wrote during his apprentice years was published. Most of it, in fact, never appeared in print. In this respect, he was caught in several unproductive patterns—trying repeatedly to re-write the classics, ignoring the day-to-day happenings that comprised his life—

patterns that were underscored by the financial stresses of the Great Depression. Steinbeck came from a modestly middle-class family: he had neither trust fund nor family support as he tried to learn the craft of writing. His two older sisters were self-supporting college graduates; his younger sister Mary found ways to encourage Steinbeck to attend the classes that he regularly missed at Stanford. When he stopped his career there, after sporadic attendance for nearly six years, his record showed a number of "Incompletes." As Robert DeMott points out, however, he was much better during the later years—from 1923 through 1925 "he earned credit in 32 out of 35 courses." He even received six *As* (DeMott *Typewriter* 9). Steinbeck later wrote Arnold Gingrich, the publisher of the new men's magazine *Esquire*, about his lack of interest in higher education, telling him "I dragged through not bravely but dully.... I thought pain could no longer strike. And then came the time—and I couldn't take it. I didn't graduate" (*SLL* 151–52).

At Stanford Steinbeck did go to writing classes and he did attend meetings of the English Club, where he often read his own fiction to the less-than-interested members. But as Benson summarizes, most of Steinbeck's writing while he was at Stanford "has to do with unusual characters and unusual situations (much less with structure or craft)." His stories reflect "the dichotomy so pervasive in his work between the romantic and the realistic." He was fascinated by the Henry Morgan story, which when expanded becomes his first novel, *Cup of Gold*. The narrative is far from historical fiction, however, and Benson points out that the Morgan story becomes a retelling of "the Grail search ... too impressionistic and allegorical to be historical romance" (Benson 76).

As Steinbeck himself told one Stanford friend, Grove Day, his first novel is "immature, full of sophomore jokes and autobiography (which hounds us until we get it said)" (*SLL* 17). He told Day about the stories that would become *The Pastures of Heaven*, calling them "a straightforward and simple attempt to set down some characters in a situation and nothing else." He added that he seems to have left behind Cabell and his ilk, and he attributes his relinquishing the popular Irish novelists for this plainer writing to his working in the mountains for two years: "I was snowed in eight months of the year and there saw no one except my two Airedales. There were millions of fir trees and the snow was deep and it was very quiet. And there was no one to pose for anymore" (*SLL* 18).[1]

By late 1931, Steinbeck had finished the accumulation of stories that would comprise *The Pastures of Heaven*, writing proudly to Albee that he liked this manuscript: "There's material for ten novels in these stories.... In the last story of thirty pages I covered three generations" (*SLL* 50). When he sent the book to Ted Miller, his sometime agent, he repeated his confidence, but pointed out, "If the reader will take them for what they are, and will not be governed by what a short story should be (for they are not short stories at all, but tiny novels).... of anything I have ever tried, I am fondest of these and more closely tied to them.... I love the stories very much" (*SLL* 51).

Steinbeck's fascination with stories continued throughout his life. Benson charts his practice of paying for stories that he thought were the stuff of fiction. Among those is a story told by Frank Kilkenny about a dying boy in Oregon who is suckled by a stranger's wife. (For this tale, Steinbeck paid Kilkenny two dollars; Benson 46–48.) Benson accurately points out that Steinbeck kept very few notes: "The storing of material, not only stories but also metaphors and even phrases, was typical of Steinbeck, and since he did not keep systematic notes, he apparently kept such things in his head for use ten or fifteen years" (ibid. 41).

It is also Benson who assesses the trap which Steinbeck's reliance on the classics, largely works in British and Irish literature, started to become. When would the aspiring writer come to a language and a style that belonged to John Steinbeck? As Benson summarized, "he loved words too much for themselves" (Benson 152). The overly romantic language of *Cup of Gold, A Life of Sir Henry Morgan, Buccaneer, with Occasional Reference to History* could never be recycled into stories of more modern times: "The crag-top house was round like a low gray tower with windows letting sight on the valley and on the mountains. Some said it was built by a beleaguered giant, centuries ago, to keep his virgins hidden while they were in that state" (*COG* 19).

In *The Pastures of Heaven* Steinbeck used language that is descriptive but not lush, almost journalistic: "To the people of the Pastures of Heaven the Battle farm was cursed, and to their children it was haunted. Good land although it was, well watered and fertile, no one in the valley coveted the place..." (*POH* 5). Influenced to some extent by the *Decameron*, Steinbeck's *Pastures* includes twelve segments—not titled, only numbered— and the author's careful positioning of each creates a world in miniature.

The book opens, and closes, with the Carmelo Mission as setting. Built around 1776, the Mission partakes in heinous cruelty to the twenty American Indians who have run away from their laboring duties for it. A hundred years later, the Mission is a stop on a commercial bus tour of the area, and the narrator explains that twenty families have come to populate the beautiful area, known throughout California as the Pastures of Heaven. As the varied stories slowly unroll, the reader learns about a myriad of tragedies—some horrible from the start, others developing into horrors as generations pass. At first the prognostication, stated at the close of Segment I, is that these twenty families would live "prosperously and at peace. Their land was rich and easy to work. The fruits of their gardens were the finest produced in central California" (*POH* 4). The successive tales, however, create little sense of peace, and the yearned-for prosperity more often than not damages the human beings who would enjoy it.

The haunted Battle farm, the uncovering of Shark Wicks' grandiose financial business, and the fantasy burials of Tularecito, digging, digging, digging to find the gnomes that plague his defective mind: the first three tales in Steinbeck's collection are already dim. The progression, however, continues to darken. After Hubert Van Deventer shot himself while hunting, telling his friends to have his wife mount him for their collection, Helen Van Deventer gives birth to Baby Hilda, a mentally damaged child. Whether that family story ends in suicide or in the mother's murder of her now-adult daughter is intentionally vague. The take-away from Hilda's death is that her mother, now alone, had found what she called "a new delicious peacefulness" (*POH* 57).

The sense of the grotesque in all humanity continues when Junius Maltby takes the son born to his dying wife and creates a family by adding the German hired man to their cohort. (He lost his first wife and their two children while he read intently during their illness from fever.) The two men and the young boy customarily sat on a favored tree branch, talking endlessly about nothing: their lives in deep poverty finally end when a school teacher points out how such living deprives the child, who has grown up to be little more than a savage.

When old Guiermo Lopez died, his daughters Rose and Maria were left penniless. They opened a restaurant in their house. The humor of the story is that for any man buying a tortilla or an enchilada, Rose will give him sex (free). When the house is closed down for immorality, the sisters leave to set up a prosperous whorehouse.

Other tales are equally fantastic, several using the device of murder by hatchet to develop plotlines. When the longest story, that of the Whitesides' sojourn, begins, Richard Whiteside decides to buy 250 acres of the beautiful land, telling his friends that he was "founding a dynasty" (*POH* 144). That story, the longest at 15,000 words, runs through three generations, and the marrying and child bearing unite several of the other families with the Whitesides. When the third generation, William, takes his bride and moves to Monterey, the family home burns to the ground.

Dedicated to Steinbeck's father and mother, *The Pastures of Heaven* shows Steinbeck turning to the reality of California life. It focuses on the American Indian population as well as on white class privilege; and it uses a reportorial style. Few judgments are made. Today's reader supposes that many of the tales are linked to real stories, and real lives, from that geographical place, between what Jay Parini called "the pale hills between Salinas and Monterey," a glimpse into the "American life category" (Parini 146). Steinbeck frequently hiked the area around the Salinas River, and in the words of his friend Bill Thomas, that river was so deep and so muddy that fish there had no eyes. The terrain was studded with distinctive rock formations such as the one Steinbeck called The Castle (Thomas in Lynch 86). This story collection was the author's introduction to the geography of the California valley that he immortalized throughout his writing career.

Steinbeck's second book was an important step into exploring his fascination with the California valley's promise—both financially and narratively. As critic Louis Owens said, *The Pastures of Heaven* prefigures *The Long Valley* and *East of Eden*. In all three books, "the stories will take place in a fallen world.... the quest for the illusive and illusory Eden will be of central thematic significance" (Owens *Re-Vision* 100).

In *The Pastures of Heaven*, Steinbeck for the first time found a voice of irony couched in actual sentiment. He seemed to be breaking out of a journalistic objectivity that many other modernist writers had found stifling. Although the collection of tales was anything but pastoral, the scenic beauty of both land and river came close to balancing the omnipresent horrors of daily living. Not all lives in the Salinas Valley were so grotesque, and without drawing attention to the timbre of the book—or to its resemblance to Sherwood Anderson's early book of the grotesque, the 1919 *Winesburg, Ohio*—Steinbeck staked a claim of which his new agents, McIntosh and Otis, heartily approved. He became their client in 1931 and early in 1932 they placed *The Pastures of Heaven* with Cape & Smith. That company's bankruptcy followed. Then Robert O. Ballou, an editor from Cape, moved to Brewer, Warren and Putnam, where *The Pastures of Heaven* was published later in 1932. A year earlier, the Robert McBride Company had rejected Steinbeck's third finished book, *To a God Unknown*. Steinbeck quickly began re-structuring this philosophical novel.

As Steinbeck's letters to friends attest, the early 1930s was a time of great creative activity for him. He and Carol Henning had married in January 1930, and they had then drifted—living at times with friends, again in cheap apartments, finally in the Steinbecks' cottage in Pacific Grove. (Pacific Grove, sometimes known as Church Town, had been founded by the Methodist Episcopal Church as a summer tent camp; flimsy as the structures were, the town was located on Monterey Bay.) John and Carol lived there rent free, supported most months by $25 gifts from John's father. When Carol could get office work, she was able to supplement that token; they also grew vegetables and fished. (Mrs. Steinbeck drove over most weekends with food for the coming week.)

Along with his serious writing, now full time, Steinbeck had met and become close friends with Ed Ricketts, whose biological laboratory was on the harbor in Pacific Grove. Engaging and quick-witted, Ricketts was an intellectual force for everyone around him: he found in Steinbeck an avid learner, eager to absorb the science that Ricketts knew so well, and just as eager to talk about books, music, philosophy, and the times. Carol had early been chosen as a "termite," one of the group of gifted children of near-genius intellect studied by Stanford psychologist Louis Terman. He followed these children through adulthood by reading their journals. Indicative of the times, when finishing college degrees was less important than following studies independently, none of these three—Ricketts, Carol, and Steinbeck—had finished a university degree. They were, however, living satisfying intellectual lives (Shillinglaw *Carol* 106).

Benson describes the inclusion of east coast philosopher Joseph Campbell in the group in 1932 as a coincidental miracle. Just as Steinbeck began rewriting his Jungian novel, *To a God Unknown*, Campbell found lodging in a house next to Ed Ricketts.[2] The three, with Carol adding a fourth, had lively and probing conversations—usually at Ricketts' lab. They talked books and ideas: Campbell was reading Goethe's *Conversations with Eckermann* and Edington's books on the new physics. He loaned Steinbeck the first volume of Spengler's *Decline of the West*. Deeply engrossed in rewriting *To a God Unknown*, Steinbeck was hungry for more conversation about myth; what he wanted to discuss would become Campbell's field of specialization, as evidenced in his later book, *The Hero with a Thousand Faces*.

Campbell remembered that Steinbeck already knew a number of the townspeople in Pacific Grove; he had a knack for talking to working men as if he were one of them. Many times the discussions in the late afternoon became parties that went on all night, or lasted for several days and nights, people deeply engrossed in substantive arguments, sharing their jugs of cheap wine along with their ideas. The group grew to include Evelyn Ott, a Jungian psychoanalyst, Francis Whitaker, a blacksmith and metal sculptor, Ritchie and Tal Lovejoy, Tal's sister Xenia and John Cage, Bruce and Jean Arris, Remo and Virginia Scardigli, Toby and Peggy Street, Toni Jackson, Beth Ingels, and others.

Benson notes that the lab parties were the models for the festive get-togethers that Steinbeck would later create in *Cannery Row*. Ricketts made liquor "with his lab alcohol, and at dawn they got into Ed's car and drove to the place where, as in the novel, the flagpole skater was doing his little dance on a platform high in the air" (Benson 224).

The close-knit group of Campbell, Ricketts, and the Steinbecks created a smaller sub-set, given to having dinners together ("turkey meatloaf, oyster stew, abalone") and, in Shillinglaw's description, "target shooting at the beach, a picnic at Point Lobos, collecting trips to Santa Cruz [to provide materials for Ricketts' lab], hikes up to Mount Toro above Monterey Bay" (Shillinglaw *Carol* 105). They read Robinson Jeffers' poetry together (Jeffers appeared on the cover of *Time* on April 4, 1932; his mother and Olive Steinbeck were friends). The group tried the Ouija board for new insights. In Shillinglaw's words, "all three men, in particular, were on an intellectual cusp, working to unite the physical and metaphysical, the immediate and the visionary.... earlier Ed and John were being drawn to the occult, the mystical, the transcendent." She called this period "a nexus.... Ricketts was writing 'The Philosophy of Breaking Through' while Steinbeck was tearing down *To an Unknown God*" (ibid.). Campbell remembered those spring months as "A beautiful time; we were all in heaven. The world had dropped out. We weren't the dropouts; the world was the dropout. We were in a halcyon situation, no movement, just floating.... So I'm coasting along" (Campbell *Open* 14).

Driving cross-country in his mother's Model T, Campbell was thinking about the far-reaching influence of Jung's insistence on the fusion of male and female; on the need for a private space—thereby to create synergy; on his recurring periods of depression. He had decided that a person's "sacred space" was necessary for successful contemporary life, and in some respects his conclusions paralleled ideas that Steinbeck had written about in 1930. Steinbeck called it getting "deeper under the surface into the black and sluggish depths of people than I ever have before. I want to show not necessarily why people act as they do, but to show the *psychological steps* which precede and clear the way for an act" (Steinbeck in Benson 202; to Wilhelmson, October 1, 1930). Both Steinbeck and Campbell were attempting not only to understand the human mind, but to figure out ways to preserve it. Applying his ideas to his writing, Steinbeck said, "There is no end to the ramification of every speech, every movement of the hand.... You see where it leads us—beyond the point where we can actually observe people, we have only ourselves to experiment with, and the possibility of our being wrong is tremendous." He then told Wilhelmson that his new and probing stories would constitute "another of my experiments," leading to a collection of fiction which "has no possibility of publication" (ibid.).

In Campbell's recollections of that wonderful year, Ed Ricketts was the central figure, a kind of repository for everyone's ideas, a synthesizer. He called Ricketts "an inter-tidal biologist. We'd go out and collect hundreds of starfish, sea cucumbers, things like that, between high and low tides, furnishing animals for biology classes and schools" (Campbell *Conversations* 14). Later that year, he was enthusiastic about sailing to Alaska with Ricketts for six weeks on a small boat ("up the Inside Passage from Seattle to Juneau ... gorgeous"). Much of the six weeks "we'd spend at an absolutely uninhabited island gathering animals while Ed made notes. The cost: twenty-five cents a day for the whole crew. We would pull into the port, all the canneries were closed, the fishing fleets immobilized—they'd throw salmon at us. Put your hand in the water and pull fish out" (Campbell *Open* 15). Campbell had learned about more than ocean life; he continued, "And the towns were supposed to be dead and they were the most *living* things. There's nothing like living when you're not living with a direction but just enjoying the glory of the moment" (ibid.).

Campbell learned a great deal about himself during 1932. This was a man who had applied for teaching positions at nearly a hundred colleges—to no avail. In 1934 he would begin teaching at Sarah Lawrence College. In the interim, in California, he had experienced "the glory of the moment" as he lived without any clear or visible "direction."

In a later conversation with poet Robert Bly, Campbell recalled about the Alaskan trip,

> you just felt this was the place of generation. This was the germ bed of our life.... The world is a mystery of the dark depths of the unconscious and the dark out of which all has come.... Goethe has a wonderful line when he's

speaking about the principles of evolution, how along the two lines of the vegetable and the world, the culminating mysteries are of the human being and the tree. One finds the nobility of nature here and the power, the *tremendum*, the *fascinans*, of the *mysterium*. (Campbell Esalan Institute 195)

Exhilarating as his weeks in Alaska were, Campbell realized that he had forfeited his deep friendship with John Steinbeck because during that spring he had fallen in love with Carol Steinbeck—and she with him. A thoroughly angry Steinbeck wanted nothing to do with either of them: he told his parents and friends about his wife's emotional betrayal.[3] As Shillinglaw described the eventual disruption, all calm shattered. "Carol and Joe dallied about in June 1932, and John simmered, eventually ordering Joe to 'disappear'—a decision that Carol and Joe had also agreed upon. The group split on June 25, after John had, in the end, ordered Campbell out of town at the point of a gun—literally" (Shillinglaw *Carol* 113).

Steinbeck's reconfiguration of the narrative appears in *To a God Unknown* so that the protagonist Joseph, his father's chosen son, is seen as a descendant of the noble tree which becomes a character in the book. This plot probably existed before the night Carol Steinbeck and Campbell declared their love in the conjoined tree scene. The healthy tree, symbolic of a fruitful land, is a staple of many mythologies, just as is the flourishing green land. Long before Steinbeck knew Campbell, he had absorbed much of Frazer's *The Golden Bough*. And the basic plan of *To a God Unknown* had already been sketched in Toby Street's play "The Green Lady," which Street had passed on to Steinbeck for whatever he chose to use from it. (Street and Steinbeck had together taken Marge Bailey's playwriting class at Stanford; Fowler in Lynch 44.) Even in Steinbeck's first version of *To a God Unknown*, he had added a significant number of characters to Street's play, and he suggested—when he explained his plan for restructuring—that little would remain of the initial drama.

To a God Unknown builds on the King James version of the Old Testament. Steinbeck's introductory materials place the father and his sons on the rocky New England homestead, near Pittsfield in Vermont. Land poor as the family is, emphasized in the novel by the refrain "There won't be enough in the land now, sir," Joseph embarks for California, planning to help support his three brothers. The journey evolves until they arrive by train "down the long Salinas Valley, a grey-and-gold lane between two muscular mountain lines." In King City, the brothers left the train and got into Joseph's buggy (*God* 229). Chicanery takes over; the dissatisfied Burton girdles the tree (with which Joseph has identified, believing it to be his now-dead father), and from then on death is omnipresent. One brother is killed for sleeping with a married woman. Joseph's wife, Elizabeth, slips on the deep moss in the mountain's secret place, strikes her head, and dies of a broken neck. Bereft, Joseph finds that it is the drought that ruins his dream of prosperity—he had paid no attention to the natural rhythms of life, he had been arrogant. He had also lost the woman who was his paired consciousness, as Elizabeth had admitted shortly before their child was born, phrased by Steinbeck as "And for the first time she saw into her husband's mind; all in a second she saw the shapes of his thoughts, and he knew that she saw them. The emotion rushed to his throat" (*God* 285). The perfect understanding of human connection was, then, lost in a second as she fell and died.

The reader is forced back to the prefatory poem from the *Veda*, each stanza closing with the interrogation that hammers home the immense ignorance of the human mind: "Who is He to whom we shall offer our sacrifice?" *To a God Unknown* impressed Steinbeck's friends and agents with its classic sonority,[4] and eventually his agents found that Robert Ballou would bring the novel out, under his own imprint, later in 1932.

Feeling relatively prosperous, but still angry over Carol's romance with Joe Campbell, Steinbeck found a location south of Pacific Grove, just above Eagle Rock, that he liked. They rented a house, and were less frequently thrown into the company of Campbell and Ricketts. Carol's half-time job with the latter had ended because money was short at the Pacific Biological Laboratory (Ricketts' wife had left him, taking what money he had), so there was no need for the Steinbecks to stay in Pacific Grove. Somewhat ironically, when they had first located to that town Steinbeck had complained, "There is no companionship of any kind here. Carol and I are marooned.... Our poverty is tiresome, but I can see no change in it. Only work. I must cut down two trees for fire wood and that will take some time" (*SLL* 50). Because of his friendship with Ricketts, Pacific Grove had taken on the aura of a definite home.

By the spring of 1932, when it seemed secure that Jonathan Cape would be publishing both *The Pastures of Heaven* and two other of his books to follow, Steinbeck cleared out what he described as over a foot-tall stack of old stories—sixty or seventy of them. He had learned that not every good story would make the transition from oral narrative to written. It was a decisive act. No sooner had Steinbeck burned those manuscripts than came the news that Jonathan Cape had gone bankrupt. He was again facing real poverty, and his agents provided little consolation (Benson 252).

As was Steinbeck's custom, he kept writing steadily, trying out stories that might possibly coalesce into a group (as he had with the dozen stories that comprised *The Pastures of Heaven*). Several of the stories were about the area known as Tortilla Flat, the paisano culture that was largely Mexican or Spanish, as well as Indian, Portuguese, and Italian, men supported by their work in fisheries and canneries. Steinbeck accepted the help of both Susan Gregory, the Spanish teacher at Monterey high school, and her older friend Hattie Gragg. Both had long befriended the paisanos and happily told their stories to Steinbeck (Benson 277–78). It was clear to Steinbeck early on that the random arrangement that *The Pastures of Heaven* had allowed would not work with this assortment of tales, so he delayed any kind of focused work on the thematic group until he had finished rewriting *To a God Unknown*.

What he was writing were stories that drew from his own emotional unrest. Just as he had in his "Murder" story, which he described as something of a pot boiler, Steinbeck found powerful metaphors that expressed underlying currents. As John Timmerman explained in his "Introduction" to Steinbeck's 1938 story collection *The Long Valley*, "Steinbeck was a daring experimenter until he found the right combinations that unlocked a story's power. If the characters didn't have the ring of authenticity at first, as was the case with 'The Chrysanthemums,' he pushed the originals aside and started over until he got it right" (Timmerman "Introduction" xxi–xxii; see Osborne and Simmonds). As part of what Timmerman called Steinbeck's "use of patterned imagery to reveal character," "The Chrysanthemums" succeeds in showing Elisa Allen's essential character, repressed, controlled, and eventually saddened by the disregard of the sycophantic peddler. The layers of metaphor, combined with the chary dialogue, subtly reveal the anguish at the heart of Elisa's adult life.

Set in the Salinas Valley during a dull December day, the story begins: "It was a time of quiet and of waiting. The air was cold and tender" (*Long* 1). Elisa, working in her flowerbed, is distanced from Henry and the two men with whom he talks. The latter wear business suits. Elisa wears "clodhopper shoes, a man's black hat pulled low down over her eyes, a figured print dress almost covered by a big corduroy apron with four big pockets." While Henry sells the thirty head of cattle, she labors in next year's chrysanthemum shoots. Growing plants is her gift; making money is his. He tells her they will go to dinner in town, maybe see a movie, maybe go to the fights.

She also can barter with the peddler who arrives in his old springwagon. Allured by his life on the road, traveling from Seattle to San

Diego and back, sleeping in the wagon, she finds some work for him to do. Their discussion of what work is appropriate—*safe*—for a woman piques her temper: *she* is strong, capable. She resists being trapped in her life as a woman. The peddler drives away, taking some shoots of her flowers with him, for a woman buyer down the road.

> In the kitchen she reached behind the stove and felt the water tank. It was full of hot water from the noonday cooking. In the bathroom she tore off her soiled clothes and flung them into the corner. And then she scrubbed herself with a little block of pumice, legs and thighs, loins and chest and arms, until her skin was scratched and red. When she had dried herself she stood in front of a mirror in her bedroom and looked at her body. She tightened her stomach and threw out her chest. She turned and looked over her shoulder at her back. (*Long* 10)

Waiting for Henry on the porch, Elisa sits quietly, her mind moving down the road with the spring-wagon.

Pleased to see his wife already dressed in her good clothes, Henry compliments her, telling her she looks "nice." She wrangles with him over his choice of words—she would rather look "strong." He does not see any difference.

On the road to town, before they drive past the peddler, she sees the dark earth-covered sprouts scattered over the tarmac; he has kept the pot but has tossed away her joy, the slips of green. Hurt to the quick, she diverts Henry's attention by asking him if they could have wine with their dinner. And then she returns to his teasing her about going to the fights. She asks him,

> "Henry, at those prize fights, do the men hurt each other very much?"
> "Sometimes a little, not often. Why?"
> "Well, I've read how they break noses, and blood runs down their chests. I've read how the fighting gloves get heavy and soggy with blood."
> He looked around at her. "What's the matter, Elisa? I didn't know you read things like that...."
> "Do any women ever go to the fights?" she asked.
> "Oh, sure, some. What's the matter, Elisa? Do you want to go? I don't think you'd like it, but I'll take you if you really want to go." (*Long* 13)

Still protected from the vagaries of life that she understands she *is* truly strong enough to handle, Elisa relinquishes her chance. She will be content with the wine... and with letting Henry keep her in her all-too-appropriate place.

Of Steinbeck's earlier stories in this period (following *To a God Unknown*), the least characteristic is one that he called a favorite, "Saint Katy the Virgin." A parable about the medieval process of canonization, this account probably began after Steinbeck had found the masterful Edward Maslin Hulme's history classes; Steinbeck adored the witty Hulme and never missed a class. According to Frank Fenton, this prose work began as a bawdy poem following Hulme's lecture on canonization (Fenton 83). Benson calls this piece the most "arch" of Steinbeck's farces, and recalls the successes that Mark Twain had with like works.

The convolution of Steinbeck's story of the pig Katy is more ribald than parodic, and comes closer to burlesque. With the saintliness described along feminine lines (as in the title), the story's definition of "virginity" itself is an elaborate joke. From the start of Katy's adult pig life, when she gives birth to a litter and promptly eats all the piglets, the rest of her machinations are predictable. Steinbeck closes the over-long story with the canonization of the pig, placed in a "gold-bound, jeweled reliquary," and, as pilgrims come to the cathedral, they are cured of both "female troubles and ringworm" (*Long* 144).

This one-of-a-kind narrative illustrates the range of Steinbeck's inventiveness—as well as his over-the-top humor—but it gives no insight into the traits of story telling that will make many of the stories in *The Long Valley* so capably written. It joins with the earliest of these mid-1930s stories, "The Murder," in showing his trying a number of stylistic approaches.

In "The Murder" Steinbeck co-opts the popularity of the detective/murder genre. Set in the Salinas Valley and approaches through the rock formation known as "the Castle," the simple story of Jim Moore's discovery of his wife's infidelity builds credible suspense. Steinbeck makes clear the cultural difference between the very American Jim Moore and his "Jugo-Slav" wife Jelka, who seems to lead "a life apart" from her husband. The beautiful woman does her wifely duties—she has his meals ready whenever he appears, she cleans, she responds minimally—but she never shows interest in his life.

Stumbling upon a butchered head of his cattle, Jim changes direction and does not head into town for an overnight stay. What he finds as he comes home hours before he is expected is his wife and her cousin sleeping together in his bed. Vomiting in anger, Jim remembers the way "his mother used to hold a bucket to catch the throat blood when his father killed a pig. She stood as far away as possible and held the bucket at arms'-length to keep her clothes from getting spattered." As he did in "The Chrysanthemums," Steinbeck here places immense weight on the seemingly disparate images. The wife complicit in slaughter, Jim's almost unconscious memory leads him to get his rifle and return to the house. There he shoots the cousin through his forehead, where the hollow-point bullet "took brain and bone and splashed them on the pillow" (*Long* 130–31). Jim then rides to town and, next morning, returns with the coroner and the sheriff.

Finding his wife hiding in the barn, he beats her. Then she makes breakfast for him. Her father's words (on his wedding night, reminding him that Slav women understand only force) return to him, and when she asks "Will you whip me any more—for this?" he understands that he must reassure her. He answers "No, not any more, for this." The story ends: "Her eyes smiled. She sat down on a chair beside him, and Jim put out his hand and stroked her hair and the back of her neck" (*Long* 134).

Violence briefly transformed by kindness does not mask the horror of Jim's vengeance. For critic Mark Spilka, Steinbeck's explaining to a friend that he wanted this story to be epitomized in "color and dream like movement" only validates the privileging of male violence against people who usurp his power. Spilka summarizes,

> To write a dreamlike story, in this deliberately obscure way is, of course, to identify with the action, the local colors, and the minimized characters, and to appropriate them for one's own dreamlike, if artistic, purposes. It amounts, I would argue, to giving oneself permission to dream this particular dream of "blameless" violence.... In some sense, that may describe Steinbeck's intentions in many of his fictions, early and late. (Spilka 248)

This critic further connects Jelka with other of what he calls Steinbeck's "troubling women characters" and speculates that all these women are "defined by their resistance to male control" (ibid. 250).

"A Murder" was published in *North American Review*—and while that literary journal paid $90 for the story, rather than the thousands *The Saturday Evening Post* was paying Fitzgerald for his fiction, it was good money for one story. Later it was included as an O. Henry Prize story in that year's anthology.

Having learned a great deal about the short story and its thousands of possible forms, and having written and written and re-written his own stories, Steinbeck was finding it hard to believe he could have done all this work with so little success. As he wrote later about the writing process,

> It is true that while a work is in progress, the writer and his book are one. When a book is finished, it is a kind of death, a matter of pain and sorrow to the writer. Then he starts a new book, and a new life, and if he is growing and changing, a whole new life starts. The writer, like a fickle lover, forgets his old love. It is no longer his own: the intimacy and the surprise are gone. (*Of Men* 158)

In retrospect, Steinbeck understood the progress he had made. Yet on September 27, 1932, he borrowed one hundred dollars from George Albee. The times were continuing to strangle him, and he yearned for some restitution so that he and Carol could live (*SLL* 65).

NOTES

1. Earlier in the letter to Day, Steinbeck confessed, "You will remember at Stanford that I went about being different characters. I even developed a theory that one had no personality in essence, that one was a reflection of a mood plus the moods of other persons present" (*SLL* 13).
2. Traveling across country after having worked on his doctorate and explored Europe and the Far East, Campbell had run out of money. In Benson's words, "Since everyone was out of work, a 'bum' was not necessarily someone who didn't want to work." The Monterey Red Cross and Salvation Army boarded the destitute in private homes, where they exchanged board for yard work and household help (Benson 223).
3. Their passionate love seems never to have been sexually consummated. Campbell wrote a dramatic scene based on Carol's sitting in one tree and his being positioned in another, with the charged dialogue between the characters telling the story of their great (and only belatedly acknowledged) love (Shillinglaw *Carol* 110–11).
4. Terry Tempest Williams admires this novel still. She recalled that the story "lives inside me and drives my own hand across the page, [trying to bring herself to] the gesture of conservation, of trying to make peace with our own contradictory nature. We love the land. We are destroying the land" (Williams *Centennial* 102).

CHAPTER 2

Tortilla Flat, the Book of the Others

By a stroke of chance, Ben Abramson, a book seller who owned the Argus Book Shop in Chicago, mentioned Steinbeck's writing to Pascal Covici, then himself a partner in the publishing firm of Covici-Friede. The name was unfamiliar to Covici. Abramson had bought remainders of both *Cup of Gold* and *The Pastures of Heaven*; he loaned the books to the young publisher. When he returned to New York, Covici phoned Mavis McIntosh and eventually brought out Steinbeck's book *Tortilla Flat* in 1935. The linked stories that Steinbeck had carved out of the Arthurian legends and given to the colorful characters of the California paisanos, the Mexicans and Mexican-Americans who worked at low-paying jobs (as Steinbeck had himself), became Steinbeck's first best-seller. What happened in the lives of Danny, Pilon, and their friends—people existing on next to nothing in the seedy streets of Tortilla Flat—seemed both relevant and comic (Benson 333). It was, after all, the heart of the Great Depression. Nobody had any money. A great many people thought that whoever could exist (and even prosper) was worth reading about.[1] And because Steinbeck's characters were not white or middle-class, recounting their sometimes pathetic, sometimes objectionable behavior took on varying shades of humor.

It began to dawn on Steinbeck that when he drew these unusual characters from people he had known or heard of, and gave them both language and thoughts that were accurate, his work was better received than when he drew conventional mainstream figures. Not that finding a

© The Author(s) 2017
L. Wagner-Martin, *John Steinbeck*, Literary Lives,
DOI 10.1057/978-1-137-55382-9_2

19

publisher for *Tortilla Flat* had been easy: the manuscript had been rejected several times before Covici became interested. Even among Steinbeck's friends, whereas Ed Ricketts shared his sense of comedy in watching the very poor and their chicanery, Joseph Campbell thought writing about these characters did little to entertain. Most of the Steinbecks' friends just observed the lives of the paisanos, accepting their existence as routine.

When Steinbeck brainstormed ways to use the stories that his friends had told him, he reverted to his long-beloved Arthurian cycle. Already competent in linking separate stories to create a collage of meaning, as he had earlier in *The Pastures of Heaven*, Steinbeck naturally turned to that technique once again. But the story of Danny as home owner took on a more integrated thrust: few of the characters in *Tortilla Flat* existed outside the group that Danny's good fortune had created. What kept the linked stories funny rather than depressingly exotic was the initial situation—that Danny, the veteran, had become a home owner, and that he knew so little about money that he was unable to make even fifteen dollars a month out of its rental. Positioning *Tortilla Flat* as a definite anti-capitalist text, Steinbeck did not lose readers who were aware of trends in contemporary fiction (whether or not the term "proletarian novel" was ever used). He would not share the fate of Ernest Hemingway, who had gone from being a well-read novelist to being the object of criticism after his bullfighting treatise, *Death in the Afternoon*, appeared in 1932, followed in 1935 by his saga of big game hunting, *Green Hills of Africa*. Even if a writer were not himself suffering during the catastrophic depression, he owed it to his readers not to flaunt his personal prosperity.

As we have seen, Steinbeck was still terribly poor—he and Carol had had to give up their rented house and move back to Pacific Grove; they were still existing on his father's gifts and his mother's supply of cooked meals. But the conditions of real poverty were by now so commonplace that they did not dampen responses still available to people throughout the United States—and, of course, throughout the world. Poverty was becoming a universal condition. In the early 1930s, in fact, Steinbeck wrote to his protégé George Albee,

> "Everyone I have ever known very well has been concerned that I would starve. Probably I shall. It isn't important enough to me to be an obsession. I have starved and it isn't nearly as bad as is generally supposed. Four days and a half was my longest stretch. Maybe there are pains that come later. Personally I think terror is the painful part of starvation." (*SLL* 47)

Mixed in with Steinbeck's hardship stories are his prolegomena about writing, as when he says at about this same time, "Fine artistic things seem always to be done in the face of difficulties.... A man's best work is done when he is fighting to make himself heard..." (*SLL* 34).

In choosing to write *Tortilla Flat*, Steinbeck seemed aware that his narrative would a pose difficulties to the commercial fiction market: how many of his readers would understand the parallels he created between the Arthurian legends and Danny's role as house owner? To expedite the reading, he used a sentence-by-sentence table of contents, which served to lead readers from point to point. Reminiscent of eighteenth-century British novels, this two-page "Chapter Headings" section summarized the book's events:

> I. How Danny, home from the wars, found himself an heir, and how he swore to protect the helpless.
> II. How Pilon was lured by greed of position to forsake Danny's hospitality. (*Flat* 371)

The chapter headings continue through to Section XVII, which recounts the demise of the surrogate companionship: Danny in his new prosperity is beneficent to all his friends, but their pettiness undermines his generosity. The elevated descriptions here, like the narrator's voice within the stories, create consistent humor.

The collection begins with a "Preface" that also leads readers:

> This is the story of Danny and of Danny's friends and of Danny's house. It is a story of how these three became one thing, so that in Tortilla Flat if you speak of Danny's house you do not mean a structure of wood flaked with old whitewash, overgrown with an ancient untrimmed rose of Castile. No, when you speak of Danny's house you are understood to mean a unit of which the parts are men, from which came sweetness and joy, philanthropy and, in the end, a mystic sorrow. For Danny's house was not unlike the Round Table, and Danny's friends were not unlike the knights of it.[2] (*Flat* 373)

The simplicity of Steinbeck's plot stems in part from the simplicity of the men who people the story. Unlettered but good-hearted, crafty, caring— and caring at all times that their good fortune be shared with friends— these characters sometimes cross the boundaries accepted in polite society. They have little tendency to work, they enjoy drinking and telling stories, they love the way being with women makes them feel. Down-and-out except for Danny's largesse, they try to lead lives that are helpful—insofar as they have the resources to be helpful. Not quite childlike, the men of Tortilla Flat have the capacity for humor. They also like to play jokes on each other. They enjoy a good fight. Their world is narrowed, however, because of their limited means.

The political correctness of the twenty-first century does not disturb Steinbeck's fictional world. No reviewer asked how the author—who was not a part of the paisano culture—understood these characters in order to write about them. The parameters of fiction allowed Steinbeck to take a great deal of license.[3] The lower-class men, often drunk, were seldom polite to women (and often referred to them as "bitches"); they were irreligious as well as unwashed, not above stealing and lying. They set up and bet on cock fights; they drank cheap wine by the gallon. In describing a party at Danny's house, Steinbeck notes somewhat coyly that "Danny had helped to dispose of one of the girls and half of the wine [after which] there was a really fine fight" (*Flat* 387). As Benson pointed out, Steinbeck here showed "his predilection to shock, often with grotesque material, sometimes humorous and sometimes simply unsavory." He calls this tendency "a personal trait," and says that the storyteller of *Tortilla Flat* illustrates the tendency in that he "savors the amoral exploits of the paisanos of *Tortilla Flat* or of the bums of *Cannery Row*" (Benson 52).

There are scenes aplenty, however, when the seemingly rough exploits lead to expressions of a kind of folk wisdom. One sequence begins with Pablo's narration of Bob Smoke's suicide attempt. Embarrassed by his failures, Tall Bob plans to construct a scene in which he sits at his kitchen table, loaded gun pointed at his head. His plan is that a friend will interrupt the act and "save" him. Unfortunately, when Charlie Meeler comes to his house, Meeler "grabbed that gun and that gun went off and shot away the end of Bob's nose. And then the people laughed even more" (*Flat* 493). Steinbeck manipulates the story-telling scene—here and elsewhere—so that a kind of commonplace energy comes through. Here, Jesus Maria takes on the role of philosopher:

> It is worse than a whipping to be laughed at. Old Tomas, the rag sucker, was laughed right into his grave. And afterwards the people were sorry they laughed.

"And," said Jesus Maria, "there is another kind of laughing, too. That story of Tall Bob is funny, but when you open your mouth to laugh, something like a hand squeezes your heart. I know about old Mr. Ravanno who hanged himself last year. And there is a funny story too, but it is not pleasant to laugh at."

"I heard something about it," said Pilon, "but I do not know that story."

"Well," said Jesus Maria. "I will tell you that story, and you will see if you can laugh. When I was a little boy, I played games with Petey Ravanno.... He had two brothers and four sisters, and there was his father, Old Pete. All that family is gone now. One brother is in San Quentin, the other was killed by a Japanese gardener for stealing a wagonload of watermelons. And the girls, well, you know how girls are, they went away. Susy is in Old Jenny's house in Salinas right now." (*Flat* 493)

In this nonchalant story telling about the deaths and imprisonment to which all these paisanos seem to fall prey, the narrator's voice echoes through the various story-telling scenes. When critic William Dow comments on the parallel between journalistic narration and stories like these, he emphasizes "the personal presence and involvement of a human witness" which ties the reader to the world of fact (Dow 225). Regardless of who becomes the story teller in *Tortilla Flat*, the sonority of Steinbeck's fictional voice threads together the separate episodes. The story of Big Joe Portagee returning from war, so drunk that he wrecks whatever house he enters, does not vilify Joe, but instead leads him to a comfortable rest in the Monterey jail ("a place to meet people. If he stayed there long enough, all his friends were in and out. The time passed quickly") (*Flat* 431).

One of Steinbeck's stylistic traits was to create an all-purpose speech for the men who cared for Tortilla Flat. When Danny asks about the fire, for example, his friends' answers show their omnipresent reliance on their religion:

"We don't know," Pilon explained. "We went to sleep, and then it started. Perhaps we have enemies."

"Perhaps," said Pablo devoutly, "perhaps God had a finger in it."

"Who can say what makes the good God act the way he does?" added Jesus Maria.

Pretending that he is satisfied with their evasive replies, Danny brings them back together in his house that night. "It is good to have friends," said Danny. "How lonely it is in the world if there are no friends to sit with one and to share one's grappa" (*Flat* 414).

Differently voiced than the speeches Steinbeck had created for his common farmers in *The Pastures of Heaven*, these speakers talk in simple yet elevated sentences. They make frequent references to God and to the Virgin and to other-worldly things. They seldom make verbal jokes, yet their lives are laced with comedy. As a method of unifying the men of Tortilla Flat, Steinbeck's prose is consistently effective.

Danny's illness as he longs for his previous freedom leads him into anguished behavior. He cannot bear the responsibility of his property; he behaves crazily; he tries to sell his house. He drinks, he leaves home for a week at a time. His friends worry. In a final burst to cut himself loose from his obligations, he falls forty feet and dies. The sorrow his good friends feel at his loss is intensified when they realize they have no appropriate clothes: they cannot attend Danny's funeral. Finally, funeral past, they allow the house to burn as if creating a funeral pyre. Yet Steinbeck makes sure the reader understands that, without Danny at the heart of their camaraderie, the group itself must disband. The story closes with this simple sentence: "After a while they turned and walked slowly away, and no two walked together" (*Flat* 527).

Tortilla Flat won few prizes; it did, however, win the annual Gold Medal of the Commonwealth Club of California for the best novel of the year about California. Although Steinbeck did not attend the ceremony, his publishers used that award to encourage Modern Library to put *Tortilla Flat* into its new series. From 1935 on, almost miraculously, Steinbeck was able to earn a modest living from his writing. For McIntosh and Otis, the deft fantasy about the poor people of Monterey remained a kind of touchstone: not only did Steinbeck know the culture, he was able to find the language and the narratives to make his readers *see* that culture. It was a kind of rebirth for the previously unsuccessful Steinbeck, and it seemed to be the reward for the crucible of pain that had come just before this breakthrough.

In February 1933, the Steinbecks had to give up their rental house and return to Pacific Grove. As Steinbeck told his agents, they were very happy there, but "we are headed for the rocks. The light company is going to turn off the power in a few days but we don't care much. The rent is up pretty soon and then we shall move. I don't know where" (*Conversations* 31). The following month, with no warning, John's mother became ill and was hospitalized. While in hospital, Olive Steinbeck had a massive stroke and was partially paralyzed. Because his sisters had families of their own, he and Carol took over his mother's care—without letting his father know how hopeless her condition was. Mrs. Steinbeck was hospitalized for several months, and John sat with her, or just outside her door, every day and night. As he wrote to Albee, "There's no change here. Mother's mind gets farther and farther from its base. She's pretty much surrounded by dead relatives now" (*SLL* 85).

When his mother was released from the hospital to return to the Salinas house in June, she needed constant care. Steinbeck wrote his friends few details, but he did tell Albee, "There are terrible washings every day, nine to twelve sheets. I wash them and Carol irons them" (*SLL* 82). The sheer physical labor involved in caring for the mother who had always taken such capable care of him was hardly as debilitating as the emotional impact of her hopeless condition. In Timmerman's words, it was "a nerve-wracking and stressful time [with] Steinbeck trapped in his boyhood home" (Timmerman "Introduction" xiii).

After several weeks of this, during August 1933, Carol moved to the Pacific Grove house with John's father, a man already devastated by what had happened to his wife. Terribly ill himself, he would live fewer than two more years.

With Carol tending to his father and he and several nurses trying to care for his mother, John wrote very little. Yet somehow in the midst of that pounding sorrow, Steinbeck began a story that would become a touchstone for his later artistic accomplishment. "The Red Pony" was written in handfuls of minutes, first outside his mother's hospital room and then in the Salinas house, John in the dining room next to his mother's makeshift bedroom, there to help the care givers with all the physical work, emptying bedpans, lifting his mother from the bed, not to mention the cooking and the laundry. As Steinbeck wrote to Albee,

> Nothing is changed here. I am typing the second draft of the pony story. A few pages a day. This morning is a good example. One paragraph—help lift patient on bed pan. Back, a little ill, three paragraphs, help turn patient so sheets can be changed. Back—three lines, nausea, hold pans, help hang bedding, back—two paragraphs, patient wants to tell me that her brother George is subject to colds, and the house must be kept warm. Brother George is not here but a letter came from him this morning. That is a morning. One page and a half typed. You can see that concentration thrives under difficulties since I have a fear and hatred of illness and incapacity which amounts to a mania. (*SLL* 83)

Steinbeck's disarming honesty makes clear that his and Carol's roles as care givers are extremely taxing. In another letter he fears that Carol may be heading for a breakdown. When critic John Seelye commented on the difficulties of writing what he here calls "the pony story" in the midst of this unalleviated torment, he broadened the commentary to conclude that Steinbeck often did his best work in the midst of such "crisis, some of his own making, as if the author thrived on emotional turmoil, escaping into the much more tidy world of his own creation yet bringing along the heightened sensibilities that conflict engenders." For Seelye, the most important source of pain was the fact that his mother lay dying, but that immense difficulty was abetted by the fact that Steinbeck also tried to keep his father's accounting business afloat. In Seelye's words, "working up long columns of figures" was a task Steinbeck had long disliked (Seelye "Introduction" viii–ix).

This critic claims that "The Red Pony" was the true beginning of Steinbeck's successful career, "a text central to [his] development as a writer." In telling Jody Tiflin's story—"a boy who has a series of painful and traumatic experiences on the threshold to adolescence"—Steinbeck is able to move from his existing personal pain at witnessing his mother's disintegration to the re-creation of the much younger character (Seelye "Introduction" viii). Evocative, human, and simply drawn, "The Gift" segment of "The Red Pony" was one of the first stories his agents were able to place: it appeared in *North American Review* in November of that year, followed in the December 1933 issue by the second of the "Pony" stories, "The Great Mountains." With an almost complete lack of sentimentality, Steinbeck wrote the story of the ten-year-old boy so that any reader who had ever rebelled against parental authority could identify. The fact that Jody had been given the colt as a "gift" was an ironic touch: the gift was the source of the boy's pain, along with the recognition that it is Billy Buck's oversight that kills the young animal. (If farmhand Billy Buck seemed to become a surrogate for Carl Tiflin, his failure as a mentor spreads across both characters.)

The heart of "The Gift"—and also of "The Red Pony" collectively—is the slow description of Billy Buck's misguided treatment of the dying colt. With each step in that treatment, Jody watches carefully. He does not leave Galiban's side, even as he recognizes the inevitability of the horse's death.

Lying beside his pony, Jody falls asleep and when he wakes, seeing that the colt is gone, Steinbeck gives the reader the core of the boy's sorrow: "The pony's tracks were plain enough, dragging through the frostlike dew on the young grass, tired tracks with little lines between them where the hoofs had dragged...." He follows the tracks, of course, and as he sees a group of black buzzards congregating, Jody runs after them, "forced on by panic and rage."

At the top of the ridge, Jody can finally see the colt. "Below, in one of the little clearings in the brush, lay the red pony. In the distance, Jody would see the legs moving slowly and convulsively" (*Long* 373).

Galiban does not simply die, however. Steinbeck gives the reader the boy's realization of his loss of "the red pony"—now nameless in its struggle, no longer *his* in its chosen return to nature. Had the story ended here, it might have seemed sentimental. But Steinbeck complicates the story with the double layers of violence to come. The first of those layers is that Jody attacks the buzzards as they settle to feed. His violence, while foolhardy—since the buzzard he eventually kills is nearly as large as he is—shows his all-too-human rage at the birds' desecration of his colt.

The second layer of violence is even more striking, as Carl Tiflin and Billy Buck argue over how Jody's rage should be interpreted. Both adult men are wrong, just as they have been wrong about how Galiban should be saved. The authority figures in Jody's life have killed his gift. Worse, they still understand nothing about the significant issues in life—and in death.

"The Great Mountains," the second of the "pony" stories, is not about Jody's love for horses. It rather shows the character of a "mean" Jody suffused with the boredom of summer on the farm, mistreating the family dog and killing a bird with his slingshot—and then beheading it; even though, as Steinbeck points out, "The bird looked much smaller dead than it had alive" (*Long* 175).

The events of the story focus on the old man, a dark-skinned paisano, who walks carefully from Salinas. Gitano is that stranger, though he tells Jody only that he has come back. He has returned to his home.

Too old to work, Gitano was born on the other side of the mountain. He tells Jody's parents that he has come back to die. Again, narratively, if the Tiflins were to allow him to stay, the story would become sentimental. Instead, Carl tells him he may stay the night, but then he must leave. By morning, Gitano is gone. He has left his belongings behind, but his steel rapier is gone. And he has been seen riding the Tiflin's old horse Easter, going directly up the mountainside. Jody absorbs the happening, and then experiences "a nameless sorrow" (*Long* 189).

The third story included in this collage of death's legitimate sadness is "The Promise." With another ironic title, Steinbeck spends most of the story describing the fact that Carl will allow Jody to have another colt—but only if the five-dollar breeding fee for Nellie comes from Jody's money. Jody then watches through the eleven-month pregnancy until Nellie, a farm favorite, is ready to deliver his colt.

Unfortunately, Jody does not obey Billy at that monumental time. Billy has promised Jody he can watch. But now complications have occurred: the colt is turned; there will be no safe delivery. Thinking that Jody has left the barn, Billy kills Nellie by hammering on her head until she dies. Jody hears "a hollow crunch of bone." He hears when "Nellie chuckled shrilly." And he sees that "Nellie fell heavily to her side and quivered for a moment" (*Long* 207). The vivid impressions not only of death but of relinquishment, of hopes destroyed and of promises broken, are drawn with simple, sharp strokes. All the consoling words in the language cannot erase what Jody has heard and seen. Yet it is still Carl and Billy who try to clarify what has happened. And the reader hears over and over Billy's apologetic refrain as he showed Jody the tiny black body, "'There's your colt. I promised.... there's your colt, the way I promised'" (*Long* 208).

Benson calls the "Red Pony" stories Steinbeck's "moral fulcrum," explaining that "these stories, with their child observer, examine the nature of life and of death and the relationship of the individual to the whole." They stem from a clear "relevance to his personal emotional condition—to his struggle to write and to publish, to the terminal illness of his parents... and to his relationship with Carol" (Benson 288).

By reaching down into the depths of his personal pain over all that was absorbing him—his mother would die in February 1934, and then his broken father would return to the Salinas house and be cared for during the next year, before his death in May 1935—Steinbeck would realize that his great dependency on his parents would abruptly end. As Shillinglaw speculated at the close of the saga of care giving that his mother's illness, and his father's disintegration, had demanded, Carol's becoming pregnant was another painful situation.[4] With her abortion, perhaps the second, the health of Steinbeck's first marriage would be more and more at risk (Shillinglaw *Carol* 14).

Notes

1. Writers who did represent Depression times tended to emphasize the sociological—the causes of poverty, the tough working conditions in farming, lumbering, and textile and other manufacturing, the sorrows of not having much to eat, especially in the lives of children. The readers who found Steinbeck's paisano stories were different from those who read

Albert Halper, Robert Cantwell, Nelson Algren, Clara Weatherwax, and the dozens of pro-Communist writers who saw little help for America under capitalism.
2. Correspondence between Steinbeck and his agents shows his questioning them about his reliance on the Arthurian legend. He has several plans for clarifying the source of *Tortilla Flat*, saying "The form is that of the Malory version—the coming of Arthur, and the mystic quality of owning a house." He later asks, "What do you think of putting in an interlocutor, who between each incident interprets the incident, morally, aesthetically, historically, but in the manner of the paisanos themselves?"(*Conversations* 31 and see *SLL* 96).
3. Steinbeck's political consciousness is clear in his "Foreword" to the Modern Library re-issue of the book in 1937. "Had I known these stories and these people would be considered quaint, I think I never should have written them.... it did not occur to me that the paisanos were curious or quaint, dispossessed or underdoggish. They are people whom I know and like, people who merge successfully with their habitat. In men this is called philosophy, and it is a fine thing" (Notes 907).
4. Steinbeck, who saw his books as children, had never pretended that he wanted to have children. Both Shillinglaw and Benson agree that he had made this clear from his early adulthood. To him, although he loved his dogs, children seemed only disruptive.

CHAPTER 3

Journalism v. Fiction

For the first time in his writing career, Steinbeck considered writing non-fiction. Increasingly during the winter of 1933–1934, California was the scene of labor unrest: even in the usually tranquil Salinas Valley, strikes and the men who organized them were in the news. Because of the American suspicion of Communism, much of the strike activity was considered illicit: police raids on workers who were trying to unionize were common, and a number of strike organizers were run out of the area, imprisoned, or killed. Among the small villages in the Salinas Valley, where union activity among lettuce pickers and fruit tramps was plentiful, Ed Ricketts' lab in Pacific Grove was well known. By 1933–1934, Steinbeck had met Ella Winter and her husband Lincoln Steffens, and although they lived in Carmel, they too were known as supporters of various kinds of radicalism.

Francis Whitaker, one of the leaders of the area John Reed Club, gave Steinbeck entry to numerous people and places. Many of the new people drifting around these sites chose to use aliases, and were members of either the John Reed Club or the Young Communist League (Benson 293–94).

Steinbeck had toyed with the idea of writing about the labor unions, or the strikes, or the organizers—being invited early in 1934 to accompany photographers into the fields. He caught a kind of fire after he had been introduced to Cicil McKiddy and Carl Williams, men who helped to run the C&AWIU local in Tulare.[1] His plan then, during the spring of 1934 (soon after the death of his mother), was to write a pseudo-autobiography

© The Author(s) 2017
L. Wagner-Martin, *John Steinbeck*, Literary Lives,
DOI 10.1057/978-1-137-55382-9_3

of a strike organizer. Long hours spent interviewing Cicil McKiddy had given him a great deal of information. But he also had traveled out into the striking groups (particularly during the lettuce workers' strike) to listen to the participants talking. Just as Steinbeck was an avid learner, he was also a good listener.

In his unsettled personal state—watching his father crumble under the strain of his mother's illness and eventual death—Steinbeck yet resumed the work habits that comforted him. The notion of writing about labor and its strikes intrigued him, but he also saw how low the pay for vegetable and fruit picking had become, and since he knew that kind of work well himself, the information pained him. He could not view the workers' difficulties as abstract. To Steinbeck, they were cruelly real.

In early spring 1934, he wrote to George Albee that he had been thinking of writing a number of new stories so that his next collection (evidently on the model of *The Pastures of Heaven*) would be "the story of this whole valley, of all the little towns and all the farms and ranches in the wilder hills. I can see how I would like to do it so that it would be the valley of the world" (Benson 264). To Albee, Steinbeck also commented that he was once again experiencing what he described as the "unspeakable joy of merging into this world I am building."

Steadying himself with his return to serious writing, Steinbeck took the occasion of the spring following his mother's burial to remind Albee that he knew himself to be an inordinately simple man. He said,

> I am so simple that I want to be comfortable and comfort consists in a place to sleep, dry and fairly soft, lack of hunger, almost any kind of food... and a good deal of work.... I just work all the time. I am writing so hard and so constantly that I am really quite happy. I don't take life as hard as you do. Some very bitter thing dried up in me last year. (*SLL* 93–94)

It was to Albee, too, that he admitted that the year watching his mother die was truly a crucible for his nerves and emotions. He told Albee,

> Two things I really want and I can't have either of them.... I want to forget my mother lying for a year with a frightful question in her eyes and I want to forget and lose the pain in my heart that is my father. In one year he has become a fumbling, repetitious, senile old man, unhappy almost to the point of tears. (*SLL* 92–93)

In this same letter, Steinbeck mentioned that he and Carol were going to Laguna with Ricketts in order to catch octopuses to be supplied to New York labs. They would be gone a week, and both of them were looking forward to leaving Pacific Grove. In another letter that spring, Steinbeck mentioned that he was going with Ed once more, but that Carol would stay home—they had money enough for only one hamburger. As Timmerman noted, one advantage of Steinbeck's trying to help with his father's accounting business was his access to the partially used ledgers: "he covered nearly every inch of the pages in his tight, tiny, but quite legible handwriting" (Timmerman "Introduction" xi). From Steinbeck's handwriting, Carol was able to type the fiction.

It is easy to forget that in the midst of Steinbeck's steady and sometimes frantic writing schedule, he had yet to make money from his publications. While *North American Review* had paid him for the two "pony" stories, *Tortilla Flat* had been rejected by several publishers, and Steinbeck's agents were hoping that the interest shown by Pascal Covici would lead to publication. While he decided where to put his writing energy in later spring, Steinbeck wrote a few stories based on the strike milieu in California—"The Raid," "The Lonesome Vigilante," and "Breakfast." These were later included in *The Long Valley* (published in 1938 by Viking).

"The Raid" is the story closest to the scenes of *In Dubious Battle*. Dialogue between the experienced labor organizer Dick and his protégé Root shows the nervousness of the younger man. They head for their evening meeting with discontented fruit pickers, and it seems as if Dick's role is to reassure Root: the younger man tells his mentor,

> "I wish I knew the ropes better. You been out before, Dick. You know what to expect. But I ain't ever been out."
> "The way to learn is to do," Dick quoted sententiously. 'You never really learn nothing from books." (*Long* 65)

Clearly drawn with journalistic objectivity, Steinbeck dispensed with nearly all description. The reader knows nothing about the two men, except that they are about the same size, nor is there much background on their circumstances. Different from most of the stories included in this collection, "The Raid" is stripped to essentials, giving readers the effect of a machine instead of an oil painting. Dick and Root are isolated from the workers they hope to recruit; they are separated from a common group identity because of their revolutionary beliefs and their willingness to fight for their ideology.

The phalanx theory that tended to pull the segments of *Tortilla Flat* together has disappeared.[2] As if giving himself permission to become a journalist, a literal reporter, working through oral history and observation, Steinbeck learns how to draw sharp dialogue.

The pervasive tone of "The Raid" is set by Root's fear of physical harm. Dick's calming explanation seems incredible, but Root in his innocence believes him: "'Listen to me close, kid.... When it comes—it won't hurt. I don't know why, but it won't. Even if they kill you it won't hurt.'" Warned by a loyal worker that a raiding party is coming (and that no one will be joining them for the meeting), Dick and Root are beaten badly.

Steinbeck breaks into the narration to show Root's regaining consciousness as he lies in the prison hospital wing. "He came near the surface several times, but didn't quite make it into consciousness. At last he opened his eyes and knew things." In his memory of the brutal beating, he reassures Dick (whose injuries are more moderate), "'It didn't hurt, Dick. It was funny. I felt all full up—and good'" (*Long* 75–76).

Steinbeck wrote the brief story "Breakfast" after he had traveled to join workers in the Salinas Valley lettuce strike, and its tone of good fellowship and tranquility shows another kind of portraiture. Simple in their wants and needs, the people around the breakfast camp are generous to the stranger who arrives. Fed by the young nursing mother, who carries and feeds the infant as she works, the men are appreciative (and in that mood they invite the narrator to join them): "'God Almighty, it's good,' the older man said. The younger said to their guest, 'We been eating good for twelve days.'"

The cotton pickers felt lavish, but as Steinbeck reported, "We all ate quickly, frantically, and refilled our plates and ate quickly again until we were full and warm" (*Long* 63). Benevolent in their prosperity, the cotton pickers radiate a spirit of good will. And as the narrator had said at the start of his story, "This thing fills me with pleasure. I don't know why, I can see it in the smallest detail. I find myself recalling it again and again, each time bringing more detail out of sunken memory, remembering brings the curious warm pleasure" (*Long* 61).

With the more complex drawing of a man who has taken part in a vicious lynching of a black man, expressed in Steinbeck's story "The Vigilante" (originally titled "The Lonesome Vigilante"), Steinbeck traced the attraction of a man's aligning himself with evil. The parameters of his characters in both "The Raid" and "Breakfast" are simple, and they are simply drawn in the story's action. But with "The Vigilante" the seemingly sympathetic man—unclear himself as to why he became a part of the lynch mob—expresses a set of differing responses to his involvement in killing another man, a man described as a *fiend* even though he may have been innocent. Mike reveals his contradictory impulses as he talks with Welch, the owner of the bar who is disappointed that other men from the lynch mob have not stopped for a beer. Set in a rigidly male world, "The Vigilante" works through minute changes in Mike's behavior to show the complexity of finding oneself a murderer.[3]

What these three short stories showed to Steinbeck the writer, usually mired in traditional narratives rather than in contemporary happenings, is that he could learn to deal with the modern world—without being didactic or stentorian. When Mavis McIntosh replied to his inquiry about her interest in a non-fiction account of strikers and labor organizations, telling him she would prefer that he wrote *fiction* about those themes, he was not afraid to begin immersing himself in the contemporary.

His usual practice of turning to the great annals of literature showed when he chose a line from John Milton's *Paradise Lost* as title. Referencing man's internal struggle between nobility and derogation, Steinbeck used as preface these lines:

> Innumerable force of Spirits armed,
> That durst dislike his reign, and, me preferring,
> His utmost power with adverse power opposed
> In dubious battle on the plains of Heaven.

It is not the characters that Steinbeck here finds interesting; rather, it is their skirmish to right wrongs, if wrongs they be. The pivot for *In Dubious Battle* is economics gone awry, and as Steinbeck prepares to write about that set of difficult circumstances, he cannot blink the fact that in *Tortilla Flat* he presented those same underdog characters as humorous rather than dispossessed.

The novel begins with a description and an analysis of the young Jim Nolan, giving up his cheap rented room to go to a strike-in-progress, but first he must see if he has passed muster to become a part of the Communist party. Steinbeck worked in journalistic order—Jim checks the time in a jeweler's window. He must walk wherever he goes. This is a man with few resources. When Harry Nilson opens the door, Jim is poised for his interview. When Nilson asks him about his father, Roy Nolan, Jim tells the story of his dad's being beaten so often (in labor conflicts) that he was punch drunk. "'He'd got an idea that he'd like to dynamite a slaughter-house where he used to work. Well, he caught a charge of buckshot in the chest from a riot gun'" (*IDB* 536). Veering away from his father's story, Jim summarized, "'My whole family has been ruined by this system.'"

Nilson sees Jim's naivete and warns him, "'you don't know what you're getting into. I can tell you about it, but it won't mean anything until you go through it.'" In return, Jim retorts, "'Did you ever work at a job where, when you got enough skill to get a raise in pay, you were fired and a new man put in? Did you ever work in a place where they talked about loyalty to the firm, and loyalty meant spying on the people around you? Hell, I've got nothing to lose.'"

Nilson's answer is a kind of amelioration: "'Nothing except hatred,' Harry said quietly. 'You're going to be surprised when you see that you stop hating people. I don't know why it is, but that's what usually happens'" (*IDB* 540).

Warren French early pointed out that Steinbeck was not a political writer, that he refused "to serve any organized party or special interest group" (and that he would never become "an ideologue"). French's assessment accurately separated Steinbeck and his efforts from a great many 1930s novelists (French "Introduction" viii). As this scene between Nolan and Nilson illustrated, Steinbeck even saw a political spectrum in relation to human need.

There is step-by-step progress through the party's approval, his training, his humble work at headquarters, and, finally, the beginning of the strike story: Jim Nolan goes to Mac's room (a "headquarters" with six cots) to be trained. There Mac introduces him to Dick the "Decoy," who earns money and food from rich women, and to Joy, the "veteran" who exists with hands crippled by often-broken bones. These three men will be the cast of strike organizers once they travel to the central California valley where the fruit pickers (peach and apple) have just had their pay lowered once again. Hungry for a strike, these workers will be manipulated by Mac (who "knows more about field work than anybody in the state") (*IDB* 544).

With painstaking deliberation, Steinbeck created the daily activities of pre-strike life. Psychologically clear, the damages from police brutality as well as hunger and sleeplessness impair whoever joins the plotline. Uppermost in the author's mind was the fact that he did not want to create more problems for McKiddy, or for anyone who had helped him to learn about strikes in the central California valley. As he said,

> I have usually avoided using actual places to avoid hurting feelings, for, although I rarely use a person or a story as it is—neighbors love only too well

to attribute them to someone.... as for the valley in *In Dubious Battle*—it is a composite valley as it is a composite strike. If it has the characteristics of Pajaro nevertheless there was no strike there. If it's like the cotton strike, that wasn't apples. (in Benson 298)

Biographer Jay Parini, more so than Jackson Benson, tried to align the circumstances of *In Dubious Battle* with the information that Cicil McKiddy had provided—seeing Pat Chambers changed directly into the character Mac. Parini noted that Steinbeck wanted to pay McKiddy and Caroline Decker for "the rights to their story" (Parini 189). French, however, said correctly that Steinbeck mixed strike stories from different times, drawing as well on labor conflicts in the lumber industry in the northwest and the longshoremans' union strike at the port of San Francisco, where "Bloody Thursday" occurred (French "Introduction" xii–xv).

After a slow beginning, bordering on the tedious, Steinbeck used the momentum of the action of planning toward the confrontational strike to carry the second half of the novel, and its quick and unexpected culmination in the macabre death of the still-idealistic Jim—his faceless body used to incite the strikers to march against the armed guardsmen—provides a shocking ending to the book. (Mac had earlier used Joy's murder by police for the same effect, but at this point in the action, conditions are much more threatening and many of the strikers have already left the scene.)

Jim's death resonates against the politics of the novel so that, rather than encourage collective action, Steinbeck's novel seems to warn against it. As Steinbeck wrote to Albee, he was unsure if this novel reflected his abilities. He commented that the novel "has a terrible order, a frightful kind of movement.... The talk, the book is about eighty percent dialogue, is what is usually called vulgar. I have worked along with working stiffs and I have rarely heard a sentence that had not some bit of profanity in it" (*SLL* 99).

The pickers are not the only victims. Burton, the care-giving doctor, has trouble deciding where his political beliefs will lead him.[4] The small landowners like Anderson and his son, Al—whose lunchroom is destroyed as quickly as the possessions of the fruit pickers—cannot hold out against the monopolistic power of the large corporations: what those corporations decide is what will happen. Their brutality in putting down the incipient strike is drawn without flinching. The "old guy Dan" becomes another victim of the ravages of poverty. As a spokesman for the misused and betrayed workers throughout the book, Dan adds humor and belligerence even as he dies broken in both mind and body.

Whether or not Steinbeck intended to be sympathetic to the strikers, *In Dubious Battle* is thoroughly so. What happens in the course of the narrative is that the title itself changes meaning. No longer focused on the interior divisions of materialistically unsuccessful men like Jim, the book absorbs some of the fragile idealism of party members who truly believed in collective action (the novel also balances its portraits by showing the hypocrisy of many of those leaders, those who are as willing to sacrifice the common people as are the large landowners). At its best the Communist party tries to be a positive force. But the reality of the times in California farming mirrors the times in most industrialized sectors of the economy: human dignity and even life will be readily sacrificed for production schedules and profits.

Steinbeck had written several short stories that seemed to be dependent on his experiences learning about strikes and their organization. He continued to fill in enough stories so that he could compile another collection: among those summer tales are "The White Quail" and "The Harness,"[5] strong stories of unspoken anger and frustration; "Flight," which captures strikingly Steinbeck's ability to mesmerize readers with a slow, detailed progression of action; and the humorous "Johnny Bear." He showed off his incipient skills as journalist by drawing "The Snake," taken from an actual event in Ricketts' lab. He brought the "pony" sequence to completion by writing the fourth story in that group, "The Leader of the People."

Even in the midst of this strangely productive summer, Steinbeck began the strike novel, and watched as it grew to its completion. He wrote to Albee that he was exhausted to finally finish the book during January 1935, having written 30,000 words in those last eight days. (Carol would type the manuscript during February, and McIntosh and Otis would then be ready to market it as a complete novel; *SLL* 99–100.)

Despite the death of Steinbeck's father, 1935 became a banner year. Covici-Friede brought out *Tortilla Flat* in May, and that same month the publisher accepted *In Dubious Battle*. With the advance income and royalties from *Tortilla Flat*, the Steinbecks traveled to Mexico City where they rented an apartment: for the first time in years, they did nothing. (Steinbeck refers to being in Mexico as a "well of just pure life.") It was the first time in three years that they had been able to leave the Pacific Grove cottage and the Salinas house. They explored the possibilities of living in Mexico, where everything was incredibly cheap; they met painter Diego Rivera. When Steinbeck learned that Paramount was offering $4000 for the film rights to *Tortilla Flat*, he and Carol drove for two weeks, traveling by car from Mexico to New York to sign the film contracts, and then returning to California.

In Dubious Battle appeared in January 1936. Except for a damaging review in *The Nation* by Mary McCarthy, reviewers praised the book. It seemed to be a combination of clear and direct writing, and timely critique of real-world happenings. (The language of the strikers did not bother most reviewers.) Sales were unexpectedly high. The Steinbecks began building a one-story house two miles outside San Jose, the planning of which both of them enjoyed. Carol was meticulous about overseeing its construction.

Encouraged by the small estate that remained after his parents' deaths, Steinbeck felt less pressure to turn out the next book, but his interest had been rekindled during the stay in Mexico: it was not long before he was drafting the play (shaped as a novel) that would become *Of Mice and Men*. After Toby, one of the many Steinbeck dogs so named, ate about half that work (and there was no copy), the writing process began all over. Steinbeck told a friend that seeing what Toby had done to his manuscript was "a little study in humility" (Benson 325). Of that undertaking, Steinbeck wrote that—given that Carol had reminded him that "Working men didn't read novels"—he was hoping that the play structure within the prose would win out, that *Of Mice and Men* could eventually be stage worthy (Benson 326). He later wrote that *Of Mice and Men* "was an attempt to write a novel in three acts to be played from the lines" (Steinbeck *Nonfiction* 159).

Again, dispossessed workers were at the center of the book. George Milton and Lennie Small were paired throughout their working years, George looking out for the large and powerful field worker, at the same time finding solace in Lennie's sheer physical size and strength. The men's aim in life comes through clearly at the start of their arrival at yet another ranch: to save enough to have their own house, to create a normal life with a yard, rabbits as pets, and safety. Rather than disguise the working men's language, here Steinbeck *featured* that repetitive talk, as George explains by rote what he and Lennie have dreamed of acquiring:

> "Guys like us, that work on ranches, are the loneliest guys in the world. They got no family. They don't belong no place. They come to the ranch an' work up a stake.... the first thing you know they're pounding their tail on some other ranch. They ain't got nothing to look ahead to."
>
> Lennie interrupts, excitedly, "That's it—that's it. Now tell how it is with us."

George went on. "With us it ain't like that. We got a future. We got somebody to talk to that gives a damn about us. We don't have to sit in no bar room blowin' in our jack jus' because we got no place else to go. If them other guys gets in jail they can rot for all anybody gives a damn. But not us."

Lennie broke in. "But not us! An' why? Because.... Because I got you to look after me, and you got me to look after you, and that's why." He laughed delightedly.

"Go on now, George!"

"You got it by heart. You can do it yourself." (*Mice* 806–07)

In the midst of this contrived pathos, Steinbeck creates a seemingly casual emphasis on *heart*. Learned *by heart*, the promise that serves to connect the two lonely working men emphasizes the caring personal bond as well as the acquisition of a home, which provides safety. As the reader comes to understand how much damage Lennie's strength has already meted out, killing mice, puppies, all things frail, and perhaps doing even greater physical damage, the irony of the men's search for safety takes hold. Throughout *Of Mice and Men*, beginning with Lennie's crushing the boss's hand, and moving to his suffocating one of the puppies and then the boss's wife, Steinbeck builds the mood of incipient disaster. In tracing Lennie's damaging strength, Steinbeck makes clear how unreal these promissory words are. There will be no safety, just as there will be no home, for the likes of Lennie.

Owens suggests that Steinbeck's choosing Soledad as setting creates an ironic "tell"—despite all the talk about partnership and home, the men will remain solitary. Again, "Soledad is a very real, dusty little town on the western edge of the Salinas River midway down the Salinas Valley." The novel's original title, "Something That Happened," reinforces the author's "non-blaming point of view." Whereas "Lennie's weakness doomed the dream it was only his innocence that kept it alive" (Owens *Re-Vision* 101, 103–04).[6]

One of the brilliant moves in this novel/play is the almost unbearable tension that Lennie's insistence demands. Lennie parrots the repetitive phrase

"An' live off the fatta the lan, An' have rabbits. Go on, George! Tell about what we're gonna have in the garden and about the rabbits in the cages and about the rain in the winter and the stove, and how thick the cream is on the milk like you can hardly cut it. Tell about that, George."

Without realizing "meaning," Lennie is lulled by the fact that George will care for him: language is in itself a panacea for their threatening lives as working stiffs, but language does not provide real answers. At the center of the numerous conflicts within the bunk house—and Steinbeck does a good job in giving readers/viewers a panoply of characteristic men, some too old to be working, another a black man who has no status at all, the leader of the troupe the more talented Slim who will survive whatever Curley, the newly married boss's son, hands out—is the shooting of Candy's old dog. Pleading the discomfort of having to smell the aged dog, one of the men takes the dog outside to kill it. Candy is bereft. The scene extends unnecessarily, but effectively: everyone is listening to hear the shot. Everyone is visualizing that bullet aimed "Right back of the head. He wouldn't even quiver" (*Mice* 830).

That middle pause foreshadows the action that George will feel forced to take at the novel's end. After the young wife's body has been found in the barn, half covered with hay, the lynch mob grows to full force. Her death must be avenged. George equips himself with the only gun and pursues Lennie, who has run away. In Lennie's distorted memory, he speaks to the only person before George who ever cared for him, his Aunt Clara; she is scolding him. She fades away and is replaced by a giant rabbit, who not only scolds him but predicts that George will leave him to starve. This transfer to scenes that might play on stage but seem only to mock Lennie's fictional dilemma leads to Lennie's calling out for George. His voice leads George to him.

As the two men sit together on a hillside, almost hidden from the searchers, they repeat the long-familiar story of their promised house, complete with rabbits and thick cream and fires and safety. The ending is drawn out by Lennie's repetition of the comfort words that have become their mantra. Their words are mixed with the sounds of the searching party crashing through the brush. George modulates the story:

"Go on, George. When we gonna do it?" [move to their house]
"Gonna do it soon."
"Me an' you."
"You.... an' me. Ever'body gonna be nice to you. Ain't gonna be no more trouble. Nobody gonna hurt nobody nor steal from 'em."
Lennie said, "I thought you was mad at me, George."
"No," said George. "No, Lennie. I ain't mad. I never been mad, an' I ain't now. That's a thing I want ya to know."
The voices came close now. George raised the gun and listened to the voices.

Lennie begged, "Le's do it now. Le's get that place now."
"Sure, right now. I gotta. We gotta."
And George raised the gun and steadied it, and he brought the muzzle of it close to the back of Lennie's head. The hand shook violently, but his face set and his hand steadied. He pulled the trigger. The crash of the shot rolled up the hills and rolled down again. Lennie jarred, and then settled slowly forward to the sand, and he lay without quivering. (*Mice* 877)

Slim arrives at the scene first; he understands George's action—but he disguises his knowledge to make it seem more reasonable for the rest of the hands. He takes George off to get a drink. Life, without any indication of its myriad complications, goes on.

The difference between this closing scene and the starkly truncated ending of *In Dubious Battle* shows immense growth in Steinbeck's aesthetic. Just as in *Of Mice and Men*, he has drawn on the heartless words of the man who insists on killing the old dog to do double duty here: as George kills his friend Lennie, in the strike novel Steinbeck allows Jim's death to stand as an unrelieved iconic etching of murder for political gain. In fewer than two hundred words, *In Dubious Battle* ends. Mac carries Jim's body into camp, carefully handling its "dripping head." As Steinbeck summarizes, "there was no face," and Mac stared at "his sticky hand." He then propped Jim's body on the platform, positioning the lantern so that its light fell on "the head." Then Mac began to speak, "'This guy didn't want nothing for himself—.... Comrades! He didn't want nothing for himself—'" (*IDB* 792–93).

Although *Of Mice and Men* would become the best selling of Steinbeck's early works (being chosen as a Book-of-the-Month Club selection and then re-written as a drama and winning awards on Broadway),[7] his turn to journalism was prompted more directly by *In Dubious Battle*. Six months after McCarthy's review in *The Nation*, Steinbeck wrote for that magazine a long and important essay titled "Dubious Battle in California." In his closely argued piece, he set what was considered *un*common labor hostility against what could now be easily seen as a revolution in farming. Once agriculture in the state had changed from hay and animals to fruits and vegetables, a shift that demanded the involvement of much more human labor, farms became either very small (several acres; that is, truck farms) or extremely large (owned usually by absentee proprietors, such as Herbert Hoover, William Randolph Hearst, Bank of America, S. J. Chandler, and others) and managed by people who had no ownership interests.

What became obliterated, said Steinbeck in his *Nation* essay, was the middle-size farm, of one hundred to three hundred acres. And along with that dramatic shift in farm size and management came the emphasis on profits alone.

Although Steinbeck could not have included all the information in this long essay in *In Dubious Battle*, "Dubious Battle in California" provided good background for the turmoil that presently existed. For Steinbeck, it was a successful foray into straight journalism.

NOTES

1. Caroline Decker, Shorty Alston, and James Harkins were other key players in the activities of the Cannery and Agricultural Workers Industrial Union in this area. Unions in the east and middle west, as well as the Pacific northwest, had concentrated on workers in manufacturing and lumbering. The C&AWIU was a comparatively young organization.
2. Intrigued by Ricketts' sense of interconnectedness within and between all strata of life—amoebic as well as human—Steinbeck had worked out a principle he referred to as "the phalanx." In 1933 he used this term rather than the phrasing of his earlier letters ("group" or "group-unit"). He wrote to Albee, man "arranges himself into larger units, which I have called the phalanx. The phalanx has its own memory—memory of the great tides when the moon was close, memory of starvation when the food of the world was exhausted. Memory of methods when numbers of his units had to be destroyed for the good of the whole, memory of the history of itself. And the phalanx has emotions of which the unit man is incapable. Emotions of destruction, of war, of migration, of hatred, of fear" (*SLL* 79–80).
3. Timmerman points out that the lynching that became the kernel of the story occurred on November 16, 1933, in San Jose, and dominated the newspapers for weeks. It was two men—John Maurice Holmes and Thomas Harold Thurmond—who were so brutally killed, and Steinbeck wrote about their lynchings under the title "Case History" (Timmerman "Notes" *Long* 229).
4. Doc Burton counters Jim's assumption that important social changes begin with violent acts. Doc tells him, "'There aren't any beginnings... Nor any ends. It seems to me that man has engaged for a blind and fearful struggle out of a past he can't remember, into a future he can't foresee nor understand. And man has met and defeated every obstacle, every enemy except one. He cannot win over himself. How mankind hates itself'" (*IDB* 724).
5. Jackson Benson points out that within *The Long Valley*, "Nearly every major character wears some kind of harness" (Benson 288). Perhaps this

assessment seems too easy; there are characters ruled by frustration and by the need for compromise as well. What Benson does not undercut, however, is that Steinbeck's stories in this collection are varied and interesting. He would make his mark on the world of the American short story.

6. Probably because *Of Mice and Men* became a best-seller, Steinbeck was often asked about the source for the character of Lennie. He usually claimed that he had worked with such a person—"for many weeks"—during his stint as farmhand on one of the Spreckels ranches. "He didn't kill a girl. He killed a ranch foreman. Got sore because the boss had fired his pal and stuck a pitchfork right through his stomach. I hate to tell you how many times I saw him do it. We couldn't stop him until it was too late.... He's in an insane asylum in California right now" (*Conversations* 9). Other of Steinbeck's accounts vary in violence from this one.

7. Directed in the film production by Lewis Milestone, who had won an Academy Award for his 1930 movie *All Quiet on the Western Front*, Steinbeck's *Of Mice and Men* was also nominated for an Academy Award for Best Picture.

CHAPTER 4

The Grapes of Wrath

As a result of his modicum of fame with the positive reception of *In Dubious Battle*, Steinbeck began his turn to journalism. Magazines were receptive to his essays. Newspapers asked him to interview impoverished workers; they asked him to comment on labor strife in California. George West of the San Francisco *News* proposed that Steinbeck write a series of articles about migrant labor in the central valley: those stories became "The Harvest Gypsies," later published in booklet form as *Their Blood Is Strong*. In less than two years, writer John Steinbeck had seemingly changed identities: he had gone from being the author of philosophical novels (such as *To a God Unknown*) to being a man in touch with the times, a writer who did not flinch from difficult topics. And even though he had realized in the writing of *In Dubious Battle* that he was not in any way prepared to take on the controversial issues of either Marxism or Communism, what he saw instead was that, in Louis Adamic's words, *everybody* was "conducting field work" (Hanley 134).

Steinbeck had hardly sent *Of Mice and Men* off to his agents before he joined the ranks of journalists and photographers out in the field. Traveling in his used bakery truck, he went first to the Gridley Migrant Camp north of Sacramento; later he would find the comparatively well-run sanctuary of the Arvin Migrant Camp ("Weedpatch") near Arvin, California. He had outfitted himself to be relatively invisible. Traveling with Eric Thomsen, the director of migrant camps in the state, he learned to see what was sometimes

© The Author(s) 2017
L. Wagner-Martin, *John Steinbeck, Literary Lives*,
DOI 10.1057/978-1-137-55382-9_4

obscured by hasty observation. Under Thomsen's guiding hand, he saw families eating dogs and rats, he saw the poverty that underlay even superficial health (Wartzman 79). From Gridley, he wrote to friends that he might soon "go south to pick a little cotton...migrants are going south now and I'll probably go along. I enjoy it a lot" (*SLL* 129).

What Steinbeck saw as he lived among the pickers was sobering. In fact, it was scarifying. Surprised at the inhumane treatment that fruit tramps and their families received—by property owners for whom they worked; by the communities in which they needed to do business; and by other similarly impoverished pickers—early in the San Francisco *News* articles Steinbeck wrote with a vengeance.

Midway through the article titled "Squatters' Camps," he describes "a family of six; a man, his wife and four children. They live in a tent the color of the ground. Rot has set in on the canvas so that the flaps and the sides hang in tatters and are held together with bits of rusty baling wire. There is one bed in the family and that is a big tick lying on the ground inside the tent." He describes the way the parents lie together, with two children between them, "Then, heading the other way, the other two children lie, the littler ones." But his narrative continues that the father is losing earning power: "he is no longer alert; he isn't quick at piecework." And he, and his children, are sullen. Steinbeck includes the backstory: "The father of this family once had a little grocery store and his family lived in back of it so that even the children could wait on the counter. When the drouth set in there was no trade for the store anymore" (Steinbeck *Nonfiction* 80).

Timmerman analyzes the first of the "Gypsies" articles as "cinematic." Like Howarth, Raeburn, Seed, and others, Timmerman describes Steinbeck's mid-1930s journalism as moving from the general to the specific, hooking readers through personal stories into the larger truths—in this case, the truth that between 300,000 and 400,000 migrants had flooded into California looking for work during the past five years (Timmerman *Eden* 52–53).

Steinbeck opened the first of his seven articles with a summary that attracted readers regardless of their prejudices about the migrants. This is his opening:

> At this season of the year, when California's great crops are coming into harvest, the heavy grapes, the prunes, the apples and lettuce and the rapidly maturing cotton, our highways swarm with the migrant workers, that shifting group of nomadic, poverty-stricken harvesters driven by hunger and the threat of hunger from crop to crop, from harvest to harvest, up and down the state. (*Gypsies* 19)

His path through his quantity of information follows a photographic strategy. In this first article, he progresses from the best circumstances that he sees within the squatters' camps. Then he moves to a more desperate family, one haunted not only by the fear of hunger but by hunger itself. That family has lost a child to starvation. In the third tier of the unfortunate, he emphasizes that all vestiges of civilization have been denied these people:

> There is no bed. Somewhere the family has found a big piece of old carpet. It is on the ground. To go to bed members of the family lie on the ground and fold the carpet up over them.
> The three-year-old child has a gunny sack tied about his middle for clothing. He has the swollen belly caused by malnutrition.
> He sits on the ground in the sun in front of the house, and the little black fruit flies buzz in circles and land on his closed eyes and crawl up his nose until he weakly brushes them away.
> They try to get at the mucus in the eye corners. This child seems to have the reactions of a baby much younger. The first year he had a little milk, but he has had none since.
> He will die in a very short time. The older children may survive. (*Gypsies* 29)

Much of Steinbeck's writing throughout *The Harvest Gypsies* moved away from strict objectivity: he used whatever images he could to make his coverage into more of a testimony, an emotional appeal to convince readers that action was needed. The migrants needed whatever help California and its various agencies could provide.

The 1930s was a time of fascination with not only film and newsreels but with photography—and a good bit of the documentation that resulted from people's deprivation was dependent on pictures. For Steinbeck, who knew a number of photographers and was becoming interested himself in the possibility of filmmaking, to explore the migrant condition with an accompanying photographer seemed ideal. When Horace Bristol approached him about collaborating, Steinbeck was interested.

Bristol, a regular photographer for *Life* magazine, was friends with Dorothea Lange and Paul Taylor, with whom he photographed migrant camps near Sacramento. *Life* was not interested in using any of the photos from the Sacramento shoots, but because of that experience, Bristol decided that he would work with a writer—hopefully Steinbeck—to produce a big picture book.

Bristol recalled that Steinbeck was "a gentle and loving man," able to "put everyone at the same level. He just talked to the migrant workers in a simple, friendly way." (Bristol in Lynch 99–100). Their large vehicle was a bit "embarrassing," Bristol thought, so they "filled up the car with cheap meats and lots of beans. It was our gift to the migrants and also our way of introduction. We would ask them to cook it up because we were hungry too" (ibid. 101). Effective as their strategy was, Steinbeck was putting together these experiences with those he was accumulating with Eric Thomsen (and with Tom Collins, who was the manager of the state-funded migrant installation at Arvin). A few weeks later, however, Steinbeck told Bristol he had to withdraw from their book because he needed to shape all these observations into a novel.

Steinbeck's *In Dubious Battle* did not fit the category of literary journalism, or of cinematic fiction, or of mixed-form writing—as did John Dos Passos' *USA Trilogy*, with its mixture of prose styles, or Erskine Caldwell and Margaret Bourke-White's *You Have Seen Their Faces*, documentary prose with photographs, leading to Dorothea Lange and Paul S. Taylor's *An American Exodus, A Record of Human Erosion*, and James Agee and Walker Evans' *Let Us Now Praise Famous Men*, as well as the collections of photographs by Lewis Hine, Arnold Rothstein, Ben Shahn, Marion Post Walcott, and others that were exhibited in cities throughout the world.

The Farm Security Administration had marshalled hundreds of good photographers, and its Washington, DC archives were full to bursting. Beyond the visual component, the actual photo montage, Steinbeck observed the relentless experimentation in prose itself—reading Meridel Le Seuer, Nelson Algren, Langston Hughes, Zora Hurston, Jack Conroy, and other writers who never reached the *New York Times* Best Seller lists. As William Howarth pointed out, Steinbeck well understood what he called "documentary"—"the wedding of reportage, the investigative methods of journalism and sociology, to new forms of mass-media imagery, especially photography.... The style tends to flourish during grave social crises (war, depression, as the New Journalism during the Vietnam War)" (Howarth 55).

In Peter Cohn's observation, when Steinbeck began assembling his knowledge, partly gained from what was becoming more and more extensive field work, he was faced with some understanding that what he had already become competent in doing—writing a terse fiction like *In Dubious Battle*, or an equally terse play like *Of Mice and Men*, or a tapestry of folk tales like *Tortilla Flat*—was not going to be adequate for a novel that tried to encompass the disaster of thousands of misplaced people.

When he finally began the big novel, he called it "The Oklahomans." Writing it felt premature. Later he tried satire. It was Carol, after typing more than four hundred pages of that book, who told him that *L'Affaire Lettuceberg* was not going to work, so he put all that manuscript away. Cohn's comparison with Steinbeck's *The Grapes of Wrath*, which was three years in the making, was that it might well be called a "non-fiction" novel. So many stories, both imaginative and journalistic, were treated in images and symbols that themselves became almost graphic—it was a true compendium of life's fragments, some pleasant, others horrifying (Cohn 70).

Steinbeck was consistent in telling readers and reviewers that "I lived, off and on, with those Okies for the last three years" (*Conversations* 19).[1] His focus had developed from the process of collecting information through his application of his knowledge in both journalism and reportage into the five-layered novel that would eventually sweep him into a permanent condition of fame.

During the fall of 1936, however, he would have preferred being less visible. The San Francisco *News* delayed publication of his "migrant" series for a time because the atmosphere in central California was so tense. When Steinbeck wrote to the Albees, he told them that "any reference to labor except as dirty dogs is not printed by the big press out here. There are riots in Salinas and killings in the streets of that dear little town.... You have six months or at most a year. I am not speaking of revolution again, but war. Every news report verifies the speed with which it is coming" (*SLL* 132). Living as they were in New York, George and Anne Albee warned Steinbeck to be careful, to stop taking chances. He assured them that he was writing no more articles. He continued, "there is practically no danger until I commit another overt act. Right now I think my safety lies in the fact that I am not important enough to kill and I'm too able to get publicity to risk the usual beating. Our house is covered by insurance against riots and commotions" (*SLL* 133–34).

Planning on using journalism to augment his income, Steinbeck was disappointed in the continuing—and worsening—political climate. He felt frustrated in many ways. Even though *Of Mice and Men* would appear in March, he predicted that it would sell few copies. Then Elizabeth Otis wrote that it had been selected for the Book-of-the-Month Club. In his stunned recognition that Carol and he could make their trip abroad after all, Steinbeck wrote to Otis that the selection of *Of Mice and Men* frightened him: "I shall never learn to conceive of money in larger quantities than two dollars. More than that has no conceptual meaning to me" (*SLL* 134).

Steinbeck would have to learn that money was going to be much more plentiful: after the first month of publication, *Of Mice and Men* had sold 117,000 copies. George S. Kaufman was to script a dramatic version, and then direct the play. (*Of Mice and Men* would open on Broadway in November and run for 207 performances. In 1938, it won the New York Drama Critics' Circle Award for best play of 1937.[2] But the previous May, 1937, *Of Mice and Men* was first produced by the San Francisco labor theater group, The Theatre Union, for sixteen weekend performances.)

Married for seven years, most of them endured in great poverty, the Steinbecks took their trip abroad. They left California by freighter and traveled for thirty-one days, through the Panama Canal to Philadelphia. Staying in New York for two weeks, Steinbeck traveled to Washington, DC to meet with Will Alexander, the head of the Farm Security Administration, about the major novel he was planning. The Steinbecks eventually sailed by freighter to Denmark and related areas, and then traveled on to Russia. In July they returned to New York, where Steinbeck dealt with the hard work of shaping *Of Mice and Men* into the drama necessary for its New York opening.

Buying a car in New York, the Steinbecks drove (on Route 66) back to California. Then Steinbeck felt secure in his plans for his migrant novel: he met Tom Collins at Gridley, and the two men, who had been exchanging reports and ideas for the past year, traveled to other migrant camps during October and November of 1937. They repeated this trip after the rains flooded Visalia early in 1938, working together during February. Then Steinbeck's article "Starvation under the Orange Trees" created deep unrest in the Salinas Valley.

The labor unrest had not improved, but Steinbeck himself was much more visible—and, accordingly, more vulnerable. As he wrote in "Starvation under the Orange Trees," California had become a land of inequity: "There has been no war in California, no plague, no bombing of open towns and roads, no shelling of cities. It is a beautiful year. And thousands of families are starving in California. In the county seats the coroners are filling in 'malnutrition' in the spaces left for 'causes of death.' For some reason, a coroner shrinks from writing 'starvation' when a thin child is dead in a tent." The old journalistic trick of naming names is one of Steinbeck's ploys here: "there are one thousand families in Tulare County, and two thousand families in Kings, fifteen hundred families in Kern, and so on. The families average three persons, by the way. With the exception of a little pea picking, there isn't going to be any work for nearly three months" (Steinbeck *Nonfiction* 83–84).

Further on in the article, Steinbeck countered the pervasive arguments—that migrants do not want to work, that they cannot learn to save. But any reader would recognize that Steinbeck was telling the truth when he wrote:

> The migrant cannot save anything. It takes everything he can make to feed his family and buy gasoline to go to the next job. If you don't believe this, go out in the cotton fields next year. Work all day and see if you have made thirty-five cents. A good picker makes more, of course, but you can't.
> The method of concentrating labor for one of the great crops is this. Handbills are distributed, advertisements are printed. You've seen them. Cotton pickers wanted in Bakersfield or Fresno or Imperial Valley. Then all the available migrants rush to the scene. They arrive with no money and little food. The reserve has been spent getting there. (ibid. 85)

Less dangerously specific than were his articles for the San Francisco *News*, this piece awoke the community once again to the subversive John Steinbeck. Now living in his new home, now making trips to Russia and, perhaps worse, to Hollywood, now mentioned in the news for winning the Best Play award for *Of Mice and Men*, now driving with Carol in their new and relatively expensive car, Steinbeck fought hard for the uninterrupted time to write his important novel. He finally began that project in earnest in March 1938.

As his letters to Elizabeth Otis showed, his dismay at the flooding near Visalia was irreparable. (Bristol and he spent several weekends mired in the grim conditions, and the photographer shot more than 2000 frames; Howarth 57.) To Otis, Steinbeck wrote,

> five thousand families were starving to death in the interior valleys... not just hungry but actually starving.... In one tent there are twenty people quarantined for smallpox and two of the women are to have babies in that tent this week.... The government is trying to feed them and get medical attention to them with the fascist group of utilities and banks and huge growers sabotaging the thing all along the line and yelling for a balanced budget. (*SLL* 158)

On what Steinbeck called "the nineteenth day of rain," he wrote, "The whole state is flooded." Several weeks later, he said, "The floods have aggravated the starvation and sickness.... The water is a foot deep in the tents and the children are up on the beds and there is no food and no fire, and the county has taken off all the nurses because 'the problem is so great that we can't do anything about it.' So they do nothing...." In that

March 7, 1938 letter to Otis, he said that all of this is "the most heartbreaking thing in the world" (*SLL* 160–61).

He also admitted there, "I'm trying to write history while it is happening and I don't want to be wrong" (*SLL* 162). He expressed what he saw as the futility of his efforts to be of any actual help: "Funny how mean and little books become in the face of such tragedies" (*SLL* 159).

Steinbeck knew that he could not write a *little* book. Angry as he was at the state agencies that might have brought help, and life, to the migrant workers, he also knew that he had to write something better than a *mean* book. He had to show the heart of the maligned and abused Americans who, through no fault of their own, had been displaced and then, accordingly, impoverished. As he viewed what was clearly the demise of the American dream, which Steinbeck and his family and friends had all believed in—and, to some extent, achieved—he contrived a piece of writing that called forth the best in its readers. Steinbeck had never aimed so high.

The Grapes of Wrath opened with the evocation of ruin throughout the Oklahoma lands. Classically drawn descriptions of the Dust Bowl existence incited reader interest: like Steinbeck, who had not traveled to Oklahoma at all, readers needed help imagining that desolation, conditions horrid enough to make families give up on their once-valuable land, and relinquish what little hope for financial recovery they had learned to have. In prose steady and almost sonorific, the novel led to the first glimpses of the people in charge of those families, women and then men, the latter in their customary positions of power. Once the men grew angry at their deteriorating circumstances, the women understood that they had to leave the farms. Chapter One ends with those men poised in the doorways of their homes, "their hands busy with sticks and little rocks. The men sat still—thinking—figuring" (*GOW* 7).

Described with a kind of erudite passivity, the human family convinces readers—of the essential closeness of family, of the grim realization that change is necessary, of the resilience to start over—but Steinbeck is not content with that introduction that already incorporates so many themes. He moves to the segment he calls "the general," in contrast to the "particular," which will drive the story of the Joad family. "Oklahoma City Transport Company" shows necessary industrial change as the driver of that truck finally relents and allows Tom Joad, just released from his prison term, to hitchhike into geography closer to his family home. It takes until Chapter 3, a description of traffic on the broken-down highway, to move the reader into a more universal theme: imaged in the persistent and agonizingly slow progress of the unsteady turtle, the people of dusty Oklahoma will make their journey.

Throughout the novel, at unexpected intervals, the mythic dimension of Steinbeck's story recurs. Most of those "general" chapters are paced carefully, with sentences constructed to lead readers, slowly, into understanding. They have been called biblical, and as a linguistically oriented critic such as Peter Cohn repeatedly pointed out, when an author writes a disturbingly political book, the use of religious ideas and language can be helpful. Cohn noted that in *In Dubious Battle* Jim Nolan's beliefs were made more palatable to readers because Steinbeck set them in his background as a Catholic; similarly, Steinbeck's use of Jim Casy in this much larger work exemplifies a similar strategy: "a radical message may find a more congenial audience if it is domesticated and familiarized by association with the sacred" (Cohn 234). That Steinbeck's prose itself emphasizes this textual influence only adds to a reader's readiness to accept the author's message.

As Shillinglaw emphasized, in explaining the alternation of a more specific section with a generalized one, "Details matter in *The Grapes of Wrath*.... Details are the grace notes of Steinbeck's prose." She recounted Steinbeck's admitting to Covici that he had had to begin with small and suggestive things, not the big picture. She quoted from an early description which Steinbeck wrote in the fall of 1936, two years before he began writing *The Grapes of Wrath* in earnest: "dust storm and the wind and the scouring of the land. And then the quiet... and the dust piled up like little snow drifts" (Shillinglaw *Reading* 15). This critic also insisted on the reasonableness of that alternation between specific and general, noting that "*The Grapes of Wrath* amplifies that insistent holistic truth: individuals belong to families, blood families are bound to other family units, and all humans are connected in spirit.... the Joad family plight as well as the generalized migrant woe revealed in the interchapters fold into even larger stories, both national and international: dispossession, power, land use, the interconnections of humans and other species, the suffering of many who can't tell their own story"[3] (ibid. xiii).

Although Steinbeck kept saying that any writer worked instinctively and less than rationally, as he did in his *Paris Review* remarks, "We work in our own darkness a great deal with little real knowledge of what we are doing," he had taken clear aim at methods of presenting the interrelated stories that his migrant novel was to explore (*Paris Review* 198). Through the months of his working on interviews and journalistic coverage about the plight of the Oklahoma farmers, he saw what an immense undertaking writing about this tragic exodus would become. What saved him from relying too heavily on facts, and what became the skeletal structure of the novel, was his belief in a story that drew from a human endeavor that was much larger than the farmers' displacement. *The Grapes of Wrath* showed to full advantage Steinbeck's innate understanding of, and sympathy with, the poorest of human beings—some American, some Mexican, others immigrants from European countries.

Steinbeck's truly original sympathy in telling the Joads' story, both that of the family and its larger incarnation as the family of man, gave him a means of reaching millions of readers. It had become a given that many American authors during the 1930s and 1940s were class-blind: the poor, despite much lip service to depicting working people, seemed to be of little literary interest. *The Grapes of Wrath* provided an almost systematic exposé of poverty, again drawing from accurate journalism. Even as observers of the United States did not want to believe that so much poverty existed in America, the trust had always been that more poverty, despite hard work and frugal living, marked the United States than it did some other civilized countries. In his pervasive concern with the lower class, Steinbeck also dealt with issues of gender, race, and religion, sometimes expressing attitudes well beyond the reach of the work's publication date of 1939.

In the purposefully chosen biblical rhythms of the novel's interchapters, Steinbeck soothed his readers, just as he did with his metaphors of flowers, fruits, and animal life. The solace provided by the determined and steadfast turtle as it crosses the highway goes a long way toward reassurance. Steinbeck's title, with all its bitter irony of promise in the American dream now rotted to the wrath of displaced farmers, parallels the kind of irony Hemingway and Fitzgerald had earlier achieved as they scrutinized their native country. And Steinbeck's insistence on the real dominance of women—as creators and nurturers of the race—links *The Grapes of Wrath* more closely to other writing of the decade by such female writers as Meridel Le Sueur, Josephine Herbst, Tillie Olsen, Myra Page, and others.

It was, of course, the roles of women in the novel that made it objectionable to some readers—the sex scenes that Rose of Sharon and Connie (as well as Jim Casy) enjoyed, the firm stance that Ma Joad took against propriety in the case of her protecting Tom Joad from the law and Rose of Sharon's giving birth in unclean circumstances, and the final horrifying close, her daughter's breast-feeding the dying stranger, to the barbaric circumstances of migrants trying to survive the flood. Steinbeck spoke ironically to that socially approved outrage in his next book, *The Sea of Cortez*, by telling the story of readers being shocked by descriptions of natural processes:

> A man we knew once long ago worked for a wealthy family in a country place. One morning one of the cows had a calf. The children of the house went down with him to watch her. It was a good normal birth, a perfect presentation, the cow needed no help. The children asked questions and he answered them.... And this was the time for their mother to come screaming down on the vulgarity of letting the children see the birth. This "vulgarity" had given them a sense of wonder at the structure of life, while the mother's propriety supplanted that feeling with dirtiness. (Steinbeck *Sea* 68, as quoted in Lisca 103–04)

There are hundreds of essays and books that critique Steinbeck's *The Grapes of Wrath*. Many echo one of the earliest commentaries, that by Peter Lisca who pointed out that the thirty-chapter organization of the novel used the foundational trinity (three sections within the thirty) to chart the drought, then the journey, and finally life in California. Lisca's drawing from biblical references and language—as well as color imagery— established one primary reading. (Lisca 162–68).

Louis Owens' reading of *The Grapes of Wrath* as Steinbeck's treatise on the westward journey to Eden, with California as the western edge of land and imagination, breaks away to some extent from the religious theme. Idealized in the human mind as naturally prosperous, the Garden supplies everything necessary for human life. To this trope Steinbeck adds the necessity for commitment from that human consciousness: nothing is given without repayment being expected. Just reaching California cannot redeem the Joads; after all, they have lost Noah, Muley, their grandparents, and, later, Connie and the baby. Their debt is clear. In Owens' words, "the old values and the old myths are dangerously, even fatally, delusive and must be discarded to clear the way for a new commitment to mankind and place, here and now. It is a depiction of and a plea for a genuine rebirth of national consciousness" (Owens *Re-Vision* 140).

For Stephen Railton, commitment implies conversion, and accrues from respect for the natural world. Prescient of the later turn in Steinbeck criticism to ecological interests, Railton emphasizes the uprooting of the Joads in terms of the corn uprooted in the Oklahoma landscape: "even human lives are caught in this pattern of being pulled up from the soil. Farmers are made migrants. Forced to sell and burn all of their pasts that won't fit onto a homemade flatbed truck, they too are uprooted, torn from their identities" (Railton "Conversion" 165). As this critic points out, there is balance: new roots will be put down as well in the truncated soil. Rather than *The Grapes of Wrath* standing as an anguished lament for what is lost, Railton sees the novel as also representing "the rhythms and laws of nature, the growth of seeds, the fermenting of grapes... this coming American revolution is inevitable, organically decreed" (ibid. 166).

Integral to the salvation of not only the Joads but their way of life, the continuity of all people regardless of geography, are the women characters. First discussed by such critics as Nellie McKay and Mimi Reisel Gladstein, Ma Joad becomes even more iconic in the recent work of Jennifer Williamson—who avoids the term "earth mother," but still sees that gender plays a crucial role in the narrative of the novel. As Williamson describes the relative power positions in the book, it is

> the domestic as a potentially revolutionary space reserved for, and run by, women. Furthermore, he [Steinbeck] presents the domestic as the universal experience connecting all human beings through the ceaseless work required to meet basic requirements for shelter and food, the need to maintain family units for survival, and the emotional connections developed through the domestic's emphasis on meeting the needs of others. Because their land and jobs have been lost, men who would leave the domestic now stay in it, relocating the center of the novel's action to this site. (Williamson 101)

This critic's larger point is that while *The Grapes of Wrath* opens with men talking about crops, or in the jailhouse, the novel shows readers that whatever safety exists lies in the domestic.

Removing his discussion from gender considerations, Marcus Klein emphasizes that Steinbeck's works drew on readers' understanding of the power of folktales. It was not that the author delineated his poor figures as objects of sympathy so much that he made them universally known, and thereby understood. The Joads, for example, "were an articulation of the folk inheritance" (Klein 177). Paralleling this reading is the earlier commentary by French modernist critic Claude-Edmonde Magny, who placed *The Grapes of Wrath* alongside what she called the universalizing comedy of Charlie Chaplin—an international film figure who never needed language to be understood. She listed the impoverished characters of *Tortilla Flat* and *In Dubious Battle*, alongside the disabled character of Lennie in *Of Mice and Men*, as interesting on an international scale. What set *The Grapes of Wrath* apart from Steinbeck's earlier works was its "serenity." The book expresses "simplicity, ease, tenderness" as it tries to mimic "the profound rhythms of natural life, [reflecting] a pre-Adam innocence" (Magny 162–63).

Closer to the home situation, large land owners and banks opposing the Fruit and Vegetable Workers local (a part of the American Federation of Labor) during the brutal 1936 strike, *The Grapes of Wrath* was seen as only hostile—and in terms of class, since the wealthy bought more books than the poor, the California market for Steinbeck's novel was surprisingly small. Most reviewers agreed that the book was an accurate picture of the California wars, and Rich Wartzman pointed out that some scenes from the novel were taken almost directly from those weekly reports written by Tom Collins serving as head manager of "Weedpatch" (Wartzman 82).[4]

Steinbeck dedicated the novel he understood to be his greatest fiction "To Carol, who willed it/To Tom, who lived it." During the five months of his actual writing—a herculean accomplishment, with Carol doing all the typing, editing, and revising as she managed to keep up with his daily production—Steinbeck continued to draw on those weekly and bi-weekly reports that Collins had made available to him during the earlier years of his research.

Wartzman agrees with British critic David Seed that a formative influence on Steinbeck's novel was the film achievement of Pare Lorentz, especially in his films *The Plow That Broke the Plains* (1936) and *The River* (1938). (Seed notes that there is some indication that *The Grapes of Wrath* might have been intended to be a "photo-text.") When Steinbeck and Lorentz met in 1938, followed by Steinbeck's trip to Hollywood traveling as a friend of Lorentz's, their similarities were obvious—they believed in the value of the picture, the photo, the film (often *sans* language), and they believed in honoring the human being at his or her most unpretentious.[5] Seed contends that Steinbeck "became a verbal camera" (Seed 194).

As William Howarth describes particularly the latter sections of *The Grapes of Wrath*, the novel works "through an intricate course of narrative 'shots,' from opening wide-angle panoramas of sea, air, and land to a tracking montage that follows the floodwaters' descent.... At the river bottom, these visual effects swiftly change from motion to contrast, an effect achieved by cross-cutting between the flood and the Joad family." Commenting on the final scenes, Howarth states that Steinbeck's narration worked in "two focal planes. The tree parallels the delivery of the baby" (Howarth 56–57).

Assessing Steinbeck's earlier journalistic writing about the migrant laborers in California, Howarth emphasizes that writing about the migrants was particularly difficult because "they were transitional and wary of strangers." Steinbeck's ability to live their lives with them was undoubtedly an asset—that and his recognition that he could not mix fantasy into their already deplorable situations. It is Howarth who mentions that Steinbeck added an epilogue, dated *Spring—1938*, to the *News* articles when they were published as *Their Blood Is Strong*. Here he described the migrants' experiences in the Visalia flood:

> And then in the rains, with insufficient food, the children develop colds because the ground in the tents is wet.... I talked to a girl with a baby and offered her a cigarette. She took two puffs and vomited in the street. She was ashamed. She shouldn't have tried to smoke, she said, for she hadn't eaten in two days. I heard a man whimpering that the baby was sucking but nothing came out of the breast.... Must the hunger become anger and the anger fury before anything will be done? (Howarth 81, note 4)

David Seed credits Lorentz's film *The Plow That Broke the Plains* with an almost direct influence on Steinbeck's *The Grapes of Wrath*, both in its stark treatment of the country and in its carefully selected language. (Seed contends that the land *is* "itself the protagonist.") The narration opens with the words, "This is a recording of land... of soil, rather than people, but of course it is a recording of the impact of the land on the fortunes of the inhabitants"[6] (Seed 194–95).

Disregarding the pro-California reviewing that seemed—at least at first—to dominate public response to *The Grapes of Wrath*, one must focus on the twenty-first-century reception, which speaks of this universally acclaimed novel always in positive terms. Richard Gray, for example, touts the "sheer sweep of Steinbeck's prose," calling the novel an apt successor to Stowe's *Uncle Tom's Cabin* in that its message demanded that "things should and could change" (Gray 226). Similarly, Janet Galligani Casey says that Steinbeck's novel "was arguably the century's most influential arbiter of Depression iconography and broadly leftist sentiment" (Casey xi–xii). She breaks down its appeal for readers then and today by explaining that the

Joads remain effective because Steinbeck draws upon "an interlocking set of assumptions and images through which the open landscape, an agrarian (and highly gendered) social system, and the notion of 'Americanness' had been compellingly conflated" (ibid. 96).

Her analysis parallels that of cultural critic Gordon Hutner, who sees the novel's appeal as resting on "several preoccupations of domestic American fiction—labor relations, regionalism, the family, public life, and, perhaps least well understood, the era's crisis of masculinism. So complete is that debt that Steinbeck's novel came to represent the fulfillment of thirties social realism, even as it emerged as a modern classic. In exposing the political and economic frameworks of the misery that migrant workers endured, *The Grapes of Wrath* immediately won recognition for its power of sympathy, its urgency" (Hutner 192). Given the *oeuvre* of what Hutner calls "middle-class fiction," he would place Steinbeck's novel in the midst of that category, rather than in any subversive political or economic grouping.

John Seelye would agree. He discounts the monolithic reputation of *The Grapes of Wrath* as being the migrant workers' novel and instead reads the book as "a tragedy centered in the breakup of a family because of bewildering changes in agricultural practices.... it is, moreover, a demonstration of inevitability that makes any kind of government palliative futile" (Seelye "Introduction" xiii).

Whatever Steinbeck's reasons for finishing the lengthy novel that would become *The Grapes of Wrath* in such a short period of time, he kept Covici fully apprised of what was happening. (The firm of Covici-Friede had gone bankrupt, but Covici had taken a position with Viking as senior editor; Steinbeck's work would follow him there.) As Shillinglaw pointed out, Viking allotted its largest advertising budget ever to the publicity campaign for *The Grapes of Wrath* (Shillinglaw *Carol* 1). In September 1938, Steinbeck had sent Covici the title, which Carol had suggested to him after hearing the way Pare Lorentz used the hymn in a radio broadcast. Steinbeck explained later that he liked the title "because it is a march, because it is in our own revolutionary tradition and because in reference to this book it has a large meaning. And I like it because people know the Battle Hymn who don't know the Stars and Stripes" (*Conversations* 39).

Even at that time Steinbeck worried, saying "I can't tell whether it is balanced. It is a slow plodding book but I don't think that it is dull" (ibid.).

Concerned about the language Steinbeck had used throughout the novel—based on what some reviewers might consider common vulgarity, irregular grammar, and his bleak choice of words—Elizabeth Otis had come to California to help him make the substitutions and cuts she thought would be necessary. She knew enough to accept what Steinbeck was willing to do; the book was sent to press soon after the Christmas holidays. There was a more significant battle with Covici over the scene of Rose of Sharon feeding the stranger, but Steinbeck held out for keeping that scene intact: he wrote,

> I am sorry but I cannot change that ending. It *is* casual—there is no fruity climax, it is not more important than any other part of the book—if there is a symbol, it is a survival symbol not a love symbol, it must be an accident, it must be a stranger, and it must be quick. To build this stranger into the structure of the book would be to warp the whole meaning of the book. The fact that the Joads don't know him, don't care about him, have no ties to him—that is the emphasis. The giving of the breast has no more sentiment than the giving of a piece of bread. I'm sorry if that doesn't get over. It will maybe. I've been on this design and balance for a long time and I think I know how I want it. (*SLL* 178)

Admitting that he is usually more cooperative about suggestions, Steinbeck continued, "I have too many thousands of hours on this book, every incident has been too carefully chosen and its weight judged and fitted. The balance is there. One other thing—I am not writing a *satisfying* story. I've done my damndest to rip a reader's nerves to rags, I don't want him satisfied.... And still one more thing—I tried to write this book the way lives are being lived not the way books are written" (*SLL* 178).

Steinbeck had fallen ill immediately after the novel was finished—with extreme pain in his sciatic nerve attributed to a dental problem, he walked like a crippled person for much of 1939. Later he explained that he had slipped a disc and an osteopath had corrected the problem. Whatever the causes, he was not well, despite the fact that the novel was set for publication early in April. (Steinbeck got his advance copies on March 31, 1939.) Reviews were immediate, and positive. As Steinbeck wrote to Carl Wilhelmson, "this book was a terrible amount of work. Never worked so hard in my life nor so long before. And I found something I didn't know about and that is exhaustion. I never thought I could get that way. But I found I could" (*SLL* 183–84).

Attributing part of Steinbeck's exhaustion to the post-publication furor, Benson remarked that the author's state of mind came through clearest in his letters to Elizabeth Otis. For example, on June 22, 1939 he wrote,

This whole thing is getting me down and I don't know what to do about it. The telephone never stops ringing, telegrams all the time, fifty to seventy-five letters a day all wanting something. People who won't take no for an answer sending books to be signed. I don't know what to do.... Something has to be worked out or I am finished writing. I went south to work and I came back to find Carol just about hysterical. She had just been pushed beyond endurance. (*SLL* 185)

The novel sold to Hollywood for $75,000, even as the films of *In Dubious Battle* and *Tortilla Flat* were in production. Late in 1938, Viking had published Steinbeck's important collection of short stories (*The Long Valley*, which included many of his best fictions), following the Covici-Friede limited-edition printing in 1937 of the three-part *The Red Pony*. In the fall of 1938, the Steinbecks purchased the 47-acre ranch outside Los Gatos (the "Old Biddle Ranch") and began building a new house. But with the appearance of *The Grapes of Wrath*, which quickly became Number One on the *New York Times* Best Seller list, Steinbeck could hardly think about working—either on the house or on his fiction. The book was banned in Buffalo, East St. Louis, and Kern County, California; it was denounced in Congress by Oklahoma representative Lyle Boren; and it became the subject of a protest meeting at the Palace Hotel in San Francisco. Herb Hinrichs, Steinbeck's high school friend, said unequivocally, "John told the absolute truth about the migrant workers. The old timers used to say 'Don't talk to Steinbeck.' He rattled too many skeletons..." (Hinrichs in Lynch 39).

The Grapes of Wrath was no sooner published than Steinbeck made good on his promise to Lorentz that he would work with him on his next film project. It was to be a movie about public health which would swing public opinion toward a comprehensive health bill which President Roosevelt wanted Congress to pass. Based on Paul de Kruif's book *The Fight for Life*, the film, with the same title, would script the dangers of childbirth. Steinbeck traveled to Chicago because the filming would occur at the Chicago Maternity Center; he was there several weeks. In June he traveled to Hollywood for another filming interval, staying nearly a month. Whether or not Steinbeck learned much about making films, he found in this work that he wanted once again to see more of Ed Ricketts. His brain was becoming involved once more with the science of the sea. In Benson's words, "the study of science became a sort of sea anchor with which he tried to ride out the storm and maintain some kind of stability" (Benson 401).

Shillinglaw traced the breakup of the marriage to Carol to the explosive stresses of writing *The Grapes of Wrath*. Despite the couple's "creative synergy," they could not survive the extreme duress of finishing that project—especially since the book's publication then let loose so much more invasive, constant work. This biographer said that "John left Carol, first emotionally, then sexually, and then through his writing" (Shillinglaw *Carol* 3). In Carol's place, Steinbeck turned to what seemed to be a casual dalliance with Hollywood singer Gwyn Conger. More permanently, he returned to the cohesive friendship he had once experienced with Ed Ricketts: "For John, Ed was a soul mate—John's philosophical friend" (Shillinglaw *Carol* 94).

Taking a harsher view, Rich Wartzman concluded,

> For a long time—before John and Carol began boozing it up too much; before...Joseph Campbell...; before he [Steinbeck] started having an affair with a long-legged band singer, eighteen years his junior, in LA; before all the hangers-on were intruding into their lives; before the fighting got too bad; before she had gotten pregnant and he insisted she have an abortion; before an abject loneliness had set in for both of them—they were happy. Broke, but happy. (Wartzman 71)

The often-erratic personalities of each partner had taken heavy tolls. On October 18, 1941, Steinbeck wrote to Toby Street, "Thank you, Toby, for everything. I know I'm socially wrong—the wife deserter and cad—but I suddenly gave up. I tried for thirteen years, did everything I could and failed. Maybe a better man than I could succeed. I wasn't good enough..." (*SLL* 234).

Carol and John did not divorce until 1943. During the time from the publication of *The Grapes of Wrath*, which won the Pulitzer Prize for Fiction as well as the National Book Award in the spring of 1940— during the months when the film made from the novel opened in theaters around the world and was nominated for seven Academy Awards—through the publication of Steinbeck and Ricketts' *The Sea of Cortez* in 1941, and of Steinbeck's *The Forgotten Village, The Moon Is Down, Bombs Away: The Story of a Bomber Team, A Medal for Benny*, and *Lifeboat*, the United States went to war. Accredited as a war correspondent for the New York *Herald Tribune*, Steinbeck saw more military action than he wanted, and returned home with burst eardrums, partial amnesia, and fatigue.

NOTES

1. He frequently wrote about his field experiences: "The death of children in our valleys is simply staggering..." (*Conversations* 38).
2. George Jean Nathan sent Steinbeck the plaque. *Of Mice and Men* had been given the award over *Our Town, Golden Boy, Prologue to Glory*—any one of which would have been a likely recipient. The award expressed the judges' appreciation of "the direct force and perception in handling a theme genuinely rooted in American life" and complimented Steinbeck "for his refusal to make this study of tragical loneliness and frustration either cheap or sensational" (Lisca 143).
3. In one of Shillinglaw's talks, she quoted from Steinbeck's reply to a college student who had asked about the alternating chapters. She agreed with the student that both "pace" and "counterpoint" were important, but then quoted Steinbeck's reply: "the basic purpose was to hit the reader below the belt with the rhythms and symbols of poetry. One can get into a reader, open him up, and while he's open, introduce things on an intellectual level which he would not or could not receive unless he were opened up" (Shillinglaw "Wrath" 159).
4. Steinbeck later wrote an essay about Collins, naming him "Windsor Drake," stressing his great attention to human values, his management style that revered the people who found refuge in his camps. In Steinbeck's words, the two men "traveled together, sat in the ditches with the migrant workers, lived and ate with them. We heard a thousand miseries and a thousand jokes. We ate fried dough and sow belly, worked with the sick and the hungry, listened to complaints and little triumphs" (Steinbeck *Nonfiction* 216).
5. Benson quotes Steinbeck saying that, rather than Lorentz's films, a more direct influence on *The Grapes of Wrath* was probably John Dos Passos' achievements in his *USA* novels (Benson 399).
6. Seed attributes the alternation between the general and the particular as well, so dominant in *The Grapes of Wrath*, to Lorentz's technique in his film of moving between "stasis and movement, settlement and civilization, peace and war" (Seed 195–96).

CHAPTER 5

The Sea of Cortez: A Leisurely Journal of Travel and Research

Richard Astro makes the point that Steinbeck's interest in the sea and its life systems did not originate with his friendship with Ed Ricketts. During one of his last summers at Stanford, Steinbeck had classes at the Hopkins Marine Station near Pacific Grove, taking a general zoology course from C. V. Taylor. Taylor had been a pupil of Charles Kofoid at the University of California, Berkeley, and both men were devoted to William Emerson Ritter, whose doctrine of the organismal conception of life influenced much teaching of biology at the time. Astro quotes from Ritter: "In all parts of nature and in nature itself as one gigantic whole, wholes are so related to their parts that not only does the existence of the whole depend upon the orderly cooperation and interdependence of the parts, but the whole exercises a measure of determinative control over its parts" (Astro *Steinbeck* 81).

This same critic aligns Ricketts' primary belief system, which he developed at the University of Chicago with W. C. Allee, with Ritter's idea "that the whole is more than the sum of its parts and that these parts arise from a differentiation of the whole," seeing similarities as well as differences. Years later, by the time Steinbeck and Ricketts were considering writing a book together, they had spent nearly a decade in conversation—some of it testy—to sort through their philosophical bases. It was clear that both Steinbeck and Ricketts believed in formal study as well as empirical observation. As Steinbeck wrote in his "Foreword" to a reprinting of Ricketts' book *Between Pacific Tides*, "The greatest human experience [is] that of observation to speculation to hypothesis. This is a creative process, probably the highest and most satisfactory we know" (Steinbeck "Foreword" vi). As biographer Jackson Benson emphasized throughout his work, the major occupation of Steinbeck's life, besides his writing, was learning. In this regard, Ed Ricketts was a terrifically influential friend. He got both the Steinbecks involved in "the day-to-day work of his lab and in the specifics of science.... Steinbeck received a fairly extensive course in practical zoology" (Benson 251–52).

In Steinbeck's friendship with Ricketts lay the foundations of their cooperative learning. Together, they studied the ocean life that bordered their coastal existences. As Steinbeck wrote in his introduction to *The Sea of Cortez*, emphasizing their cooperative thinking about their discoveries of the natural world,

> "We have a book to write about the Gulf of California.... We have decided to let it form itself: its boundaries a boat and a sea; its duration a six-weeks charter time; its subject everything we could see and think and even imagine."
>
> Focusing factually on "the marine invertebrates of the littoral," Steinbeck worked hard to bring excruciating detail to this "expedition" of the Ricketts–Steinbeck fusion of maritime knowledge within an envelope of several strands of Western philosophy. (*Sea* 751)

It was Thomas French, studying Steinbeck's relationship with his editor and publisher Pascal Covici, who commented accurately that "Ricketts was in many ways as important for John Steinbeck as was Pascal Covici," in that Ricketts early on "helped Steinbeck crystalize his 'non-teleological' thinking" (French 10).

Astro also commented that many of Steinbeck's more unusual characters in his fiction were illustrative of Allee's beliefs that animal behavior changed from living in isolation to participating in groups. Ricketts described his intertidal study as working with "the good, kind, sane little animals," the marine invertebrates of the Central California coast, that themselves took on human characteristics (Astro "Introduction" xi–xiii).

Steinbeck's primary motivation in undertaking the 4000-mile journey to the Sea of Cortez between the Mexican and California coasts may have been escaping from the inferno of publicity that *The Grapes of Wrath* had ignited. He admitted that he needed to bring his mind under control, focusing on new and interesting work; he had to literally shed the vestiges of his knowledge about the migrant workers. While Carol was encouraged to come along—ostensibly as cook, but more regularly as the woman on board given to storms of pique and anger, and finally as just another crew member—no one saw the six-week expedition as a reconciliation trip for the Steinbecks.

Both Steinbeck and Ricketts were planning another *Beagle* voyage, modestly similar to the trip Charles Darwin had executed to the Galapagos archipelago. In the words of critic Brian Railsback, who traced much of *The Sea of Cortez* to Darwinian roots, "*The Origin of Species* illustrates the kind of process Ricketts and Steinbeck made an ideal: it shows a man's attempt to find truth by abandoning popular beliefs, making observations firsthand, gathering the facts together, and making the inductive leap to discover a great principle." In this observer's comparison, Darwin's *Origin* is an example of Ricketts' *is* thinking (Railsback *Environmental* 131).

For Stanley Brodwin, *The Sea of Cortez* is a beginning rather than a copy of another work. Brodwin describes *Sea* as a unique design, saying that it "transcends simple narrative descriptions by forming hypotheses and speculating on their relationship to broad natural functions." Steinbeck "recaptures the poetry in scientific thinking" even as he sees "the hypothesis as a work of art 'beautiful and whole' in its own right" (Brodwin *Environmental* 142).

It is good to have these positive assessments. When the reader begins *The Sea of Cortez*, what Steinbeck emphasized from the start was the planning, assembling the supplies and the crew, equipping the *Western Flyer*. (It was, after all, his money, as it was his dream of becoming a genuine scientist.) He paid close attention to all the details. As he described their collecting equipment in the first chapter of *The Sea of Cortez*,

> Shovels, wrecking-and-abalone-bars, nets, long-handled dip-nets, wooden fish-kits, and a number of seven-cell flashlights for night collection.... Containers.... Wooden fish-kits with heads; twenty-hard-fir barrels with galvanized hoops in fifteen—and thirty—gallon sizes; cases of gallon jars, quart, pint, eight-ounce, five-ounce, and two-ounce screw-cap jars, several gross of corked vials in four chief sizes. (*Log* 11)

More importantly, as Steinbeck was later to write in his essay "About Ed Ricketts," "Very many conclusions, Ed and I worked out together through endless discussion and reading and observation and experiment. We worked together, and so closely that I do not now know in some cases who started which line of speculation since the end thought was the product of both minds. I do not know whose thought it was."[1] In a later section of reminiscence, Steinbeck continued,

> We worked and thought together very closely for a number of years so that I grew to depend on his knowledge and on his patience in research. And then I went away to another part of the country but it didn't make any difference. Once a week or once a month would come a fine long letter so much in the style of his speech that I could hear his voice over the neat page full of small elite type. (*Log* 263)

Frederick Feied described *The Sea of Cortez* as a book that "summed up and gave philosophical finish to ideas" shared by Ricketts and Steinbeck. In Steinbeck's mind, it was never to be a "break" from his Depression novels—*In Dubious Battle* and *The Grapes of Wrath*—but was rather an integral part of the "cycle of work that has been biting me for many years" (Feied 12). Steinbeck thought in such terms—seeing all his work, fiction or non-fiction, journalism or philosophy, as "work" proper—throughout his career. It differed little from the kind of intensity the three friends had experienced in 1932, that miraculous year—in Campbell's words, "an Earthly Paradise"—when Joseph Campbell had joined the Pacific Grove culture. Because Campbell and Ricketts had remained friends, after Ed sent Joe a copy of *The Sea of Cortez*, Campbell responded with his former eagerness:

> I think that the book form discovered by you and John is perhaps as close to the life form itself as [a] book could possibly be to life. The on-and-on carelessness of the first two hundred pages, with the cans of beer and the vague chewing the fat; and then, emerging out of all this, the great solid realization of "non-teleological thinking": and then again, the moment just before the entering of Gueyamas, when a realization of two realistic worlds, in the most moving way presenting itself; gradually, meanwhile, the dominant theme of the work is emerging, and from this remark and from that, we understand that society itself is an organism that these little intertidal societies and the great human societies are manifestations of common principless.

As if he contributes the third and relatively fused voice in an ongoing discussion, Campbell—who had not yet published any of the "hero" work which would bring him worldwide attention—continues their conjoined thought: he writes "more than that: we understand that the little and the great societies are themselves units in a sublime, all inclusive organism, which breathes and goes on, in dream-like half consciousness of its own life-processes, oxidizing its own substance yet sustaining its wonderful form" (Shillinglaw *Environment* 12–13, from Campbell December 26, 1941, Stanford University archives, and see Campbell *Fire* 172).

There is an ebullience in this reaction that typifies that excitedly rapt conversation people remember about the men's interactions (sometimes as a twosome, sometimes as a threesome, usually during the late afternoon and evening and days-on-end parties). In Audry Lynch's book of oral interviews, for example, several people claim that no parties then or later came close to the excitement of those in the early 1930s, usually in Ed Ricketts' lab. Ruth Duval remembered feeling "like I was in fairyland. There was lots of good conversation. They'd talk about all sorts of things. They had a great idea.... I was just happy to be around all that creativity" (Duval in Lynch 63). She also saw Steinbeck as the center of the discourse: "They all looked up to Steinbeck. He was the one who made things happen.... At the parties he always seemed like the person in charge."

The Lynch interviews also provide information about the *Western Flyer* trip on which *The Sea of Cortez* is based. Flora Woods (later Dora Flood) recalled that her husband Tex, who crewed on the expedition, called it "the trip of a lifetime." He and Steinbeck "often shared wheel watches, when they would talk for hours on end." Had the war not begun, they were planning to buy a boat together (Woods in Lynch 80, 83).

Both Parini and Benson confirm that Steinbeck had placed a lot of faith in the fact that the expedition, with Ricketts, would bring sanity to his future. Benson explained that this was a trip Steinbeck had to make for himself. He was sober; he saw all its implications. "He needed to bring his life and work back into focus." In doing so, "he was fulfilling a pattern established in recent years of obtaining material for writing on the basis of the observations of a field trip.... It led to the objective sort of writing he was most comfortable with" (Benson 439).

Given that *The Sea of Cortez*, while published in 1941, took on an extended life when it appeared in 1951 as *The Log from the Sea of Cortez*, Steinbeck's pride in his and Ricketts' accomplishment was not feigned. Because Pascal Covici seemed unaware of the centrality of this philosophical/scientific treatise to everything else that Steinbeck wrote, he kept denigrating the co-authorship; Steinbeck had to fight hard to have Ricketts listed as co-author.

In the words of Wes Tiffney, the book was unique in that Ricketts and Steinbeck "were pioneer ecological thinkers." He considered both men "advanced early ecologists, not only evaluating organisms in relation to the physical environment, but also considering living populations, including man, in relation to each other" (Tiffney 4). Benson adds that the exploration yielded at least thirty-five new species (Benson 482). For Stanley Brodwin, who viewed *The Sea of Cortez* as an important scientific travel narrative, "The goal of the quest into the Sea of Cortez and its world was somehow to test and explore these assumptions in scientific collection, encounters with nonindustrial cultures, and metaphysical hypothesizing." He found that Steinbeck and Ricketts had provided "an imaginative poetic theology," reminding readers that "the two modes of creation, the scientific and the artistic, spring from the same deep source" (Brodwin 158, 160).

The trip itself ran only from March 11, 1940, through the *Western Flyer*'s return docking in Monterey on April 20, 1940. For all the hard physical work of the collecting and processing, Steinbeck wrote to Elizabeth Otis that, on his return, "I have more of a sense of peace than I have ever had."

There are long passages of prose that reflect this stasis. (Although Steinbeck was using Ricketts' journal as the basis for his account, the language and the tone were entirely that of the observer who was often less than scientifically objective.) When the boat came to Cape San Lucas, for instance, Steinbeck's narrative voice is both thrilled and thrilling:

> The exposed rocks had looked rich with life under the lowering tide, but they were more than that: they were ferocious with life. There was an exuberant fierceness in the littoral here, a vital competition for existence.
>
> Everything seemed speeded-up; starfish and urchins were more strongly attached than in other places, and many of the univalves were so tightly fixed that the shells broke before the animals would let go their hold. (*Sea* 49)

At times, Steinbeck recounted experiences with an eye to providing humor for readers. Here he described their extensive collecting in the inner bay of Puerto Escondido, a location

> incredibly rich in fauna. Here, where the water rushes in and out, bringing with it food and freshness, there was a remarkable gathering. Beautiful red and green clusters of a solitary soft coral-like form in great knobs and

heads.... Caught against the rocks by the current was a very large pelagic coelenterate, in appearance like an anemone with long orange-pink tentacles, apparently not retractable. On picking him up we were badly stung. (*Sea* 141)

Steinbeck added a caveat to that story, "So very many things are poisonous and hurtful in these Gulf waters: urchins, sting-rays, morays, heart-urchins.... One becomes very timid after a while" (ibid.).

Much of the narrative has to do with locations, and with the simple chronology of leaving and arriving. Chapter Thirteen opens,

> We sailed in the morning. The mustached old pilot came aboard and steered us out, then bowed deeply and stepped into the launch which had followed us. The sea was calm and very blue, almost black-blue, as we turned northward along the coast. We wished to stop near San Jose Island as our next collecting station. It was good to be under way again and good to be out from under the steady eyes of those ubiquitous little boys who waited interminably for us to do something amusing. (*Sea* 106)

Years later, novelist Jim Harrison spoke to the power of *The Sea of Cortez*, saying that he "was amazed at [Steinbeck's] knowledge of the natural world, to which I must add his broad knowledge of the world at large that far surpassed his fellow writers at the time. Steinbeck never seemed to use characters as tools to prove a point as did Dos Passos and Hemingway" (Harrison *Centennial* 39–40). Novelist Russell Banks echoed this respect, saying that in some ways he wrote *Continental Drift* "to enter into a dialogue with Steinbeck... to test his insights and understanding against the social and economic realities of a different time" (Banks *Centennial* 7). In the annals of literary history, whatever Steinbeck wrote and published once *The Grapes of Wrath* had won its prizes put Steinbeck at the top of people's reading lists.

In 1941, as *The Sea of Cortez* was published, readers were either dismissive of the book or confused by it, probably assuming *it* would be fiction. In the world of science, however, *The Sea of Cortez* became a model for what Wes Tiffney termed "a fine description of ecological field biology." In this period, the Gulf of California was virtually unknown territory for marine biologists, so the book grew more and more valuable (Tiffney *Environment* 5).

One of the best critical readings of the book occurred in Frederick Feied's study, where he parsed the segments of story to connect philosophy with natural science.

Focusing on the issue of Japanese shrimpers denuding the shrimp beds, Feied began with the opening illustration of what Steinbeck and Ricketts called "is" thinking. Feied began with exposition, noting that the men passed through "various stages of thought... as they attempt to approach or approximate a sense of the whole." Feied's question was whether the Japanese are "committing a true crime against nature and against the immediate welfare of Mexico and the eventual welfare of the whole human species."

The second stage of interrogation that Feied projected onto Ricketts and Steinbeck had them going beyond their human tendency to blame. What can they do to preserve this valuable food source? They propose that the "Mexican Ministry of Marine" should make a "careful study" of the situation, so as not to lose potential food. The aim would be to maintain the supply, keeping it in "balance."

The third level spoke to "a more philosophical nature in which, leaving out their own notions of what ought to be," they tried to predict the long term effects of the Japanese fishermen's acts. They concluded that, using organismal thinking, "to the whole, there is no waste" (Feied 106–07). To emphasize this level, Feied quoted from Steinbeck's assessment in *The Sea of Cortez*:

> In the macrocosm nothing is wasted, the equation always balances.
>
> The elements which the fish elaborated into an individuated physical organism, a microcosm, go back again into the undifferentiated macrocosm which is the great reservoir. There is not, nor can there be, any actual waste, but simply varying forms of energy. To each group, of course, there must be waste—the dead fish to man, the broken pieces to gulls, the bones to some and the scales to others—but to the whole, there is no waste. The great organism, Life, takes it all and uses it all. (*Sea* 263)

As Steinbeck concluded near the end of the narrative, "Life has just one commandment for living things! Survive!" (*Sea* 241). That edict occurred after he had cogently asked,

> What was the shape and size and color and tone of this little expedition?.... This trip had dimensions.... It was a thing whose boundaries seeped through itself and beyond into some time and space that was more than all the Gulf and more than all our lives. Our fingers turned over the stones and we saw life that was like *our* life. (*Sea* 223)

Admitting that this expedition, for all their hard work, was "makeshift" in strictly scientific terms, Steinbeck yet saw the narrative as a way to garner acceptance for Ed Ricketts' ideas (with the help of friends, he had tried to get Ricketts' essays published, but they were written in difficult prose and Ed had not developed an audience). So for the Easter Sunday entry, dated March 24, Steinbeck included much of Ricketts' essay about "is" thinking. (In his Introduction, Astro refers to this section as a "sermon.") The essay restatement concludes,

The whole is necessarily everything, the whole world of fact and fancy, body and psyche, physical fact and spiritual truth, individual and collective, life and death, macrocosm and microcosm... conscious and unconscious, subject and object. The whole picture is portrayed by *is*, the deepest word of deep ultimate reality, not shallow or partial as *reasons* are, but deeper and participating, possibly encompassing the Oriental concept of *being*. (*Sea* 125)

Throughout *The Sea of Cortez*, Steinbeck mentioned the people of Mexico—clearly, part of his interest in the expedition to the Sea of Cortez hinged on his ongoing fascination with Mexico. In one passage, for example, he challenged the trite belief that "Mexicans are contented, happy people." Steinbeck's conclusion to his inquiry is that an observer understands that "the channels of their happiness or unhappiness are different from ours, just as we know that their time sense is different" (*Sea* 81, 83). Soon after returning to Monterey, Steinbeck went back to Mexico with filmmaker Herb Klein, beginning to work toward the documentary film already scripted called *The Forgotten Village*. A testimony to the efficacy of progressive thought in even a small Mexican village, the well-received film followed the bravery of a young Mexican boy as he searched for—and found—good medical help available through the Rural Health Service. Juan Diego has watched his brother die, and his sister become ill, even as the village witch doctor is ineffectual. The microbial virus in their water supply will soon sicken everyone.

More conclusive than Steinbeck often was, the message in *The Forgotten Village*, according to Jackson Benson, was that science must be utilized to save lives. Becoming a "propagandist for science," "here, in regard to health, the situation seems clear: science and education are the way out of disease and the pain of grinding poverty" (Benson 237–38).

This last foray to Mexico helped establish Steinbeck as a writer conversant with Mexicans and Mexico, a possible filmmaker as well as a novelist and a science writer, and, probably most important, a man still furiously curious about the life that surrounded him.

NOTE

1. Within the primary text of *The Sea of Cortez*, Steinbeck at times included extensive passages from Ricketts' two unpublished essays, "The Philosophy of Breaking Through" and "A Spiritual Morphology of Poetry" (Astro "Introduction" xxv).

CHAPTER 6

World War II

Steinbeck never wrote the great American novel of World War II, nor had he planned to do so. What he did do, immediately after leaving from a June trip back to Mexico, was travel to Washington, DC to suggest to President Roosevelt that he establish an Office of War Information, to begin countering the Nazi propaganda already being generated. In Steinbeck's opinion, such Fascist influence was especially effective in Central and South America.

Steinbeck's life for the next several years was frantic and, accordingly, the writer himself was irascible and frustrated. To begin with, *The Forgotten Village*—from the earliest days of fund raising through filming to the later stages of arranging distribution and countering censorship—was an enormous amount of work. Simple as the process had seemed when he observed Pare Lorentz making his films, Steinbeck did not have an experienced crew of any kind—and his funds were limited. During the years 1940 and 1941, to illustrate this stressful existence that stemmed from the completion of the six-week Ricketts–Steinbeck trip to the California Baja peninsula, Steinbeck faced writing that entire narrative. It was in itself a daunting task.

He had, however, also begun other projects that demanded his attention. He had promised to script what would be the film of *The Red Pony*. (Late in 1939, both the films of *Of Mice and Men* and *The Grapes of Wrath* opened in Hollywood and New York—*Of Mice* on December 22, 1939 in Hollywood and two months later in New York, *The Grapes of Wrath* on

January 24, 1940. Such openings were themselves frenetic, especially because the Sea of Cortez expedition was planning to leave in March 1940.) All of Steinbeck's books were being sold, and in some cases resold, for films that would plausibly continue to be box-office hits. The pressure on him to develop a screenplay for *The Red Pony* was a part of that hysteria; it was also a favor to the same director, Lewis Milestone, who had done such great work on the film of *Of Mice and Men*.

Difficult to sort through the commitments that had to be slated for work, Steinbeck moved erratically through various lists. He took some flying lessons during the fall of 1940. But that September he once again visited FDR, leaning on him to consider building a legitimate propaganda office, one that would aim to create pro-United States sentiment in the Western hemisphere. Had Steinbeck been privy to the FBI files, he would have realized that Roosevelt had little choice about putting *him* in charge of anything connected with government. From the time *In Dubious Battle* was published, the Steinbeck file grew and grew. When he was one of the sponsors of the Western Writers Congress, held in San Francisco during November of 1936, he had entered the FBI's sights. Whereas Steinbeck did not go to Spain, he did support the rebels during the Spanish Civil War. He had written for the publication *Writers Take Sides*. He was considered "Red" in both *In Dubious Battle* and *The Grapes of Wrath*, so even if his comments (as in *Writers Take Sides*) were meant to be ironic, government investigators would read them "straight."[1]

Early in spring 1941, Steinbeck bought a modest house on Eardley Street in Monterey. He then confessed to Carol about his affair with Gwyn, and moved out. Later that spring Gwyn moved to Monterey to live with him. *The Forgotten Village*, with stills from the film, was published as a book in May. And Steinbeck wrote and wrote—all of *The Sea of Cortez* narrative, a complete screenplay for *The Red Pony*, and a number of radio speeches for the Foreign Information Services, the agency directed by Robert E. Sherwood. He also helped with the screenplay for the film of *Tortilla Flat*, abandoned the idea of scripting a musical (*The God in the Pipes*), and wrote the novella, complete with film script, for his first war fiction, *The Moon Is Down*. He considered *The Moon Is Down* his second "play-novella" and paired it technically with *Of Mice and Men*.

By March 1942, Viking realized that it had another best-seller in press. *The Moon Is Down* was chosen as a Book-of-the-Month selection, and advance sales were twice what they had been for *The Grapes of Wrath*. After it had been in print less than six months, *The Moon Is Down* had sold half a million copies. Later it would sell to Hollywood for $300,000, twice as much as Hemingway's *For Whom the Bell Tolls* a few years earlier and the highest price ever paid for a novel. Roy Simmonds explained that *The Moon Is Down*, originally titled *The New Order*, "served its purpose during the war by extolling the courage of the patriots in the occupied countries of Europe and by helping to comfort and inspire those members of the Resistance fortunate enough to read clandestine copies of the book circulating under the noses of the Germans" (Simmonds 296).

Capturing the mood of the times, drawing readers in to the European conflagration even though the United States had barely declared war on Japan and the Nazi powers after Pearl Harbor, *The Moon Is Down* was an even greater success as a play than as a novella. Steinbeck had written the text so that stage directions and camera angles were already in place. At only 30,000 words, the slim book by its very appearance gave off a sense of urgency: tightly crafted, with characters who were almost undifferentiated, *The Moon Is Down* took on features of an Everyman production.

Reviewers disagreed about the novella's effectiveness: James Thurber referred to it as "Mr. Steinbeck's gentle fable of War in Wonderland" (*New Republic* 1942), even though John Chamberlain defended the way Steinbeck wrote this marvel of Allied propaganda (*New York Times* 1942). The book seemed to be written in pastel colors: executions and murders were all off-stage, few voices were raised. Yet *The Moon Is Down* was translated into countless languages and smuggled into all the occupied countries. German forces executed people who had copies of the forbidden book. Steinbeck later wrote, "The Germans did not consider [the work] unrealistic optimism. They made it a capital crime to possess it, and sadly to my knowledge this sentence was carried out a number of times. It seemed that the closer it got to action, the less romantic it seemed" (Steinbeck "Lunar"). In November 1946, the author was invited to Oslo, Norway, where "he was awarded the Haakon VII Cross for the account he had given of Norwegian resistance." (Simmonds' view of this presentation—to which Steinbeck traveled—was that the event was memorable. The cross had never before been given to anyone who was not a soldier; Simmonds 117)

The Moon Is Down would have been less compelling had Steinbeck written it later in the war. Part of the work's effectiveness is the confounding naivete of the common people of Norway (they allow their town to be occupied during one morning; it takes only a few hours for the Germans to "conquer" the town). Six of their twelve soldiers are shot and killed immediately; three others are injured. The remaining three desert.

This single conflict occurs early in the novella. It is presented without authorial commentary.

The deaths and executions that happen later in the occupation are given more attention; they come as the result of planning, even if the plan is only Molly's putting her sharp scissors inside her bodice before opening the door to the German officer. They also occur with more and more frequency because the villagers learn fast: they know how to take a life, how to place dynamite effectively, how to disappear to England themselves.

The action of the novella is consistently subdued; yet, with effective dramatic irony, its very peacefulness grows more and more ominous. The early snowfall underscores the town's very lack of normalcy. Part of the work's sense of hesitation comes from the mayor's speech patterns. He says more about the coming snow than he does about the German occupation. When he must contradict the officious German colonel, he does so in language that resonates with the common sentiments. Early on, the mayor explains to the man now living in his house as his superior officer, "The people don't like to be conquered, sir, and so they will not be."[2] When the mayor does speak, usually to his close friend Dr. Winter, his understated opinions are clear. He knows he will die at the hands of these conquerors. All he can do while he still has life is to spirit away the deserters, or those who will be executed for their acts against the Germans.

Mayor Orden tells the two brothers who are fleeing (their third brother has been executed by the Germans a few hours earlier), "Doctor Winter and I have tried to think—there's so much talk about justice, injustice, conquest. Our people are invaded, but I don't think they're conquered." Progressing on from that seemingly long-delayed statement, Orden then suggests that, if they were armed, the townspeople could resist more effectively. This is a scene that reverses the action of the novella:

> Orden began slowly. "I want to speak simply. This is a little town. Justice and injustice are in terms of little things. Your brother's shot and Alex Morden's shot. Revenge against a traitor. The people are angry and they have no way to fight back. But it's all in little terms. It's people against people, not idea against idea."
>
> Winter said, "It's funny for a doctor to think of destruction, but I think all invaded people want to resist. We are disarmed; our spirits and bodies aren't enough. The spirit of a disarmed man sinks." (*Moon* 72)

Urging the brothers to ask for small arms—something that could be dropped by planes—the mayor and the wise doctor put an effective plan into operation. When the blue-wrapped sticks of dynamite, sweetened with pieces of good chocolate, drop during the night, the townspeople carefully hide away their arms. From then on, the mood of the novella switches to emphasize the fearful behavior of the now-paranoid Germans. The occupying forces collapse in upon themselves. That both the mayor and the doctor will die at the end of the narrative does not matter. Success for the occupied people is implied.

Steinbeck wrote this novella/play using only two sets: the peacefully out-of-date "palace" where the mayor and his wife live—a residence taken over by the German invaders, even as the mayor continues to live there— and Molly's sitting room, where readers see her grief over her husband's execution as well as her beginning a plan to kill Germans. No scenes occur outside the dwellings (although shots and explosions are heard). Keeping attention on the actual settings for people's lives, Steinbeck takes what might have been a highly charged discussion of "justice" and brings it into the realm of the everyday.

The movement of *The Moon Is Down* becomes one of waiting. Everything about the snowy village bespeaks normalcy—except that the village no longer belongs to its people. Despite all the sabotage the miners can create inside the mines the Germans are so hungry to control, very little has changed in the town. Except... except there is a continuous threat of violence. As W. H. Frohock pointed out decades ago, Steinbeck was more compassionate than he was angry. Even here, as in *In Dubious Battle*, which Frohock thinks Steinbeck's best work, Jim Nolan's "self-subordinating single-mindedness [becomes] a sort of radical sainthood." Even though there is "violence to spare" in Steinbeck's 1936 strike novel, the reader focuses on the hero and his outcomes (Frohock 136). The point of violence in Steinbeck's fiction is to make sympathetic characters *more* sympathetic, not to destroy them for the sake of shocking readers.

Tensions in *The Moon Is Down* work in the same way. From the first appearance of Mayor Orden, an honorary figure characteristic of a leader for a do-nothing people, readers know he will die. What changes in the course of the narrative is that readers begin to see the occupying Germans as people without confidence: shut off from reliable news from their homeland, isolated within a population that hates them and will strike whenever possible. Steinbeck's harsh focus on the German invaders softens. As Simmonds explains, "the predicament of troops, far from home and their loved ones, who find themselves policing territory inhabited by a resentful and actively antagonistic population" is an unexpected dimension to Steinbeck's narrative tapestry. Even the German Colonel Lanser takes what wisdom there is in Mayor Orden's behavior; by the end of *The Moon Is Down*, he is treating his soldiers with a modicum of understanding.[3]

Like most Americans in 1942, Steinbeck wanted to help win the war. He wanted only to help fight the Axis power and Japan—his suggestions to FDR showed his willingness to work for the United States in any one of several unpaid positions, or simply to volunteer when he was needed. As Lewis Gannett pointed out, the idea for *The Moon Is Down* came from Steinbeck's "long discussions with Colonel William J. Donovan of the Office of Strategic Services, about techniques for aiding resistance movements in the occupied countries of German-held Europe." It also incorporated what he had learned from talking with refugees who had escaped from those occupied countries. Similarly, Steinbeck's other war publication, *Bombs Away: The Story of a Bomber Team*, was suggested by "a number of conversations with General 'Hap' Arnold of the Army Air Forces" (*Conversations* 40, Benson 488). To do research for the latter journalistic book, Steinbeck, with photographer John Swope, visited more than twenty air bases throughout the United States. As usual, he saw this book as the product of thorough investigation. Even this non-fiction book, when released, captured the imagination of the film world; although the movie was never made, a studio paid $250,000 for the film rights.

As Steinbeck worked hard on the news release stories, and on whatever the federal agencies asked him to do, he was watching his married life with Carol end. On March 12, 1942, Carol was given "an interlocutory decree" in Salinas; her divorce from Steinbeck would be valid one year from that day. Her settlement was over $100,000 in bonds and stocks, along with cash in the amount of $111,922 (Simmonds 118). Unfortunately, Steinbeck's living with Gwyn in the Eardley Street house made them privy to all of the hard feelings this settlement had unleashed, so they moved to the east coast a few months later.

Steinbeck's divorce from Carol was final on March 18, 1943; the judge then awarded her another $220,000 property settlement. Steinbeck married Gwyn Conger on March 29 of that year. But because he had become so frustrated with his indeterminate status as a writer for the United States services, he had accepted an offer from the New York *Herald Tribune* to become a war correspondent. Less than two months after his wedding to

Gwyn, he traveled to London on a military troopship. His series of eighty-six dispatches for the newspaper (and for numerous syndicated re-publishings, as well as London papers) ran from June 10 through December 15. This series of war dispatches made Steinbeck one of America's most famous journalists—but it created a disappointing beginning for his married life with Gwyn.

Although Steinbeck had never written systematically or regularly for a newspaper, he had no qualms about wearing a journalist's credentials. He had seen himself as an investigative reporter throughout his work on both the migrant novels and the marine biology treatise *The Sea of Cortez*. As he wrote to the office of the United States Information Services,

> What can I say about journalism? It has the greatest virtue and the greatest evil. It is the first thing the dictator controls. It is the mother of literature and the perpetrator of crap. In many cases it is the only history we have and yet it is the tool of the worst men. But over a long period of time and because it is the product of so many men, it is perhaps the purest thing we have. Honesty has a way of creeping in even when it was not intended. (Howarth 53)

Steinbeck noted that the professional journalists in the war zones seemed to distrust him, but he was not coasting on his comparative fame as a novelist: his assignment for the New York *Herald Tribune* was to write human-interest stories, not to cover "straight news." As he recalled in his Introduction to *Once There Was a War*, a 1958 book that collected many of the dispatches he had written, other reporters "were very kind to me and went out of their way to help me and to instruct me in the things I didn't know. For example, it was [Robert] Capa who gave me the best combat advice I ever heard. It was 'Stay where you are. If they haven't hit you, they haven't seen you'" (Steinbeck *OWW* xvi).

That retrospective introduction gives a sense of the loneliness Steinbeck felt during war. He was a man who often worked collaboratively; sometimes Carol was with him, sometimes Ed Ricketts, sometimes a photographer or a film director. He had not only never been to war, he had seldom ever worked alone. The experience unnerved him, as did the lack of mail from his young second wife. Steinbeck felt very isolated.

He did write his dispatches with dispatch: in fact, he wrote ahead of deadlines, at least at the start of the six-month contract. He sailed on the troopship in early June and his first article ran in the *Herald Tribune* on

June 20. From then on, until the last dispatch appeared on December 15, 1943, Steinbeck was prompt and careful with his writing. As he commented,

> We edited ourselves much more than we were edited. We felt responsible to what was called the home front. There was a general feeling that unless the home front was carefully protected from the whole account of what war was like, it might panic. Also we felt we had to protect the armed services from criticism, or they might retire to their tents to sulk like Achilles. (Steinbeck *OWW* xvii)

Steinbeck's first dispatch made him relatively famous. Titled simply "Troopship," it began with a focus on the young troops, caught in helmets, armed with assorted kinds of rifles:

> The troops in their thousands sit on their equipment on the dock. It is evening, and the first of the dimout lights come on. The men wear their helmets, which make them all look alike, make them look like long rows of mushrooms. Their rifles are leaning against their knees. They have no identity, no personality. The men are units in an army. The numbers chalked on their helmets are almost like the license numbers on robots. Equipment is piled neatly—bedding rolls and half-shelters and barracks bags. Some of the men are armed with Springfield or Enfield rifles from the First World War, some with M-1s, or Garands, and some with the neat, light clever little carbines everyone wants to have after the war for hunting rifles. (Steinbeck *Nonfiction* 282)

In one of his longest pieces, Steinbeck captures the steady movement of groups onto the ship, the process punctuated with voices announcing the "embarkation." The reader feels the immensity of the project, and the presence of literally thousands of men: "The tennis courts on the upper deck are a half-acre of sleeping men now—men, feet, and equipment. MPs are everywhere, on stairs and passages, directing and watching." The last scene Steinbeck draws is the commanding officer and his adjutant, working hard in the staff room, as the dispatch concludes: "The ship remains against the pier and a light breathing sound comes from deep in her. The troops are cut off now and gone from home, although they are not a hundred steps from home..." (ibid. 284). The six dispatches Steinbeck wrote about the troopship crossing were among his strongest; another sequence that was collectively strong was the set of nine pieces about the bomber stations in England. Simmonds observes that all of Steinbeck's articles are of "remarkably high quality," but he finds some difference within the groupings (Simmonds 203).[4]

One of the best of Steinbeck's bomber dispatches was dated July 4, 1943, and described the behavior of the "dogs, most of which are of uncertain or, at least, of ambiguous breed." The crew owned the dogs, and after the bomber had taken off the animals "wander disconsolately about the field. The life has gone out of the bomber station." In the midst of checking the time—knowing that the attack was slated for 9:52 and that the bomber was due back at 12:43—the reporter had little to focus on except the dogs, quietly waiting for the return of their ship. Titled "Waiting," the dispatch included a story of another strike, told ostensibly by the crew before it departs. The reader's attention, however, remained on "A small dog, which might be a gray Scottie if his ears didn't hang down and his tail bend the wrong way." In the midst of what Steinbeck referred to as "the longest set of minutes imaginable," this dog hears his bomber coming. Impossible as it seems, in the midst of several landings, the dog understands which of the ships is his: "The little dog seems hardly to touch the ground. He streaks across the field toward the landed ship. He knows his own ship" (Steinbeck *Nonfiction* 285–87).

In that same thematic grouping, Steinbeck wrote a column that included several important stories. "Stories of the Blitz," dated July 10, 1943, recounted Londoners' tales in the format of oral history. "'It's the glass,' says one man, 'the sound in the morning of the broken glass being swept up, the vicious, flat tinkle.'" Another person Steinbeck interviewed could describe what kind of bomb did which damage to the downtown buildings. Another told of "passing Hyde Park...and going down into the gutter." Still another commented that "People save such strange things. One elderly man lost his whole house by fire. He saved an old rocking chair." Steinbeck's point in the amalgam of narratives was that each of the story tellers used the same ending, "a little simple thing that stays in your mind, a little incident." As he concluded, "The bombing itself grows vague and dreamlike. The little pictures remain as sharp as they were when they were new" (Steinbeck *Nonfiction* 289–90).

Until the battles in Italy, Steinbeck's dispatches rarely included battles. They were more likely to praise the unending energy of entertainer Bob Hope, or the origin of a popular song, or the young girls who served as lookouts on the coast of England, or the waiting bomber crews whose "care of the guns is slow and tender, almost motherly." Once he was assigned to a US invasion force commanded by Douglas Fairbanks, Jr., however, Steinbeck saw action in Palermo, Sicily and on Ventotene off the Italian coast—his physical injuries occurred there. Historian Doug Underwood, in fact, compares Steinbeck's behavior during those weeks with Hemingway's later involvement in war:[5]

> Steinbeck demonstrated the same eagerness to jump into the action. He would wait in the landing boat until there were few witnesses and an extra tommy gun would be brought up so he could carry it. 'John, to his everlasting glory and our ever-lasting respect, would take his foreign correspondent badge off his arm and join in the raid.... We had great admiration for him,' said the boat's commander, Douglas Fairbanks, Jr. (Underwood 154)

By mid-October, however, Steinbeck negotiated a return to the United States. He told the *Herald Tribune* that he would fulfill his contract by writing the last month of dispatches from his notes. (He also refused the offered contract that he go to write about the Pacific front.) In Simmonds' words, "Battered by his near escape from a German bomb on Red Beach, both eardrums broken, he'd had enough of war" (Simmonds 278). Louis Owens agreed, calling Steinbeck's "nervous system shredded, his hearing deadened" (Owens *Re-Vision* 201). Owens quoted Steinbeck's writing to Louis Paul that "People here at home like to think of the war as an heroic thing where nobody gets hurt, whereas it's a dirty thing where everybody gets hurt in one way or another" (ibid. 202).

Months after Steinbeck's return to New York, he wrote to Dook Sheffield that he had finally gotten medical help for his ears. Dated April 12, 1944, his letter described not only his burst eardrums but

> probably little vesicles burst all over my body, in the head and under the skin and in the stomach. He says that in some cases where post mortems have been performed the vesicles even in the marrow of the bones were found to be burst. Anyway it will take from a year to two years for the little clots to absorb and it just has to be weathered. I can hear quite well now so the drums are healing or are healed but the others, the nervousness, dreams, sleeplessness etc. have to take their own time. I took a very bad pasting in Italy but oddly enough was not hit at all. It occurs to me that there are about fifty thousand men who are having the same trouble. There is going to be a frightening amount of it after the war.

NOTES

1. Steinbeck had not learned to be cautious. His brief statement in the 1938 booklet discussed what he termed his being "treasonable enough not to believe in the liberty of a man or a group to exploit, torment, or slaughter other men or groups." How would one read the word "treasonable" for a positive effect? In that same essay, he commented that he believed in "the despotism of human life and happiness against the liberty of money and possessions" (Steinbeck *Nonfiction* 88). Steinbeck's more cheerful news was that their baby was expected in July; that he planned to make a film of *The Pearl* in Mexico; and that he was working now on "a silly book that is fun" [*Cannery Row*] (SLL 268–69). He closed by telling Dook that he was happy to leave "the cosmic foolishness of war" behind, and that he was proud of the fact that *Cannery Row* "never mentions the war" [and] "is a relief to work on" (*SLL* 270).
2. The sonority of the mayor's speech sets a pervasive tone: as Steinbeck told an interviewer in 1947, one pathway into the reader's mind is "the sound of words, in a kind of lulling with syllables" (Steinbeck *Conversations* 44).
3. As well educated as are the mayor and the doctor, Colonel Lanser participates in the dialogue from Socrates' *Apology*. The two townsmen had performed that set of speeches forty-six years earlier. They reprised them as they went to their executions.
4. Simmonds usefully describes nine thematic categories, ranging from four dispatches to eleven—with some single pieces that appeared separately. He finds some of Steinbeck's best writing in the late group of articles which cover "Task Group 80.4."
5. Underwood compares Steinbeck's need to take part in military action with Hemingway's, as does Mimi Gladstein in "Mr. Novelist Goes to War."

CHAPTER 7

Cannery Row and *The Pearl*

In Steinbeck's eyes *Cannery Row* was a "silly" release of his war terrors, a return to the days when he visited Ed Ricketts and the occupants of Cannery Row nearly every afternoon. To friends, he wrote about "a funny little book that is fun." When he had finished writing it in the early summer 1944, from New York, he told Ritchie and Tal Lovejoy, "I just finished a crazy kind of book about Cannery Row and the lab, etc. All fiction of course but born out of homesickness. And there are some true incidents in it" (Benson 553).

When *Cannery Row* was published, critics disliked it thoroughly. They took it back to *Tortilla Flat*; they talked about obsolescence. As Roy Simmonds said, correctly, the book was so far from the war and its seriousness, and now from the expectation of postwar prosperity and its promise, that readers could not figure out *why* the book had been published at all. They saw the novel as an "apparent inconsequential series of episodes that constituted what they saw as the light-weight, antisocial and somewhat bawdy *Cannery Row*. Never has any important twentieth-century American work of fiction been so misunderstood and undervalued at the time of its publication" (Simmonds 296).

Whereas Steinbeck knew that the writing and publishing of *Cannery Row* was a means of getting back into a healthy life, forgetting his blackouts and his injured body, and returning in all possible ways to his new young wife and her concerns, he also knew why the critics disliked the novel. He told Pascal Covici that criticism always turned away from his paisano fiction, and that it never paid attention to the finesse with which stories were told. As Benson pointed out, *Cannery Row* was "a very experimental novel. Nearly every element—language, form, imagery, and characterization—expressed a non-teleological view of the world. The novel was a great personal risk, and much of Steinbeck's hurt and anger came not from getting bad notices, but from the feeling that in the callous hands of uncaring and insensitive reviewers, the book's fragility and intimacy seemed to be constantly violated" (Benson 565).

Cannery Row was Ed Ricketts' book, just as *The Sea of Cortez* had been. Rather than comedy, this postwar novel deified the role that Ricketts—disguised here as "Doc"—played in the daily existences of the inhabitants of the Row. Philosopher savant as well as medicine man, Doc gave so much good to everyone who knew him that the entire plot of *Cannery Row* is based on the theme of giving Doc a party, repaying him for all his kindnesses and all his knowledge. Mack and his friends work hard toward that end. Yet after the first party turns into a disaster—leaving the absent Doc to come home so as to clean his house and restore order—there is a second, much more successful party. Few novels have ever followed such a simple plotline. The effectiveness of the men's desire to make Doc happy comes through even more clearly because they are themselves close to inarticulate, their language not only truncated but expressed as much through silence as through words.

Steinbeck from the beginning builds in bridges back to *The Sea of Cortez*, and to Doc's identity as a marine biologist. At the close of *Cannery Row*'s brief preface, Steinbeck as author explains,

> When you collect marine animals there are certain flat worms so delicate that they are almost impossible to capture whole, for they break and tatter under the touch. You must let them ooze and crawl of their own will onto a knife blade and then lift them gently into your bottle of sea water. And perhaps that might be the way to write this book—to open the page and to let the stories crawl in by themselves. (*Cannery* 102)

As significant a metaphor for truthful writing as was the persistent turtle at the start of *The Grapes of Wrath* a metaphor for a people's strength, Steinbeck signaled that his writing skills—unlike his body—had not been impaired by war.

The first lines of the novel are themselves a stunning experiment. Steinbeck begins, "Cannery Row in Monterey in California is a poem, a stink, a grating noise, a quality of light, a tone, a habit, a nostalgia, a dream." Direct and incisive in its impact, this opening leads the reader through the street, and then bifurcates into divided opinions: "Its inhabitants are, as the man once said, 'whores, pimps, gamblers, and sons of bitches,' by which he meant Everybody. Had the man looked through another peephole he might have said, 'Saints and angels and martyrs and holy men,' and he would have meant the same thing" (*Cannery* 101). Dedicated to Ed Ricketts, the book straddles that line that Steinbeck had walked before—between the "vulgar" speech of the real people who catch the sardines and work their processing, and the writer's approximation of that speech.

Steinbeck relies on realism here as he draws the universe of Cannery Row (where, in the heyday of the sardine industry, that street alone had eighteen canneries and the sardine fishermen harvested 200,000 *tons* annually). First, the sardine fleet brings in its catch. "Then cannery whistles scream and all over the town men and women scramble into their clothes and come running down to the Row to go to work."

Next, "shining cars bring the upper classes down: superintendents, accountants, owners who disappear into offices. Then from the town pour Wops, Chinamen and Polaks, men and women in trousers and rubber coats and oilcloth aprons."

"The whole street rumbles and groans and screams and rattles while the silver rivers of fish pour in out of the boats..." (*Cannery* 101).

Finally—empty—Cannery Row becomes "itself again—quiet and magical."

Into that calm atmosphere comes the authoritative Steinbeck voice. Whereas Ed Ricketts is the protagonist of the novel, there are three kinds of characters besides Doc. There are the bums sitting on the rusty pipes in the vacant lot, the girls from Dora's, and the duality of Doc—first strolling from the Western Biological Laboratory and then crossing the street to Lee Chong's grocery for two quarts of beer, as well as Doc as he returns home and links these separate elements into the collective that is Cannery Row. A memory account, Steinbeck's description of these mixed elements of the street—the bums, the workmen, the women, Doc, the culture—are nostalgically based: he has moved away from California and he fears he may not return.

Cannery Row drew from Steinbeck's techniques and tactics in *The Red Pony*. Whereas the author considered the pony stories both a memorial to his parents' lives—since they were written during Steinbeck's watch outside his mother's bedroom as she was dying—as well as his important entry to commercial publishing, here he downplayed his technical skill in order to create a story that was intentionally enjoyable. As Benson and Parini confirm, the street that housed Ricketts' biological laboratory had been the center for much of Steinbeck's satisfying emotional life, and the friendships that grew in that place were remarkably enduring. Throughout his history with Ricketts, whenever Steinbeck needed to leave Carol's bed, he spent nights in Ricketts' biological laboratory; being in that surrounding, even when Ricketts was elsewhere in his own home, was comforting. The central structural episode of the novel, giving Doc a party, was also autobiographical, though the community effort at giving a party was the celebration of *Steinbeck*'s birthday, not Ricketts'. In Steinbeck's "Conversations" he recounted that "the boys had a birthday party for me. It was a wild and raucous thing that went on for three days and nights. Each man had five gallons of beer to drink" (*Conversations* 87; *Cannery* 105).

Cannery Row from the start tells stories of death and suicide, however, providing a tension that underlies and darkens the seemingly comic tone. No sooner has Lee Chong opened his store than Horace Abbeville, deeply in debt to Chong, appears. To cover his debt, he offers the storekeeper ownership of a warehouse that is his property. After the deal is made, Abbeville walks into the building which he had formerly owned and shot himself. Aside from the drowned young girl that Doc finds in his tide pool, and several other dead bodies that give the residents much reason to gossip, the aura of life as lived, complete with unexpected death, does not vary throughout the novel. In fact, that aura increases the men's need to give Doc a party.

Doc had "become the fountain of philosophy and science and art." He was the center of both physical life and emotional life for the street—not because his own life was exemplary, but because he had the capacity, and the wisdom, to listen to the men and women who lived there with him (*Cannery* 122). Steinbeck reinforces Doc's role by surrounding him as he moves through his careful life as collector and shipper of marine life, again as visiting good spirit when someone falls ill. As he had in his earlier paisano fictions, Steinbeck drew from people he had known, telling stories he had heard in an earlier life. He told an interviewer in 1937 that "all the characters in *Of Mice and Men, Tortilla Flat* and his other books have been people he has known" (Steinbeck *Conversations* 7). *Cannery Row* is no exception: in many cases he uses real names in his text (as if he were rewriting *The Sea of Cortez*, Steinbeck gives his readers characters named Red Williams, Sparky Enea, Tiny Colletti, Jimmy Bruscia, and others). He also describes a number of marriages that are far from satisfying—Mack and Henri's liaisons have been "terminated," and the relationships for Gay, Richard Frost, Tom Tolbert, and Sam Malloy are "troubled." Only Dora Flood and her happy hookers are, in Simmonds' words, "fully exempted from the latent antagonism directed against the book's other female characters" (Simmonds 238).

Like Mack, Doc is spared these cumbersome pairings. *Cannery Row*, for all its attention to Dora Flood and her girls, is a male province. Much attention goes to describing the biological laboratory, for instance, although no conventional house bears attention:

> It is a low building facing the street. The basement is the storeroom with shelves, shelves clear to the ceiling loaded with jars of preserved animals. And in the basement is a sink and instruments for embalming and for injecting. Then you go through the backyard to a covered shed on piles over the ocean and here are the tanks for the larger animals, the sharks and rays and octopi, each in their concrete tanks. There is a stairway up the front of the building and a door that opens into an office where there is a desk piled high with unopened mail, filing cabinets, and a safe with the door propped open. (*Cannery* 116)

Literally leading his reader with his use of the traditional "you," Steinbeck continues for several more pages of detail; the unopened mail and the propped-open door of the safe have already shown Doc's unconventionality.

Other descriptive passages place Doc as he does his work of collecting in his tide pools. One of his favorites is the Great Tide Pool on the tip of the Peninsula,

> a fabulous place when the tide is in, a wave-churned basin, creamy with foam, whipped by the combers that roll in from the whistling buoy on the reef. But when the tide goes out the little water world becomes quiet and lovely. The sea is very clear and the bottom becomes fantastic with hurrying, fighting, feeding, breeding animals. Crabs rush from frond to frond of the waving algae. Starfish squat over mussels and limpets, attach their million little suckers and then slowly lift with incredible power until the prey is broken from the rock. And then the starfish stomach comes out and envelops its food. Orange and speckled and fluted nudibranchs slide gracefully over the rocks, their skirts waving like the dresses of Spanish dancers. And black eels poke their heads out of crevices and wait for prey. The snapping shrimps with their trigger claws pop loudly. The lovely, colored world is glassed over. (*Cannery* 117–21)

Hand in hand with the beauties of the natural world comes Doc's own set of systematic beauties: his prowess and his care as collector. The methodical man "worked down the flat after the retreating sea. He turned over the boulders with his crowbar and now and then his hand darted quickly into the standing water and brought out a little angry squirming octopus which blushed with rage and spat ink on his hand.... he got twenty-two little octopi. And he picked off several hundred sea cradles and put them in his wooden bucket. As the tide moved out he followed it while the morning came and the sun arose." Doc's habits of observation are as ingrained as his habits of collecting: "He had about what he wanted now and the rest of the time he looked under stones, leaned down and peered into the tide pools with their brilliant mosaics and their scuttling, bubbling life. And he came at last to the outer barrier where the long leathery brown algae hung down into the water. Red starfish clustered on the rocks and the sea pulsed up and down against the barrier waiting to get in again" (*Cannery* 170).

In such descriptions, Steinbeck creates a montage of the unexpected. This is the scene during which Doc finds the drowned young girl, untouched as yet by the marauders of the ocean and by time. Still beautiful, her floating body haunts him, but he first has to wait for someone else to arrive so that the death can be reported. Doc does not wait for any reward; he quietly leaves the site.

Benson calls *Cannery Row* "that strange, neglected, often misunderstood little book" that uses "the ecology of the seashore as its central metaphor" (Benson 432). It does that, but as the above excerpts suggest, *Cannery Row* is not a simple book.

Using what he had learned in organizing multiple stories within *The Grapes of Wrath*, Steinbeck here alternated narratives. Many of the "extra" chapters in the work—those not directly involved with Mack and his friends giving Doc a party—have little to no relationship to that pervasive theme.

The alternating chapters are more visible at mid-point. Chapter Twelve features Monterey's recognition of Josh Billings' literary greatness, and describes his death, embalming, and burial. Chapter Fourteen marks the appearance of two tired soldiers and their two equally tired girlfriends. Chapter Sixteen traces the prosperity (and parallel exhaustion) of Dora Flood and her girls during the March peak of the sardine season. Chapter Nineteen tells the story of the flagpole skater (and his waste can) sponsored by Holman's Department Store. Chapter Twenty-four is devoted to Mary Talbot's practice of giving parties, even if she has neither food nor funds for that activity. Chapter Twenty-six is a dialogue between the boys

Joey and Willard, the former being teased because his father had suffered an agonizing death after he took rat poison—he had been unemployed for more than a year.[1]

Even as Steinbeck had described the early stages of *Cannery Row* as "silly," the work had evolved into a much more nuanced portrait of the town, complete with the ravages of economic war as well as military. Its lynchpin was the character of Ed Ricketts, existing as he did on hamburgers and pineapple pie, driving his old car, caring for the townspeople as well as for his work among the living objects of Monterey Bay and La Jolla. He had chosen to live where "There is a beautiful view from the Carmel grade, the curving bay with the waves creaming on the sand, the dune country around Seaside and right at the bottom of the hill, the warm intimacy of the town" (*Cannery* 164). Yet, as Mack observes, "In spite of his friendliness and his friends, Doc was a lonely and a set-apart man."

Louis Owens was among the earliest of Steinbeck's critics to connect the author's fascination with the sea during these years with his earlier study of Jung, Weston, and Frazer: "Steinbeck was acutely aware of the sea as a symbol of death and the unconscious—an awareness that is amply illustrated in the war dispatches he wrote." Owens sees these dispatches as showing "a remarkable unity, a unity that depends almost solely upon Steinbeck's fascination with the sea as symbol of the unconscious. In the dispatches, Steinbeck's soldiers make a 'night-sea crossing' in a ship unmistakably symbolizing the belly of the whale,' and they slip into a deeply unconscious dream-state from which they do not emerge during the dark violence of war. The sea shifts and sighs beneath the writing of the dispatches."

Owens identifies Steinbeck's own immersion in the violent truth about war as the reason he leaves his work for the *Herald Tribune* early, and upon his return is able to write *Cannery Row* in only six weeks. Searching once again for a belief system that he can use to cope with what he has so thoroughly observed and learned of war, Steinbeck reverts to the earlier wisdom he thought he had then shared with Ed Ricketts as well as with Joseph Campbell (Owens *Re-Vision* 160–61).

Now discharged from the army, Ricketts resumed his life in Cannery Row—and Steinbeck was himself resuming his plan to move back to Monterey, once his and Gwyn's baby was born in August 1944. All the assorted bitterness from his wartime experiences came to a head in the memorial essay he wrote after Ernie Pyle's death, an essay those responsible for the correspondent's memorial chose not to publish. Exhausted from his continuous reporting, Pyle had not wanted to return to the Pacific theater of war, but Washington put pressure on him: for his millions of readers, Pyle was synonymous with the American soldier.

Shot by a Japanese sniper on Ie Shima, Pyle had earlier spoken with Steinbeck of his hatred of the war, according to Steinbeck's essay, "It's just piled up dead men.... millions of them." Steinbeck re-told one of Pyle's stories: "There was a soldier with only one leg, on the hospital ship. He was hopping about like a cricket—up and down stairs. It was wonderful. I can't stand hurt men. I'm going to Albuquerque and forget the whole damned thing" (Steinbeck *Nonfiction* 214). Had Ernie Pyle followed that inclination, he would probably have been alive much longer.

As if to temper his mixed emotions while he wrote *Cannery Row* and refused to think about the re-publication of his New York *Herald Tribune* dispatches, Steinbeck began writing the story and screenplay for the Mexican film he had long planned to shoot with Mexican director Emilio Fernandez. *The Pearl of La Paz*, which appeared as a story titled "The Pearl of the World" in *Woman's Home Companion* for December 1945, was a Mexican story Steinbeck had mentioned briefly in *The Sea of Cortez*. Part of the approbation he felt for the country and its people, this narrative held a fascination for Steinbeck that overrode his agents' sense that *The Pearl* would not serve as any kind of war novel—just as *Cannery Row* did not fill that purpose. In Steinbeck's mindset during 1944, he had no plans to write a novel about war, regardless of when the warfare occurred. Although he may not have admitted it to himself, Steinbeck was in retreat.

As much as Steinbeck wanted to move back to Monterey, he also wanted to spend some time in Mexico. His first son's birth in early August delayed the move to the Soto house, but it was not long after the young family arrived in California that Steinbeck wanted Gwyn to go with him for a meeting with Fernandez about the filming of *The Pearl*. He had decided that music would be a crucial part of the film's effect and he understood that Gwyn, trained as a singer, could bring important insight to the selection—or the composition—of that element.

In the words of critic Joseph Millichap, "Mexico always had been an important symbolic place for Steinbeck. As a native Californian, he had been aware of his state's Mexican heritage. Even as a boy, he sought out Mexican-American companions, fascinated by their unconcern for the pieties of WASP culture; he also befriended Mexican fieldhands at the ranches where he worked" (Millichap 94).[2]

Millichap pointed out that John and Carol had earlier spent several months in Mexico, considering it as a possible permanent home, as soon as Steinbeck had received royalties from *Tortilla Flat*. Then he and Ricketts had chosen to use the Sea of Cortez as the site for their maritime expedition. Steinbeck had also involved himself frequently in the filming of his documentary *The Forgotten Village*, so that he again spent weeks in Mexico. Now he was intrigued with the opportunities that filming *The Pearl* would give him, once again necessitating his return to Mexico.

In Millichap's view, "Mexico was everything modern America was not; for him Mexico possessed a primitive vitality, a harsh simplicity, and a romantic beauty.... [and the country] was still alive with social concern.... For Steinbeck, Mexico came to represent the artistic purity and social purpose he had lost after World War II" (Millichap 95).

Steinbeck referred to the writing of *The Pearl* as "a strange piece of work... full of curious methods and figures. A folktale, I hope. A black and white story—like a parable" (Steinbeck *Conversations* 41). His confusion was understandable: he had had to juggle writing a screenplay with the regular narrative prose form (the publication of *The Pearl* was tied to the release of the film; therefore, it would be 1947 before *The Pearl* would see print). What he understood from the start was that the language he used should convey a disciplined tone, a voice-over speech pattern completely removed from anything Mexican, American, or Spanish, native or educated. The voice of a people's history should convey the tragedy of Kino and Juana and Coyotito. The specifics of the story were tied to the all-too-human quest for safety for loved ones, but the story itself was larger than any specific happening.

The language of *The Pearl* resonates with a kind of pacific stateliness that may have stemmed from the interchapters of *The Grapes of Wrath*. It also shared the same intense choices of nouns that Steinbeck had found effective in the dialogue scenes in *Of Mice and Men*. Reminiscent of early English, when an emotional quantity had only one word that expressed a condition, dialogue in *The Pearl* relied on such nouns as "fear" and "evil." The complexity within a condition is left to readers and viewers to interpret.

Soon after Kino has found and hidden the great pearl, Steinbeck brings the reader into his hut to watch his behavior under the aegis of fear:

> Kino squatted beside the little glowing coals in the fire hole and listened to the night sound, the soft sweep of the little waves on the shore and the distant barking of dogs, the creeping of the breeze through the brush house roof and the soft speech of his neighbors in their houses in the village. For

these people do not sleep soundly all night; they awaken at intervals and talk a little and then go to sleep again. And after a while Kino got up and went to the door of his house.

He smelled the breeze and he listened for any foreign sound of secrecy or creeping and his eyes searched the darkness, for the music of evil was sounding in his head and he was fierce and afraid.... And Juana, sitting by the fire hole, watched him with questioning eyes, and when he had buried the pearl she asked, 'What do you fear?'" (*Pearl* 41)

Days and nights pass. Juana quickly understands the danger, and her own fear brings her to speech: "'This thing is evil,' she cried harshly. 'This pearl is like a sin! It will destroy us,' her voice rose shrilly. 'Throw it away, Kino. Let us break it between stones. Let us bury it and forget the place. Let us throw it back into the sea...'" (*Pearl* 43).

The stark rage of the woman's imperatives does not shake Kino's ambition. This dialogue has itself spelled out the entire narrative, and part of the reader's/viewer's own fear accrues from it. To finally rid themselves of the pearl by throwing it back into the sea will not undo all the sorrow they will have experienced: Juana as sage claims her role only through her language as she delivers it to the deaf Kino.

The Pearl as Steinbeck finally wrote it was not the story he had heard in Mexico, the gist of which appears in *The Sea of Cortez*. Based partly on his own comprehension of what being a father to Thom, his first born, meant, Steinbeck changed the story he had been told in order to create the modest folk family of Kino, Juana, and their baby. As he had heard the tale originally, the boy who found the pearl was young, eager to have money to give himself pleasure. A simpler story, the Mexican tale made the large point that selfishness is never a worthy motive. In Steinbeck's telling, Kino's motives for trying to capitalize on the value of the enormous pearl are more complicated: he wants to have the resources to give his son an education, so that he can leave the poor life his parents know. Altruistic rather than hedonistic, the urge for money is transformed into a story the world recognizes—a father's demand that his children's lives be better than his own. (The author's other great novel of the postwar period, *East of Eden*, would work with those same self-defining themes.)

With Steinbeck's change from the pearl's satisfying Kino's individual pleasure to its becoming a vehicle for the education of their child, and (one assumes) for the family's rise in social and economic position, he makes the Mexican folktale a parable about the American dream. In both versions of the story, he counted on readers' recognition of the biblical "pearl of great price," the jewel for which the merchant trades everything he owns—hoping to attain Heaven—although this acquisition does not transport anyone into bliss.[3] Similarly, in Steinbeck's parable, when "the great pearl, perfect as the moon... as large as a sea-gull's egg" is found, Kino must look past its rare beauty to see what lurks within. When Steinbeck had completed writing about his mixed-race characters in *Cannery Row*, Mack and his friends, he admitted to readers of that work that the traits he loved about the paisano, or Chicano, figures—"kindness and generosity, openness, honesty, understanding and feeling"—were the traits most likely to lead to their *failure* within the United States' dog-eat-dog capitalistic system.

More intent than usual on creating empathy between whites and paisanos, Steinbeck did not mention the recent riots in California. During 1942 and 1943, Los Angeles was racked by race riots. In the east-side barrios, Mexican and Mexican-American adolescents had formed *pachucos*, or gangs, and uniformed themselves in wide-brimmed hats, long-tailed coats, and ankle-length watch chains. Dressed in these zoot suits, the Mexicans were targets for racial discrimination. The trial of twenty-four *pachucos* in the summer of 1942 for the murder of Jose Diaz led to many convictions, and the men had served two years of their sentences before the second-degree murder convictions were overturned for lack of evidence. Even more visible were the ten days of the so-called Zoot Suit Race Riots in June 1943, when servicemen from the Navy training facility in the barrio attacked the zoot-suited Mexicans. Abetted by police, the servicemen went free while the Mexicans were arrested. Like the unreasonable persecution of the Okies, this turn against people of non-American background puzzled and angered Steinbeck.

Much of his work on *The Pearl* stemmed from his writing the narrative for *The Sea of Cortez*, a project for which he had studied Mexican history. His naming of Kino, for instance, suggested the historical figure of Eusebius Kino, the Jesuit missionary and explorer in the Gulf region, who proved that lower California was a peninsula—a *baja*—rather than an island. Veering away from the particular, Steinbeck chose Juana—*woman*—to name Kino's wife. As he had in *The Grapes of Wrath*, dividing the power of the family between Pa and Ma Joad, here Steinbeck associated Juana with wisdom and common sense. She is also the mother of Kino's most prized possession, his son, Coyotito. Steinbeck's sophisticated use of musical themes ("The Song of Evil" less significant than "The Song of the Family," the latter scored as "this is safety, this is warmth, this is the *Whole*") leads Kino in his deliberations.

Narratively, Steinbeck complicates the parable of the family when he adds the vulnerability of the baby. The child's helplessness is introduced in the scorpion scene, which provides the first exposure of the voracious medical doctor—he will treat the baby only if he is given the pearl. The pearl traders repeat his avariciousness as they collude to rob Kino of his valuable jewel. The vehicle for the chicanery, however, is Kino's self-defined motive—to give Coyotito a life beyond anyone's dreams. Despite this self-justification, the content of *The Pearl* becomes more and more non-verbal. (Benson reminds the reader that Steinbeck was reading folktales in Spanish as he wrote the script, building a tonal base that would help convey non-verbal meaning.)

Now considered one of Steinbeck's best novellas, *The Pearl* did not have immediate success when it was published in 1947. The film was widely shown, however, and became a marker in the annals of film history—directed by a Mexican director, enacted by a Mexican cast, it set an important precedent for future global filmmaking. The fame that re-introduced Steinbeck to a postwar audience came from the 1945 *Cannery Row*, a novel which became a best-seller immediately (although it was not critically acclaimed). Advance sales for the novel were between 90,000 and 95,000 copies. Soon after Steinbeck heard those surprising figures, Covici told him that he had arranged an unusual deal with the Book-of-the-Month Club: it would offer a special printing of Steinbeck's *The Red Pony* as a dividend book to members. Steinbeck would automatically receive a fee of $16,000 for this arrangement.

Notes

1. See Simmonds 321, note 15, for an exhaustive description of what Steinbeck called these "little interchapters."
2. A reader might add, given that Steinbeck's mother Olive paid tribute to WASP allegiances throughout her life, that freedom from the white, middle-class world was a continuing dream of the young Steinbeck.
3. Steinbeck drew as well on the fourteenth-century alliterative poem *Pearl*, an elegy by an anonymous poet for the death of his young daughter before she was two years old. In the 1212-line poem, the poet sees a vision of his child as she would have become. Because of this mystical vision, he plunges into a river, wanting to join her. His journey, a trip into the dark night of the soul, leads to his eventual acceptance of the child's loss. The poem closes with his renunciation of his earthly pain: "Upon this hill this destiny I grasped,/ Prostrate in sorrow for my pearl./ And afterward to God I gave it up."

CHAPTER 8

The Ed Ricketts Narratives

Whether or not Steinbeck understood the way he was hiding behind his writing, he realized that in many ways his second marriage was leaving him more dissatisfied than had his first. Gwyn was a city person; she had enjoyed living in Los Angeles. She did not mind their various rented houses and apartments in New York; at least there, friends came from the worlds of theater and film. But she had not expected the long bouts of Steinbeck's leaving her alone—as he had during the nearly five months of his writing about the war soon after they had married. His repeated trips to Mexico, and to other possible film sites, made her increasingly angry. She found herself enraged on a long Christmas Day when she was in bed with the flu and her spouse went to his older sister's for a family get-together.

High on Gwyn's list of grievances was Steinbeck's very visible friendship with Ed Ricketts. Once the Steinbecks had returned to Monterey and Ricketts was discharged from the military, the two men resumed their almost daily visits and conversations. Steinbeck's absence left Gwyn alone first with one baby, and then with another baby and a toddler.

Neither she nor Steinbeck had ever learned how to parent.

None of her life as *Mrs. John Steinbeck* was what she had anticipated.

When Gwyn had met Steinbeck he was a world-famous writer, trying to avoid the fame and visibility—and the threats—that followed the publication of *The Grapes of Wrath*. Besides the money, there was the notoriety. There was then a quick succession of profitable films and theatrical productions—*Of Mice and Men, Tortilla Flat, The Grapes of Wrath, The Moon Is Down*, not to mention *The Forgotten Village* and *The Pearl*.

Gwyn herself was barely twenty when they met. She was a singer who also danced, and she had a lithe and well-cared-for body. After the two Caesarian section deliveries of the boys, she could not regain the youthful beauty she assumed Steinbeck admired. She saw her marriage as little but a downward spiral, and a lonely spiral at that. (Benson records that Gwyn hated John's traveling; Benson 582.)

Although she did not claim to be any kind of literary person, she could not help but notice that there was very little of Steinbeck's writing that related to her—as either lover or wife. He wrote about war; he wrote about Ricketts' laboratory in Monterey,[1] complete with the good-for-nothing characters that populated Cannery Row; and he wrote about a Mexican couple who had found a precious jewel. There was no outright love story anywhere in Steinbeck's recent *oeuvre*, although he dedicated *The Wayward Bus* in 1947 to Gwyn. There is little indication that she would have appreciated that work's humor.

Steinbeck did not notice the omission of any work about romance. He seemed oblivious to Gwyn's state of mind, although he knew that she preferred living in New York in the brownstones on East 72nd Street, with the Benchleys as close neighbors, to any locations in California. Later, in writing to his sister Mary about his divorce from Gwyn, he said, "I don't want you to think this is all Gwyn's fault.... I do have to work and it is my work that finally seems to destroy marriages. So maybe I will have no more wives. I can't cut the work off because that is all I am and incidentally that is why they want to marry me in the first place" (Shillinglaw *Carol* 255). As self-justifying as any breadwinner's letters about his "work," Steinbeck here seemed to have quickly erased what he had preached in writing *The Pearl*: a man's livelihood cannot destroy his human role as man, husband, father. The family—which demands both parents—should constitute a man's greatest good.

When Steinbeck here pleads his "work," he does not tell Mary much about the particulars. He does not enumerate how many afternoons and evenings his "work" leads him to spend time in Ricketts' biological laboratory, how often their talk obviates all thought of work. He also does not mention his long absences from home. (He seems to have forgotten that when Carol—at his insistence—filed for their divorce in 1942, she listed those many absences, both long and short, as part of the "mental cruelty" she claimed.)

Steinbeck had felt his marriage to Gwyn begin to fray as soon as he returned from Italy. Writing to Pascal Covici in that early spring of 1945, he admitted "there is no home coming nor any welcome. What there is is jealousy, hatred and the knife in the back. I'm beginning to think I made a mistake" (Benson 567). His feelings of remorse were no doubt intensified because Carol had re-married just a few months after his wedding to Gwyn. Even though friends told him they thought Loren Howard had married Carol for her money, he still had to realize that the woman who had been so much a part of his life—and of his *writing* life—was no longer available to him.

The consistency in Steinbeck's existence was his friendship, his sheer camaraderie, with Ricketts. That, of course, was why he had written *Cannery Row*. That was the reason he was planning another expedition with Ricketts and their crew for the summer of 1948. Literarily, as Shillinglaw and Benson pointed out, male friendship was

> the relationship that Steinbeck explored most often in his fiction, Lenny and George, Mac and Jim, Tom and Casy, Mack and the boys, Adam Trask and Lee.... In all of these stories of male bonding, there was, either as one of the friends or as a sage looking on, a figure of serene demeanor and broad understanding. That character was always modeled on Edward Flanders Ricketts. He was a natural object for Steinbeck's interest. He was self-contained without being arrogant; extremely competent at his work...; knew things that Steinbeck didn't know well enough." (Shillinglaw and Benson *Nonfiction* 176)

Steinbeck took a brief hiatus in his use of Ricketts as a figure of guidance in his fiction. He had thoroughly explored Doc's privileged and steadying role throughout Cannery Row in his 1945 novel titled simply *Cannery Row*. When he returned from another filming trip to Mexico, seeing *The Pearl* nearly finished, he began to write a book that he knew Ricketts would enjoy. Using a battered bus as his comic vehicle, setting the narrative on the winding roads of Mexico, Steinbeck once again returned to the journey plot from earlier literatures.

His plan was to write "the story of a busload of Mexican peasants and American tourists making a difficult pilgrimage across the sierra." He thought it would be a long story, comprising many narrative strands, and he remarked that it might be as long as *The Grapes of Wrath*. It would, however, be comic, perhaps even ribald.

In fact, from Cuernavaca, he wrote to Covici (July 12, 1945) that his current book might be something all the *Mexicans* who had been so kind to the film company could themselves enjoy: "*The Wayward Bus* could be something like the Don Quixote of Mexico. The more I think of it the better I like it and the better I like it the longer its plan and the wider its scope until it seems to contain the whole world. From the funny little story it is growing to the most ambitious thing I have ever attempted" (*SLL* 284).[2]

He spoke tenderly to his publisher Pascal Covici about "my bus...a cosmic bus holding sparks and back firing into the Milky Way and turning the corner of Betelgeuse without a hand signal."

It could be that the Mexican bus driver, Juan Chicoy, would resemble Ricketts. In Steinbeck's mind, Juan was the dominant character, "all the god the fathers you ever saw driving a six cylinder broken down, battered world through time and space. If I can do it well *The Wayward Bus* will be a pleasant thing."[3]

Writing the bus narrative took much less time than Steinbeck had expected, perhaps because he dictated it and gave the discs to a typist. During his work on the manuscript, he told Charles Brackett, who wanted to produce the film, that the title was misleading. He had wanted to use the Spanish term *vacilador*, signifying "aiming at some place, but you don't care much whether you get there." The mood Steinbeck suggested was more aimless than illegal (*SLL* 284).

Steinbeck's life with Gwyn was anything but aimless, however, once their second child—another boy, this one named John IV—was born in June 1946. Against Gwyn's protests that *she* never got to travel, that *her* life was a continuous shifting from New York to California and back to New York, whereas Steinbeck's life was spent in exotic places (always without small children), Steinbeck realized that he and Gwyn needed to take trips themselves. Accordingly, he promised her that as soon as he had finished writing *The Wayward Bus*, they would take a leisurely trip through the Scandinavian countries. Five weeks of travel were planned for the fall of 1946.

In August 1946, however, Steinbeck received several letters from Ricketts, letters which evidently showed the despair his friend was experiencing. Steinbeck replied immediately, inviting Ricketts to visit New York—to get away from old faces, old situations—and enclosing a check for "anything you want or need it for."

> I am writing immediately. The matter of death is very personal—almost like an idea—and it has to be discovered and accepted over and over again no

matter what the age or the condition of the dying. And there is nothing for the outsider to do except to stand by and maybe to indicate that the person involved is not so alone as the death always makes him think he is... in all of this there is some necessity of saving yourself." (*SLL* 292)[4]

The changes that occurred in *The Wayward Bus* may have been influenced by Ricketts' situation, but generally, when Steinbeck finished the novel in October 1946, it was still about the somewhat strange group of travelers on the broken-down bus, traveling through California (though at the edge of Mexico—42 miles below San Ysidro, in a village called Rebel Corners). The property, owned by Alice, boasted two outhouses and two great oak trees, as well as a lunch counter. Despite Alice's fondness for drink, her redeeming quality was that "she loved him [Juan]. She really did. And he knew it. And you can't leave a thing like that. It's a structure and it has an architecture, and you can't leave it without tearing off a piece of yourself. So if you want to remain whole you stay no matter how much you may dislike staying" (*Bus* 72).

The buffoonery that occurs before boarding the bus, and after the bus breaks down, is mock-heroic. Although *The Wayward Bus* was considerably shorter than Steinbeck's comments had originally predicted, it still began with the prologue from medieval lore, and it showed Juan's wily cunning as a Mexican-*Irish* character, using accented speech that would appeal to the American tourists, flirting with American women—despite his love for Alice. Juan himself was a mock-heroic character, less Hispanic than Irish, less cavalier than capable. There seem to be few of Ricketts' traits embodied in this figure; Juan may more sensibly be considered a take-off of Steinbeck himself.

When the novel was finally filmed in 1957, a decade after its publication as a book, the mixed-race Juan disappears completely from the script: the film becomes a typical Hollywood comedy, with actor Dan Dailey as one of the young white travelers and Jayne Mansfield as the beautiful prostitute Camille. Racial issues are non-existent, though the privileges of wealth are clearly visible.

Published in February 1947, *The Wayward Bus* sold half a million copies, and was chosen as a novel to be sent to servicemen. It also was a Book-of-the-Month Club selection. As critic Gordon Hutner pointed out, for months it placed just below Frank Yerby's novel *The Vixen*, at seventh on the *New York Times* Best Seller list (Hutner 263). Once again, the Steinbeck household felt rich.

Success in writing did not translate into marital success, however. Benson described the Steinbeck household in no uncertain terms. Even after their Scandinavian trip, and even aware that *The Wayward Bus* would bring in another round of unexpected wealth, Gwyn and Steinbeck lived with "constant tension—irritability, sulking, and retaliation. Each was trying to out-do the other in flirting with others, feeding with jealousy the mutual antagonism that was building between them" (Benson 597). Gwyn took the boys to California for a month; Steinbeck waited several weeks and then went out to retrieve his family.

The next hurdle to be faced was Steinbeck's planned trip with photographer Robert Capa to make an extensive photo-documentary book focused on the common people of Russia. To pacify Gwyn, Steinbeck proposed that she and he would first spend two weeks in Paris. Then, Capa would join them, and he and Steinbeck would tour Russia (the government having given them rare permission to do so) for their journalistic work. That was the plan. But a few weeks before the couple were to leave for Paris, Steinbeck fell through the second-story railing of the New York house, and in the fall broke his kneecap. There were other injuries. The kneecap was operated upon, and—too soon—the Steinbecks set off for France. Steinbeck knew he would be in great pain for the duration of his travels in both France and Russia.

Again, the four months Steinbeck was gone wreaked havoc with his wife's feelings. Once he returned in late October 1947, Gwyn claimed illness and went to bed. Steinbeck then watched the boys' nurse leave for her long Christmas holiday. As he wrote the New York *Herald Tribune* columns from the Russian trip and tried to care for his ailing wife, he was also the person in charge of the two little boys. In Benson's words, "the children were now becoming for him a positive nuisance" (Benson 608).

Early in 1948, Steinbeck made the research trip to Salinas that he had planned: he was about to begin work on his big California novel, and the history for generations back of his family—as well as other families—needed to become the foundation of information for his text. While there, he visited his two older sisters; but he also spent a great deal of time with Ricketts. It was during this visit that Ricketts and he planned their next expedition, this time to the northern areas of the Pacific; hopefully, they would be ready to sail once more early in the summer of 1948.

At the beginning of May, however, those ebullient plans changed. Ricketts, still driving the old Packard that behaved erratically, set off from his laboratory to drive a few blocks for some dinner. The car, however, stalled on the tracks and was hit by the Del Monte Express coming in from San Francisco. The train dragged the car several hundred yards down the track. Still alive and conscious, Ricketts told those who found him, "Don't blame the motorman." The doctors operated where they could, but internal damage was extensive. Four days later, Ricketts died.

Steinbeck told Nat Benchley the night before he left to travel to San Francisco, "The greatest man in the world is dying and there is nothing I can do" (Benson 615).

Steinbeck arrived in time for the funeral, but he and many of Ricketts' friends had their own service out by the tide pool—and then that group went to a small Mexican restaurant for dinner. In Benson's words, "John sat during the meal without speaking or even moving, completely rigid with grief and drink" (ibid.) Because Steinbeck was an executor for Ricketts' will, he stayed on several weeks. With George Robinson, he spent days in Ricketts' lab. It was at that time that he burned his letters to Ricketts, though he kept many of his friend's notebooks and essays. He also made what restitution he could for Ricketts' debts.

When Steinbeck returned to New York, so sad he could scarcely function, Gwyn met him with the totally unexpected news that she wanted a divorce. She told him she had not loved him for several years. From his room at the Bedford Hotel, Steinbeck wrote his friends the Lovejoys that the impact of Ricketts' death was "all dulled out." He continued, "Wouldn't it be interesting if Ed *was* us and that now there wasn't any such thing or that he created out of his own mind something that went away with him. I've wondered a lot about that. How much was Ed and how much was me and which is which" (Benson 616). As Steinbeck later told an interviewer, Ricketts "was my partner for eighteen years—he was a part of my brain. When he was killed, I was destroyed" (Steinbeck *Conversations* 68).

The Steinbecks' divorce was final that October. It was uncontested. Because Gwyn never remarried, Steinbeck paid alimony and child support for decades.

Nearing a breakdown, Steinbeck returned to the Pacific Grove house—without a typewriter, his books, or his clothes. Gwyn demanded everything; she would not allow him to take any of his books. In his eyes, she became an inhuman monster. Benson described those 1948 fall months in California:

> Visitors to the little house reported Steinbeck as by turns silent, irascible, and absent, or garrulous and manic in rationalizing a style of living that

featured a hermitlike defiance of the world and a rejection of his previous habits of regularity. One visitor, an old friend from Los Gatos, found the atmosphere bizarre, with Steinbeck in a kind of melancholy stupor and Ed Ricketts' microscope enshrined under glass and set in a position of reverence in the center of the room. (Benson 624)

Steinbeck gardened in the wild yard, and tried to clean the derelict house. He could not write. Sometime during 1948, he and Carol spent time together—her divorce from Loren was already final. Although Steinbeck wrote to his friend Bo Beskow that there was no bitterness between them, he also told him that Carol "was still unhappy, still tended to blame others for her problems." He told Beskow he would not go back to her (Shillinglaw *Carol* 256).

It took months for Steinbeck to begin writing the third of his novella-plays, a text of the order of *Of Mice and Men* and *The Moon Is Down*. This one was titled *Burning Bright*, and it featured a powerful yet reticent character known as Friend Ed. When it was produced early in 1950, the play ran for only sixteen performances, but it satisfied Steinbeck's relentless need to express his grief at the death of his friend.

Divided into three parts, *Burning Bright* took its title from William Blake's "Tyger" poem, the elusive glimmer of life within the animal's glowing eye. The first, and most developed, segment is set in a circus among a group of acrobats—the middle-aged Joe Saul, his partner Mordeen, and the young Victor. Joe Saul had lost his beloved wife Cathy three years earlier; his cousin Will had fallen to his death only eight months before. The troupe, accordingly, is built from his losses. He remains sorrowful and what Friend Ed calls "nervy."

Intent on having children, Joe Saul laments the fact that he has had no children with either Cathy or with Mordeen. With an Irish flamboyance, he challenges his surroundings to provide him heirs. The observant Friend Ed realizes that Mordeen may take the situation into her own hands—she may find a way to become pregnant despite Joe Saul's impotence. In this first scene, Friend Ed is the perceptive, caring observer: the clown of the circus, walking the earth with his senses attuned to all of life, especially that of his friend Joe Saul.

The second part of the play is set on a farm, but the plotline repeats. In both of the two opening sections, Joe Saul is fixed on the fact that blood is the important criterion for judgment—the acrobats learn their skills because they are born to them, just as the farmers intuitively understand the land. The audience reads Joe Saul's insistence on the truth of blood as an opening for dissension once he discovers that Mordeen has slept with the young Victor so as to give Joe Saul—her husband—the child he desires. The apparent dramatic irony is that a child *not* of Joe Saul's line will lead only to tragedy.

Burning Bright works through this and other examples of dramatic irony; only Friend Ed seems to recognize all the forces at work, even those that are well-intentioned. Friend Ed says very little; the loquacious, and often beautiful, speeches come from Joe Saul.

Act Three is divided into two scenes: the first, titled simply "The Sea," shows Victor as captain of the ship on which they travel. Seemingly intent on forcing Mordeen to come away with him, since it is his child she is carrying, Victor yet trusts Friend Ed—and the latter character kills him by shoving him into the sea. Even when Joe Paul returns from his medical appointment and faces the realization that he is impotent, as Scene Two, titled "The Child," makes clear, he will love any child borne to him and Mordeen. Friend Ed, watching this unlikely resolution, stays in character as the silent but always devoted friend. As he says at the close of the penultimate scene, "I've given you everything a friend can give" (*Burning* 292). But perhaps Joe Saul's closing lines are more revealing. He says then to Mordeen, "I had to walk into the black to know—to know that every man is father to all children and every child must have all men as father" (*Burning* 296). Even in Friend Ed's absence, Joe Saul has righted himself.

Burning Bright when published in 1950 was dedicated to Elaine Scott. In the two years since his divorce from Gwyn, Steinbeck had come to understand that his life was still viable—and he had written successful, if slight, works that in one way or another commemorated Ricketts and their undying friendship. The fact that Steinbeck wrote comparatively few letters after Ricketts' death marked an abrupt change from his usual methods of achieving stability. When he did begin writing once more, relinquishing some of the sorrow that exhausted him, he wrote about Ricketts, or a Ricketts-like character. Much of what he wrote constituted a threnody to Ricketts.

Even before his friend's death, Steinbeck had made the turn back into the history of his life in California with the publication of *Cannery Row* in 1945. While he often explained that the soldiers he had known in Europe asked him to write something comic, something *not* war related, he would not have been able to make that return in subject matter had he not been following his own heart.

The Wayward Bus, in its staged and convoluted narrative, is a kind of continuation of Steinbeck's impulses in *Cannery Row* to create a language of praise for the Ricketts character often named "Doc." In *The Wayward Bus*, more broadly comic than Steinbeck's paisano fictions, the competent though risqué bus driver assumes that façade.

Remaining intrigued by the form Steinbeck thought of as his own creation—the "play-novelette" that brought him such success in the cases of both *Of Mice and Men* and *The Moon Is Down*—it was after the agony of his personal loss of both Ricketts and his second wife began to diminish that Steinbeck wrote the third of his play-novelette pieces. *Burning Bright* was a step forward into innovation, since it provided a resolution for the forces that had nearly swamped him. The work commemorates the "life force" that Ricketts would have privileged—what Shillinglaw describes as his belief in "participation," the fact that "humans must see themselves in relation *to* other species, not *above*" (Shillinglaw *Homer* 164). She justifies Steinbeck's immense respect for Ricketts as she continues in this essay: "Ricketts was a visionary thinker and scientist who spent his career considering man's plan in nature—what he called full participation." Shillinglaw further equates the substance of Ricketts' first book, *Between Pacific Tides*, with Steinbeck's achievement in *The Grapes of Wrath*, saying that both books "really embrace, instruct, inspire and enlighten the audience and help readers see that humans *occupy* a world. They do not dominate that world" (Shillinglaw *Homer* 165).

When Shillinglaw considers Steinbeck's writing in the early 1950s, she notes that his translation of Ricketts' scientific principles gave him the thrust of *Burning Bright*, that "all children are his children or, more widely based, that any human being is a part of all the physical world" (ibid.).

The next year, 1951, Steinbeck published his essay for Ricketts as an integral part of the new version of *The Sea of Cortez*. To allow the copyright separation from the 1941 publication, which was registered—correctly—to the joint authors John Steinbeck and Edward Ricketts, this 1951 edition is titled *The Log from the Sea of Cortez*. This book begins with Steinbeck's commemorative essay, "About Ed Ricketts." (In subsequent editions of *The Log from the Sea of Cortez* the Ricketts essay appears as an appendix.)

Steinbeck as journalist appears as the writer of this 150-page essay: as if to cut through the emotional fabric that the details of the essay reveal, the writer's stance here is objective. The essay begins, and ends, with the characterization of Ed Ricketts as a living person. At the start, it describes his leaving his lab and driving out for his supper; journalistic in tone, the essay does not delve into motivation (some of Ed's friends thought his death was a suicide, but his closest friends did not believe that any kind of intentionality led to the accident). Similarly, at the end of the long essay, Ricketts appears in the writer's imagination as he existed alive: a listening and loving person, a man who cared about his relationships with everyone who crossed his modest path: "no one was ever cut off from him. Association with him was deep participation *with* him, never competition."

The primary tone of the essay is puzzlement. Steinbeck gives up his assumed authority as author for his expression of incredulity: what will he do without Ed Ricketts? What will the people of Cannery Row do? Steinbeck's answers are meant to be partial, suggestive: he writes "Everyone who knew him turned inwards.... everyone was related to him." Ricketts was a man passionately interested in music, said Steinbeck: "He thought of it as deeply akin to creative mathematics." As a sentient organism, Ricketts "was interested in everything. His mind had no horizons."

Firm in his likes and dislikes, Ricketts hated "reasonless cruelty" and often defended animals that were being mistreated. The natural world was as real to him as the philosophical world was. Even as Steinbeck wrote about the fusion he had experienced when his thoughts merged with those that Ricketts expressed, he did more than insist on the symmetry between their conclusions. He instead illustrated the ways in which their minds joined. Steinbeck described what he called their "game," a process they termed "speculative metaphysics. It was a sport consisting of lopping off a piece of observed reality and, letting it move up through the speculative process like a tree growing tall and bushy. We observed with pleasure how the branches of thought grew away from the trunk of external reality. We believed, as we must, that the laws of thought parallel the laws of things.... an enjoyable exercise on the instruments of our minds."

In another node of the essay, Steinbeck described the reason Ricketts was given to creating unusual terms linguistically. He described his friend as "walled off a little, so that he worked at his philosophy of 'breaking through,' of coming out through the back of the mirror into some kind of reality that would make the day world dreamlike...." Again, Steinbeck moved toward a conclusion by counting the ways in which Ricketts related to everyone who knew him. He described this as the "ability to receive, to receive anything from anyone, to receive gracefully and thankfully and to make the gift seem very fine.... Receiving... requires a fine balance of self-knowledge and kindness... of humility and tact and great understanding of relationships...."

Some sense of the several reasons why Steinbeck was so bereaved by the death of Ricketts comes through in these comments. Never intended to close the door on personal reflection, Steinbeck's essay hoped to allow the same kind of openness that Ricketts himself valued to resonate through the memories evoked by his friend's life. Almost as a negative coda, Steinbeck ends the essay with the sense of unwilling relinquishment; he says that writing this essay has not "done what I hoped it might. It has not laid the ghost."

> The picture that remains is a haunting one. It is the time just before dusk I can see Ed finishing his work in the laboratory. He covers his instruments and puts his papers away. He rolls down the sleeves of his wool shirt and puts on his old brown coat. I see him go out and get in his beat-up old car and slowly drive away in the evening.... I guess I'll have that with me all my life.

Steinbeck's commemoration of his friendship with Ricketts was not completely finished—later, in 1953–1954, he wrote a sequel to *Cannery Row*, a postmodern treatise on the way an author tries to claim valid understanding of his characters. In *Sweet Thursday*, he attempted to finish the narratives of Cannery Row, an area now devastated by the end of the prosperous fisheries and their employees, an area hit hard by postwar conditions that may have improved the financial situation of many Californians—but not those of the people of the short stretch of Monterey's "Row." Narrated by Mack, the book begins with a Prologue in which Mack suggests changes to *Cannery Row* itself: chapter titles must tell the reader more about what will be happening in any segment; the text should include less description because, in Mack's words, "I kind of like to figure out what the guy's thinking by what he says." Perhaps the most telling change that Mack suggests is that the novel needed to "break loose with a bunch of hooptedoodle.... Spin up some pretty words maybe, or sing a little song with language" (*Sweet* 299).

Mack's narrative begins with the war itself, and he points out retrospectively that Doc was drafted when World War II began. He did not return for nearly two years after the war had ended, and when he did his lab was dusty and in disrepair. What Steinbeck had earlier described—"Life in Cannery Row was curious and dear and outrageous"—was only a shadow of itself. To console himself as he remembered the glory days, Mack bought himself a second-hand Geiger counter.

Much longer than *Cannery Row*, *Sweet Thursday* pivots on two central chapters in which Doc is maneuvered into a meeting with Suzy—but the setup falls flat. The novella continues through another season, replete with its bevy of strangely assorted Cannery Row characters, before it finally ends with another "Sweet Thursday" meeting, this one again pre-arranged. Doc has been seemingly content with his previous science-devoted life, but now he finds that he has unexpected needs. In the fulfillment of some of those needs, just as in the earlier fulfillment of giving Doc a birthday party, the community of Cannery Row is both satisfied and united.

Louis Owens pointed out that *Sweet Thursday* was "a bittersweet farewell... to Cannery Row and to Monterey, to California and to Steinbeck Country." (Owens *Re-Vision*, 190). After the novel was published in 1954, Steinbeck turned to other locales.

NOTES

1. Benson points out accurately that much of Steinbeck's fascination with Ricketts was dependent on that man's life work. He sees *Cannery Row* as a "professional tribute" to Ricketts, shown through the detailed descriptions of his work.
2. Within the letter Steinbeck qualified what he meant by "funny:" "Not that it won't be funny but funny as Tom Jones and Tristram Shandy and Don Quixote are funny." Steinbeck, with Ricketts, enjoyed all those tales (*SLL* 284).
3. Steinbeck's choice of the name of the woman Juan had married, Alice Chicoy, may have reflected the woman Ricketts was to marry in 1947, Alice Campbell. Even though Ricketts' divorce from his first wife, Anna, was never final, he married the Berkeley graduate student at the end of that year.
4. Ricketts had for some years been living with the journalist Toni Jackson, whose daughter Kay was slowly dying with an inoperable brain tumor. This letter may refer to those conditions, or it may refer to Ricketts' depression itself. According to the notes in the *Letters*, Ricketts seems not to have visited New York.

CHAPTER 9

East of Eden and the 1950s

In some respects, Steinbeck found solace abroad. After Ricketts' death and Gwyn's filing for divorce, he shed elements of his mournful grief and traveled to Mexico, where he researched much of his planned screenplay for *Viva Zapata!*, the film Elia Kazan would be directing. True to his life patterns, if Steinbeck could find meaningful work to do, he plunged into that work. (See his June 24, 1941 letter to his agent Elizabeth Otis, where he admits to not liking his own current behavior—but explaining to her that he can avoid this personal dislike "as long as there is work for me to do"; *SLL* 231.)

Working hard in Mexico, a place he had come to love, got him through the summer. He returned to the United States. Then, in the fall of 1948, with his depression worsening again, Steinbeck went with Kazan back to Mexico; the two men repeated that visit in February 1949.

From what Steinbeck then considered his permanent home in Pacific Grove, California, he learned that he had been elected to the American Academy of Arts and Letters. He was also pleased with Lewis Milestone's film of *The Red Pony*. Then over Memorial Day he met Elaine Scott; within months, she had filed for divorce. By the autumn of 1949, Steinbeck had moved to New York, living with Elaine and her daughter Waverly in a large apartment on East 52nd Street.

The year 1950 was devoted to finishing the *Viva Zapata!* screen play and writing *Burning Bright*. With Kent Smith and Barbara Bel Geddes in the play's leading roles, it opened—and closed—in October; the book appeared in November. On December 28, 1950, Steinbeck and Elaine Anderson Scott married.

Throughout not only this two-year period but much of the past decade, Steinbeck had been planning the novel he thought would be his major work. Writing to Toby Street, he described it in 1948 as "My long novel... the Salinas Valley one," which he had been "practicing" for about thirty-three years (*SLL* 408). A year earlier he had confessed to George Albee, "It seems to me that for the last few years I have been working on bits and pieces of things without much continuity and I want to get back to a long slow piece of work." He estimated that this novel would take half a million words to finish.

Throughout Steinbeck's writing career, he had commented about his family's history (all branches of that family), wound as it was throughout California history. He had already mined as much family history as there was: he was serious about making *his* history the core of the novel. In John Timmerman's 2014 book, that critic accords *East of Eden* a central place in the development of Steinbeck's moral philosophy, terming the novel "a focal point for the moral views about human kind and human relationships that he had been developing since the early thirties" (Timmerman *Eden* 78). In his discussion, Timmerman quotes much of the novel's Chapter 34:

> I believe there is only one story in the world, and only one, that has frightened and inspired us, so that we live in a Pearl White serial of continuing thought and wonder. Humans are caught—in their lives, in their thoughts, in their hungers and ambitions, in their avarice and cruelty, and in their kindness and generosity too—in a net of good and evil. I think this is the only story we have and that it occurs on all levels of feeling and intelligence.... A man, after he has brushed off the dust and chips of his life, will have left only the hard, clean questions. Was it good or was it evil? (Steinbeck *East* 747)

Thrown off-balance by Steinbeck's professed interest in this kind of far-reaching morality, critics were unanimous in describing *East of Eden* as a historical novel. It was dramatically different from Steinbeck's Pulitzer Prize-winning *The Grapes of Wrath*, his other long treatise about individual and community. In the earlier novel, characters shied away from anything resembling philosophical discussions.

In *East of Eden*, amid the sometimes confusing array of characters and their decisions, moral choices seemed to be put front and center. For example, readers questioned whether Cathy deserved her eventual suicide. How evil was a mother who abandoned her babies, or who murdered her friend, a woman whose property she desired? Even as opinion about Steinbeck's major novel was somewhat divided, most readers felt that his portrait of Cathy—later known as Kate—was indescribably evil (and therefore exaggerated). In a postpublication letter to Dook Sheffield, before the full array of criticism had appeared, Steinbeck somewhat self-consciously explained,

> I'll speak of Cathy for a moment.... You won't believe her, many people don't. I know know if I believe her either but I know she exists. I don't believe in Napoleon, Joan of Arc, Jack the Ripper, the man who stands on one finger in the circus. I don't believe Jesus Christ, Alexander the Great, Leonardo. I don't believe them but they exist. I don't believe them because they aren't like me. You say you only believe her at the end. Ah! but that's when, through fear, she becomes like us. This was very carefully planned. (*SLL* 459)

Contrasting with this antiseptic description is the powerful central scene of Cathy Trask as feral bitch, giving birth to her unwanted children. For most readers of *East of Eden*, the scene of Samuel Hamilton's playing Good Samaritan to aid in Cathy's delivery is irrevocable: long put off by Cathy's unresponsive behavior when he visited with Adam Trask, Samuel is stunned when she stares at him with sheer hatred, "unforgiving, murderous hatred" (*East* 189). In the throes of her physical pain, she bites through and into his hand, tearing and clamping down on his injured flesh so that he can scarcely retrieve his hand. In Steinbeck's stunning description, it reads like a travesty of human behavior:

> Her head jerked up and her sharp teeth fastened on his hand across the back and up into the palm near the little finger. He cried out in pain and tried to pull his hand away, but her jaw was set and her head twisted and turned, mangling his hand the way a terrier worries a sack. A shrill snarling came from her set teeth. He slapped her on the cheek and it had no effect. Automatically he did what he would have done to stop a dog fight. (*East* 512)

Finally, to free his hand, Samuel chokes her. Later, to himself, he compares her behavior to that of a collie bitch he had once delivered of pups.

Steinbeck intensifies the scene of physical damage by later describing what the wise Chinese houseman Lee must do to save Samuel's hand and arm: Lee is described as he carefully cuts the scraps of wounded flesh with his "wedge-shaped Chinese razor." Then he "cut deeply into the hand, opened the flesh around the toothmarks front and back, and trimmed the ragged flesh away until good red blood flowed from every wound." After bringing Samuel a cup of strong coffee, Lee said obscurely, "I think I'll go away.... I never went willingly to a slaughter house" (*East* 515).[1]

The pact between Lee and Samuel has been made. Yet when Samuel tries to get Lee to agree that Cathy's behavior is demonic, the Chinese man demurs. He does, however, admit to her sinister characteristics. One of these is the scar on her forehead, which changes intensity at times, almost glowing with her effort to achieve her aims. Its appearance becomes metaphoric, taking the reader back to Milton's *Paradise Lost* or to Melville's *Moby-Dick*: a mark of evil.[2]

In the context of Samuel's delivering the Trask babies, Steinbeck creates an unexpected pause in the action when he has Samuel discussing William James' *The Principles of Psychology*. Lee tells Samuel he also owns the two volumes. Again, the pact between the educated readers—Lee and Samuel—is reinforced. One implication is that to follow Cathy's behavior requires knowledge of the incipient science of psychology. It also requires that one be a reader. Samuel has referred to James as "an Eastern man," suggesting the isolation of California from the acknowledged centers of academic learning. Repeatedly, Steinbeck describes California history as separate and apart from more generally known United States history.

The physical impact of Cathy's attack on Samuel lingers through much of the novel, inexplicable. No reader believes her excuse that the pain had brought about her savagery: nothing else about the woman reflected pain; she lived through her ordeal without murmur. The context of the Trask story made clear that Cathy was not protecting her babies. She did not even want her twin sons, and a week after they were born she dressed herself to leave Adam's house. In preparation for her abandonment, she sent Lee away for the weekend; when Adam tries to lock her into her room, bewildered as he is by her threatening to go, she shoots him in the shoulder with his Colt.44.

Samuel Hamilton recovers from the fever her bite has given him; Adam Trask eventually recovers from the gunshot. But neither of them will confess to the demonology Cathy seems to represent. Her attacks upon them leave both Samuel and Adam infected, fragile, and depressed. It will be more than a year before Adam has the will even to name the little boys that Lee, alone, has so carefully tended.

Susan Shillinglaw was among the first to see characteristics of Ed Ricketts in the fictional Lee: "He is always the character who sees broadly and most fully...." He maintains what she calls "a symbiotic relationship" with "the work's protagonist" (Shillinglaw *Homer* 177). In DeMott's reading, the fact that Lee and Adam Trask, as well as Samuel Hamilton, are intellectuals—or at least, readers—creates a male-oriented narrative that forms the spine of the novel. DeMott links this structure, achieved through these three male characters, to what he reads as Steinbeck's primary discipline as writer. DeMott calls this Steinbeck's belief that "literature is built on borrowing" (DeMott *Reading* xxxix). Any great writer must have, at some time, been a great reader. For this critic, Steinbeck's belief in the power of reading stemmed from the example of Melville who, said DeMott, "swam in libraries" (DeMott *Typewriter* 10).

Following Jackson Benson in many ways, DeMott presented the most succinct descriptions of Steinbeck's aims in creating *East of Eden*, taking readers from the biblical Cain and Abel narrative in Genesis through the unusual arc of viewing the novel as personal history. Many critics have provided a religious exegesis, but placing the heart of *East of Eden* within the Salinas Valley keeps more personal interpretations germane. The novel's opening two sentences provide its foundation:

> The Salinas Valley is in Northern California. It is a long narrow swale between two ranges of mountains, and the Salinas River winds and twists up the center until it falls at last into Monterey Bay. (*East* 309)

Steinbeck as character immediately takes over the story: "I remember my childhood names for grasses and secret flowers. I remember where a toad may live and what time the birds awaken in the summer—and what trees and seasons smelled like—how people looked and walked and smelled even. The memory of odors is very rich."

From these boyhood days through the author's present half-century mark, he made no secret of the fact that half his years had been spent in the Salinas Valley; even his 1941 *The Sea of Cortez* was set in Monterey Bay. Yet in this dramatically poised description, Steinbeck made clear that the Salinas Valley is being presented anew: *East of Eden* is John Steinbeck's return to a place that had been his personal sources of both knowledge and comfort. In his second paragraph, he brought the physical description into a characterization of his mind as the narrating consciousness.

The sense of generational memory underlay Steinbeck's phrasing here. The lexicon of a family is layered over the generations of the valley. The description continues,

> From both sides of the valley little streams slipped out of the hill canyons and fell into the bed of the Salinas River. In the winter of wet years the streams ran full-freshet, and they swelled the river until sometimes it raged and boiled, bank full, and then it was a destroyer. The river tore the edges of the farm lands and washed whole acres down; it toppled barns and houses into itself to go floating and bobbing away. It trapped cows and pigs and sheep and drowned them in its muddy brown water and carried them to the sea. (*East* 310)

Much of the first chapter of *East of Eden* is a naturalist's description of the ecology of the land, the terrain itself, and the patterns of rains and droughts. Toward the end of the section, Steinbeck lauds the richness of the land, but points out that

> there were dry years too, and they put a terror on the valley. The water came in a thirty-year cycle. There would be five or six wet and wonderful years when there might be nineteen or twenty-five inches of rain, and the land would shout with grass. Then would come six or seven pretty good years of twelve to sixteen inches of rain. And then the dry years would come, and sometimes there would be only seven or eight inches of rain. (*East* 311)

As he had built his story blocks around this natural cycle in *The Pastures of Heaven* and *The Long Valley*, here Steinbeck made paramount nature's control of human circumstances.

Finally, he introduced the people of the Salinas Valley—the Indians, then "the hard, dry Spaniards," followed by the "greedy" Americans. Among those was Steinbeck's grandfather, who "brought his wife and settled in the foothills to the east of King City" (*East* 308). There are no adjectives to describe this character, but Steinbeck trusts his readers to understand that the rapacity of the human inhabitants would parallel the voracious river's destructive bent. The author reminds his readers that the natural world is as violent as the human.

Layering the biblical tropes within the natural, focusing repeatedly on the Valley characters, Steinbeck achieved what DeMott called his "metamorphosis" not in only theme, but in "vision, technique, and temperament."

He was, in a sense, beginning all over, reinventing himself as a writer and as a person." No longer was he drawing his knowledge from reportorial observation; he was veering far away from what reality his knowledge of people provided. In Samuel Hamilton, his "Ishmael" figure, who was also the root of John Steinbeck's character—or so the novel presumed—Steinbeck could create a loving, searching man who benefited from both his wide reading and his powers of observation. In Steinbeck's *Journal of a Novel: The "East of Eden" Letters*, he described to Pat Covici how significant Samuel was to be:

> I want to make a fine thing of this. I will tell you now what I intend. I want Samuel to become a kind of a huge fiber of folklore. For that reason I am not going to take the reader to his death.... In this way I will keep him partly alive like a frog's heart in saline solution or like the memory of a man. (*Journal* 140)

Most critics of the novel said little about individual characters. It was difficult, in fact, to find commentary about Adam Trask's twin sons, Cal and Aron, as if the book ended well before the Trask babies had grown up.

Most critiques were thematic and broadly based. In DeMott's words, for example, *East of Eden* was "a partly historical, partly fictional epic tale, based on the Cain-Abel story, of several generations of fictional California Trasks.... and quasi-real-life Hamiltons (Steinbeck's matrilineal family) whose lives run parallel, then contiguously, in a sixty-year period from 1862 to 1918, mostly in California. Each successive generation of Trasks is fated to repeat the sins of its fathers" (DeMott *Typewriter* 80). Steinbeck spoke to his novel's structure, too, in *Journal*, as if anticipating critical objections to his use of the two family narratives. He explained that

> he had written about one family and used stories about another family, as well as counterpoint, as contrast in pace and color.... Samuel represents the man who has accepted the fact of the Fall and thus the responsibility for life as it really is, both good and evil. Adam, in contrast, clings to the Eden myth and seeks an unfallen garden in a fallen world. Samuel, like his biblical namesake, is the prophet and judge: Adam, like his namesake, is man on trial. (*Journal* 180)

Another dimension about *East of Eden* that comes in for consistent critique is the author's use of the Hebrew term "timshel" ("Thou mayest"). Here the division between the several sets of paired male characters hinges on each character's ability to ask—and receive—forgiveness (DeMott *Typewriter* 82).[3] In other explanations, *timshel* is God's gift of free will to human beings who do not fear making significant choices. In this novel, Adam Trask chooses a path different from that of his brother Charles, just as Aron chooses to decide for himself—leaving his family— while Cal supposedly profits from both his choice and Aron's. The gist of the gift lies in its offering of freedom.

Timmerman assessed the importance of *East of Eden* as a clearly drawn bifurcation between kinds of human responses to ethical decisions. Of the paired male characters, one may be situated in the light, the other in the dark. For the first time in this novel, Steinbeck "clearly depicts how individual choices affect communities" (Timmerman *Eden* 79). This critic sees Steinbeck's 1952 novel as a turning point in his *oeuvre*.

> If ethics is concerned with individual responsibility and communal justice, then we can trace a clear trajectory in Steinbeck's ethical beliefs through the early 1950s. His early ethics are firmly rooted in naturalist thinking and Darwinian biology. Without a transcendent being responsible for providing a code of ethics for his creation..., life, of which humanity is one part, must follow the principles of survival, protection, and reproduction. An act is right or wrong only as it corresponds to one of these three principles.[4]

DeMott describes what he sees as the immense change in Steinbeck's belief system as being the result of his shifting direction for his writing life, ultimately contributing "density and thickness" to his published work. Starting with *East of Eden*, DeMott says, Steinbeck illustrates the enactment of "this uneasy (but no less real) choreography between expression and construction, reflexivity and mimesis, self and world. Indeed ... the struggles of the writing/reading life become a ground of presence for Steinbeck, and writing—conceived of in its largest sense as a mode of narration, a style of perception, and a habit of mind—becomes a way of being and acting in the world" (DeMott *Typewriter* xxx).

For Benson, *East of Eden* was more a continuation of Steinbeck's pervasive beliefs than it was any abrupt departure. He describes those basic beliefs as the premise that "man is but a small part of a large whole that is nature and that this whole is only imperfectly understood by man and does not conform to his schemes or wishes. Furthermore, as part of nature, man often obscures his place and function...by putting on various kinds of blinders..." (Benson 668). Steinbeck's best biographer connects *East of Eden* with the author's own growing sons, whose consciousnesses he found himself trying to shape, particularly during the summers when the boys often lived with him and "Aunt Elaine." Throughout *East of Eden*, it was hard to escape the importance of one primary question, "is there any chance for the individual to effect his own destiny?" (ibid.)

Steinbeck probably knew how unrepresentative *East of Eden* would be considered; the early polite reviews the book received were acceptable to him. It was decades later that critics began calling his 1952 book a changed, and a changing, process; they then used the term "postmodern." Whereas critics contemporary with the book's initial publication seldom commented on his inclusion of the writer's consciousness, later critics saw this tactic as part of the self-referential effect that brought the novel into a different categorization. The opening of Chapter Seventeen, for example, appears in recent theoretical discussions by such observers as Henry Veggian and others:

> When I said Cathy was a monster it seemed to me that it was so. Now I have bent close with a glass over the small print of her and reread the footnotes, and I wonder if it was true. The trouble is since we cannot know what she wanted, we will never know whether or not she got it. If rather than running toward something, she ran away from something, we can't know whether she escaped. Who knows but that she tried to tell someone or everyone what she was like and could not, for lack of a common language. Her life may have been her language, formal, developed, indecipherable.
>
> It is easy to say she was bad, but there is little meaning unless we know why.
>
> I've built the image in my mind of Cathy, sitting quietly waiting for her pregnancy to be over, living on a farm she did not like, with a man she did not love. (*East* 503)

When Veggian discusses the possibility of Steinbeck's *East of Eden* not only being a part of the 1950s American fictional mainstream, but also having wide influence among the books of the early 1950s, he makes the case for what he calls the novel's "conversation" about bio-political themes. It is not only Steinbeck's use of seemingly autobiographical segments so much as his incorporation of traditional literary markers: fiction later in the twentieth century was beginning a slow turn back to elements of the nineteenth century novel. For example, Steinbeck's incorporation of the Trask history is reminiscent of Hawthorne's interest in historiography. Veggian notes:

> Steinbeck composed *East of Eden* before Marquez, Morrison, and Pynchon wrote their major genealogical novels, and is therefore not in conversation with them. But the novel converses at length with certain precedents, and in particular the writings of Hawthorne, Melville, Adams and Faulkner. As Hawthorne had before him, Steinbeck sets the early American history of the Trask family in New England in order to appeal to established authority. As in Henry Adams' late writings, *East of Eden* stands literary prose in a succinct critical relation to the anonymous blur of institutional power. (Veggian 103)

In Veggian's summary conclusion: "*East of Eden's* self-conscious relation to the history it represents, its mixed narrative style and its author's integrated commentaries on the unfolding narrative, justify the postmodernist revaluation of the book" (Veggian 102).

Bruce Ouderkirk similarly discusses the patterns of the novel in relation to Steinbeck's strategies of using narrative history. He points out that in this novel of "moral exploration, with Cathy and Adam Trask serving as antitheses and Samuel and Lee serving as moral mediators," *East of Eden* becomes an effective book. He sees that it is both Lee and Samuel, along with the first-person narrator, who speak for Steinbeck's moral values: "The qualities that set Lee and Samuel apart from the other characters are a propensity to probe moral questions deeply, a willingness to accept empirically perceived realities, and a strong orientation toward others. As a result, Lee and Samuel develop a moral philosophy that enriches their own lives and exerts a positive influence on those around them" (Ouderkirk 241).

Steinbeck worked diligently on the novel that Covici thought was overlong and cumbersome. He did not allow the book to be cut. In fact, as he was nearing the end of his work, he wrote to Covici, "I keep wondering what I will do when I finish this book. It will be a terrible job to put down the last words. I'll have to have something very soon like right away to sop up the sorrow and something very different.... I would hate to be left high and dry without anything when *Eden* is done" (Benson 700). That Steinbeck placed the manuscript entire in a specially carved wooden box, which he had made for Covici, and presented it to his editor marked the novel—and his process of writing it—as a truly memorable accomplishment. He gave Covici the thousand-page manuscript, which contained 265,000 words, on September 16, 1951 (*SLL* 431, 433).

East of Eden was published in 1952, and Warner Brothers made a good offer: Elia Kazan would direct the film, despite the lengthy and intricate content of the novel. With Paul Osborne developing the screen play, the text became a truncated portion of the families' history: the story was that of Cal, played by James Dean, and the film was much more contemporary than readers remembered of the book. The characters of both Lee and Samuel have disappeared from the text, and although the film was nominated for four Academy Awards—best picture, best director, best actor, and best supporting actress—it won only the latter. Jo Van Fleet, who played the character of Cathy/Kate, won the award.

Despite the fact that *East of Eden*, both book and film, had returned Steinbeck to something like his earlier levels of fame, it had not given him projects for the years ahead. He was disappointed in both the novel's reception and audience reaction to the film. He tabled his plans to write a sequel to *East of Eden*, bringing the Cal and Aron stories into the present day. He worked on other projects and finished *Sweet Thursday*. He saw a psychiatrist. He learned to vacation with Elaine, and for a time they lived in France while he wrote a number of articles about his experience as an American leading a European life.

Those years following *East of Eden* became years of friendship. Elaine was a sociable and talented woman, who knew how to draw people out; she compensated for Steinbeck's inherent shyness, and the pleasure in socializing that he had enjoyed decades ago in California, when he and Carol had had many friends, returned to the more mellow writer. He sometimes remembered those deep friendships—and not only with the Ricketts crowd. He missed his vintner friend, Martin "Rusty" Ray, who had bought the Paul Masson winery and, together with his own, staved off possible bankruptcy during Prohibition. As Eleanor Ray recalled, Steinbeck was curious about and interested in all aspects of the winery. He would come out afternoons, when his writing day was finished, and help Rusty with whatever tasks were to be done: "from pruning the vines in the spring to harvesting them in the fall to doing all sorts of strenuous cellar work alongside Ray." (Eleanor Ray in Lynch 115–16.) Because both the men were great storytellers, their hours together were generally interesting. Eleanor recalled that Steinbeck signed one of the first copies of *The Grapes of Wrath* to Rusty, "My vintage for yours." She also recalled that

Steinbeck and Carol brought Ed Ricketts and other friends to their afternoon get-togethers. And because actor Charlie Chaplin was one of those friends, Rusty designated vintage #117 as "Reserved for Charlie Chaplin."

Among the new friends Elaine and Steinbeck made in their travels were Barnaby Conrad, Ernest Martin and Cy Feuer, Catherine and John Kenneth Galbraith, Adlai Stevenson, and other political and theater acquaintances—Arthur Miller, Terrence McNally, Edward Albee among these. Traveling for PEN and for various United States agencies, Steinbeck came to know John Dos Passos, William Faulkner, John Hersey, Erskine Caldwell, and other writers. Because there is only one volume of Steinbeck's letters published, even though he wrote several letters to friends nearly every day of his mature life, readers cannot track the range of his friendships; hopefully, that lack will be remedied eventually. But given the diligent work that Benson, Parini, and Demott did as they prepared their biographical or bibliographical works, readers already have large amounts of information about the wide circle of the Steinbecks' friends.

Like Steinbeck himself, Elaine was an inveterate traveler. The Steinbecks found ways to travel together to augment their incomes—she acting as a photographer for his travel essays. During the first years after *East of Eden* appeared, they toured Europe and spent four months in Paris, while Steinbeck wrote a series of seventeen essays for the French morning paper *Le Figaro*. Earlier in 1956, he had covered both the Republican Convention and the Democratic Convention for the *Louisville Courier-Journal*. (A year later he would write essays for that paper about the couple's European travels.)

Steinbeck quickly learned that travel writing was different from war reporting. He developed skills in recounting stories, using the idioms of each country and featuring colorful characters. He varied styles to reflect mood and action. For instance, in his "Positano" essay, he used as the opening for the central description of the village on the Amalfi coast, "The history of Positano is rich, long, and a little crazy." But the essay itself begins with an exciting description of those frightening mountain roads their driver negotiated to get the Steinbecks to that coast:

> Flaming like a meteor, we hit the coast, a road, high, high above the blue sea, that hooked and corkscrewed on the edge of nothing, a road carefully designed to be a little narrower than two cars side by side. And on that road, the buses, the trucks, the motor scooters and the associated livestock. We didn't see much of the road. (Steinbeck *Nonfiction* 252)

With similar aplomb, in his essay on Florence Steinbeck relied on the important sentiment connected with Easter week. He emphasized the good feeling for other people that the religious celebration evokes: "a week of gift-giving; small, thoughtful presents, baskets of gold-wrapped chocolate eggs and many flowers. We went nowhere without carrying some small gifts, an embroidered handkerchief or a potted flowering shrub. And our apartment is overflowing with the gifts our friends have brought to us. It is a gentle, pleasant custom" (Steinbeck *Nonfiction* 259).

Some of Steinbeck's enjoyment in this kind of writing may have stemmed from his parallel turn to serious work that was in itself lighter. At the back of his writer's planning board was his move to continue writing a modern-day English version of the Arthurian legend. But he knew that such a project would require months of study. So as an interim task, he drafted the brief novella that he titled *The Short Reign of Pippin IV*. He traveled with Elaine, sometimes accompanied by his younger sister, Mary Dekker. He wrote. And he, rightly, saw this as the interval between what would become his major later fictions.

NOTES

1. Another pivotal scene of Cathy at her worst occurs when Steinbeck describes her slow poisoning of her mentor Faye. Once she has convinced the owner of the "better" house of ill repute that she has become like a mother to her—so that Faye has left her entire estate to "Kate"—she begins a steady poisoning (of both Faye and herself) that will eventually sicken her and kill Faye. Kate has also shown in her sadistic sexual dealings with her customers that she enjoys other people's suffering. Her behavior toward Faye fits that "inhuman" pattern as well.
2. Robert DeMott in his *Steinbeck's Typewriter* made the strongest case for the influence of *Moby-Dick* on the character of Cathy, suggesting that from Melville Steinbeck had come to acknowledge "the malevolence in the universe" (DeMott *Typewriter* 77).
3. In *Steinbeck's Reading*, DeMott calls him "a negotiator of inner vision and outer resources, a mediator between internal compulsion and external forces" (DeMott *Reading* xxx).
4. Timmerman continues, "While not forsaking his essential naturalist view, in the late 1930s and early 1940s, Steinbeck began to define more clearly an agency of evil or wrong. This was manifested in the huge nameless conglomerate of *The Grapes of Wrath* and in more particularly agents such as the doctor and the pearl buyers in *The Pearl*" (Timmerman *Eden* 91–92).

CHAPTER 10

The Winter of Our Discontent

After Steinbeck's first heart attack, his body seemed unable to recover fully. He wrote fewer letters; he tempered his enthusiasm for new projects, especially those that led to the New York stage; and he wrote only one more novel. Steinbeck maintained his identity as a man who was always writing, however, whether he was covering the Republican and the Democratic conventions for the *Louisville Courier-Journal,* writing up wry jokes for the British humor magazine *Punch,* or writing essays in his new role as "Editor-at-Large" for *Saturday Review.*

Months passed. Years passed. The sobering changes to Steinbeck's health continued. There were periods of mysterious illness. There was arthritis along with back and hip pain. There was a detached retina. There was the suspicion of small strokes; there was a minor heart attack. Above all, there was depression, anger at his two maturing sons, anger because Gwyn asked for more alimony.

Finally, in April 1960, Steinbeck sat down at his New York apartment desk and began writing the novel that would be published the following year as *The Winter of Our Discontent.* He wrote steadily and with little fanfare on the moral dilemmas of his chary protagonist, Ethan Hawley.

Most reviewers did not admire *The Winter of Our Discontent.* For John Timmerman, however, this book was a definite step forward from what Steinbeck had attempted in *East of Eden.* In this critic's opinion, in *East of Eden* Steinbeck had "created an agency of evil in human nature, [but] in

Winter of Our Discontent he demonstrates the effects of a broken, and positive, ethical virtue—commitment. Hawley... does not so much act in evil desires, thereby harming community, as he lapses into a morose inaction and isolation" (Timmerman *Eden* 96).

Rather than separate *East of Eden* from *The Winter of Our Discontent*, Timmerman here links the two, pointing out that *Winter*

> also places us at the heart of the ethical conundrum of interested versus disinterested actions. Cathy Ames [in *East of Eden*] represents the interested pole; that is, she uses people and things to satisfy her own desires and ends. Samuel Hamilton represents the disinterested pole; that is, he sets his own interests aside to form a holistic view of the wellbeing of others. By extension, we might say that Ethan Hawley drops in the middle to the murky bog of the uninterested. His sordid little life passes before us without light, without commitment or significant action, and virtually without meaning. (ibid. 97)

For an accomplished writer of fiction, Steinbeck's creating such a nonentity to serve as protagonist runs the risk of leaving readers completely disconnected from Hawley—and, therefore, from the novel itself. At least within *East of Eden* Cathy provided a strong, if evil, character and readers could assess her actions in relation to those of the entire community—and most especially to those of Lee, Samuel Hamilton, and her husband. In *The Winter of Our Discontent*, however, Hawley is primarily a character who repels his readers. He "forswears all such obligations, other than to himself.... It is an ethics of abdication" (Timmerman *Eden* 98).

By setting *The Winter of Our Discontent* in his ethical framework for an evaluation of Steinbeck's success as novelist, Timmerman necessarily draws on the author's conception of why he wrote the book. Quoting from Steinbeck's correspondence with Elizabeth Otis, he points out the author's aim—"to illuminate" contemporary life—but notes that Steinbeck was never a philosopher. Steinbeck is a *writer*, an artist who works through indirection and through compelling scenes of action. There is, according to this critic, too little action (as well as very little indirection) in *The Winter of Our Discontent*. Steinbeck owes it to his readers, says Timmerman, to remember his role. Here, as a writer, he relies too often on vapid dialogue; his narration is visibly awkward; and he has forgotten how to tell stories (Timmerman *Eden* 103).

Writing to Elizabeth Otis shortly after his heart attack at Sag Harbor in December 1959, Steinbeck took on the task of explaining why his recent work had not been up to his expectations—and his assumption was that Elizabeth shared his view of his current writing.

> True things gradually disappeared and shiny easy things took their place. I brought the writing outside.... The fact that I had encouragement is no excuse.... I tell you this because if I am able to go back, the first efforts will be as painful as those of a child learning to balance one block on top of another. I'll have to learn all over again about *true* things. (*SLL* 657)

While Steinbeck never mentioned his early success writing "The Red Pony" stories while he and Carol took physical care of Olive Steinbeck during her months of dying, he surely understood that lack of the "shiny easy" approach. Truth lies hidden within the writer's being: it is an "inside" quality and it exists in private. Bringing his writing "outside," to use his language, so that his admirers could see it was a simple mistake— he enjoyed being praised by those admirers. He enjoyed working with them to create new writings. (At base, Steinbeck was a fundamental partner in all enterprises; he would miss Ed Ricketts and his generous companionship for the rest of his life.)

Writing was the one activity that Steinbeck savored privately—*good* writing. As he wrote to an interested college student about this same time,

> A man who writes a story is forced to put into it the best of his knowledge and the best of his feelings. The discipline of the written word punishes both stupidity and dishonesty. A writer lives in awe of words for they can be cruel or kind, and they can change their meanings right in front of you. They pick up flavors and odors like butter in a refrigerator. (Steinbeck *Paris Review* 182)

Perhaps his first admission of his somewhat sycophantic friends' influence on his art, Steinbeck's statement here makes his turn to both journalism (and his repeated returns to the *Tortilla Flat/Cannery Row* narratives) somewhat understandable. After early years of trying to publish, after years of having his work rejected and choosing that he and Carol live in poverty, the ready markets that journalism provided were appealing. Even more appealing was the social acclaim of theater producers and film producers— many of them his neighbors in both New York and Sag Harbor—who encouraged Steinbeck to carve musical production ideas out of much of his writing. For as he continued in his statement above,

> A writer out of loneliness is trying to communicate like a distant star sending signals. He isn't telling or teaching or ordering. Rather he seeks to establish a relationship of meaning, of feeling, of observing. We are lonesome animals. We spend all life trying to be less lonesome. One of our ancient methods is to tell a story begging the listener to say—and to feel—"Yes, that's the way it is, or at least that's the way I feel it. You're not as alone as you thought." (Steinbeck *Paris Review* 183)

Timmerman draws from these various motivations in describing what he thinks Steinbeck was trying to convey, even as he carefully drew a man like Hawley, a man difficult to like: "In writing the novel it appears that Steinbeck saw himself as a physician, probing a sick and dying body called civilization and trying to determine an etiology for its disease." When he began the book in the spring of 1960, he was considering one theme: "a deep sense of loss—of moral fiber, of battling for a way of life, even a loss of moral fortitude" (Timmerman *Eden* 98). Steinbeck wrote to Elizabeth Otis that, as he went in and out of consciousness during his hospital stay in 1959, he saw a door opening. He ran to it but he did not enter it. Somewhere within himself, he chose *not* to go through the door; more significantly, he saw his decision to write as well as he could as an answer to his moral dilemma. He decided that he would save his life by "taking it right and true. The mind does not tire from true work.... Only frustrations weary one to death" (*SLL* 657).

In retrospect, Steinbeck told an interviewer for his *Conversations* that he assumed the novel would be much shorter than it turned out to be. He drew from Shakespeare's *Richard the Third*; he knew what his over-arching theme would be.

But he was aiming for no more than 60,000 words. As he described the process, he began the book at Easter 1960 and finished on July 10. "The action runs from Easter through July 9, the day before I finished it.... It's about 'immortality... taking out more than you are willing to put in'" (Steinbeck *Conversations* 74).

Part of the less-than-enthusiastic reception of *The Winter of Our Discontent* stemmed from the literal dating of the novel's events. Steinbeck opens the book with Ethan Hawley making his (comic) "frog mouth" at his awakening wife, Mary. When she mentions that "it's Good Friday," Ethan replies "The dirty Romans are forming up for Calvary." Quickly moving to discuss his boss Marullo's practice of closing the grocery story between noon and three of the holiday, Hawley notes in a self-pitying undertone, "Would my great ancestors be proud to know they produced a goddam grocery clerk in a goddam wop store in a town they used to own?" (*Winter* 505). Riffing on the prestigious Hawley family line—which included Pilgrim Fathers as well as whaling captains—Hawley uses a scatter-shot conversational technique to criticize Mary's friends, his own position in the town, and the seemingly religious envelope of dailiness that surrounds him.

While his comments to Mary are sprinkled with corny terms of endearment, his private thoughts more somberly reflect on the house he walks away from, "his father's house and his great-grandfather's, white-painted shiplap with a fanlight over the front door, and Adam decorations and a widow's walk on the roof" (*Winter* 507). Steinbeck makes clear that Hawley considers himself a fallen man; such an identification continues as he walks to his store with Red Baker, the neighborhood setter. Joining Hawley next is Joey Morphy, bank teller at New Baytown bank.

Entering the grocery, Hawley pauses for a soliloquy that points again to his lowly social and financial position:

A clerk in a grocery story—Marullo's grocery store—a man with a wife and two darling children. When is he alone, when can he be alone? Customers in the daytime, wife and kiddies in the evening; wife at night, customers in the daytime; wife and kiddies in the evening. "Bathroom—that's when," Ethan said loudly, and right now, before I open the sluice. Oh! The dusky, musky, smelly-welly, silly-billy time—the slovenly-lovely time, "Now whose feelings can I hurt, sugarfoot?" he said to his wife. "There ain't nobody nor nobody's feelings here. Just me and my unimum unimorum until—until I open that goddam front door." (*Winter* 513)

Wearing his grocery clerk apron, Hawley walks through his fantasy life, speaking formally to cans of fruit and condiments: "Hear me O ye canned pears, ye pickles and ye piccalilli," he intones (*Winter* 512). Surrounded by the established propriety of the New England village, governed by its bankers and church elders, Hawley prefers playing the role of irreligious bad boy. Readers may have problems with his caustic humor, with his clear anger that seeps through his conversations with the businessmen of New Baytown; seemingly, however, the character of Ethan Hawley never troubled his creator.

As Steinbeck worked on the novel—a process that moved quickly and easily to its close—he was more concerned about the movement of the underlying narrative than he was about readers' possible reaction to that narrative. He wrote, somewhat self-consciously, to Covici that he had changed the methods of his writing for this work. Not only did he write "daily" about a named day that occurred both in Steinbeck's life and in Hawley's existence, he also changed the rhythm of his personal days:

> I've made a little change in method which is very great. I used to get the papers in the morning and read them before I went to work. Now I get up at six, hear fifteen minutes of news and go directly to work unconfused and undefeated.... Few people know how completely the attention must be concentrated. (*SLL* 676)

To preface a reading of *The Winter of Our Discontent* with this specific statement is to ironize the novel's plot. Describing Hawley's Good Friday as a progression of insults—although hardly life-threatening insults—Steinbeck shows the character being patronized by the wealthy banker who, unfortunately, knows his financial business (and shames him for his timorous handling of money), being urged to accept a 5 % kick-back on selected grocery orders (Mr. Biggers is new to the area, but Mary's friend has sent him to Hawley), and then being denigrated by his wife who tells him the town thinks his lack of success proves his lack of will.

The scope of these insults leaves even the most diligent reader somewhat bewildered. Although Steinbeck had created a moving opening scene of Hawley's sweeping the sidewalk around the grocery door, dressed in his clean white apron, the thrust of dismay that a *real man*—Hawley, a brave veteran—so dressed and so employed evokes seems fantastic. Even if Hawley is descended from the great families who shaped the town, the goodness of hard work hardly needs to be set up as the villain for Steinbeck's moral dilemma. Supposedly in fun, Hawley asks Mary whether or not he should rob a bank in order to get them out of their financial dilemma. As ineffectual as his earlier comic sayings have been, this question does not carry the weight of actual thought: Ethan Allen Hawley is not in any way a criminal, nor does he attempt to become one. He is not a law-breaker. He is, rather, a man stifled by the sameness of his unchanging job, but he remains a man who does that job well. *The Winter of Our Discontent* does not seriously introduce any moral dilemma that might change Hawley's life for either good or ill.

The real hinge of the moral narrative within the novel is the fact that Mary's friend has read her palm, and has "discovered" that Hawley is to come into great success and great prestige: he is soon going to be important to the town. Life is going to change. Mary's expectations jar Hawley into seeing that their community of friends—people with whom they have lived and socialized for years—have ulterior motives, and are not above making jokes about Hawley's heretofore seriously moral life.

Hawley's initial dialogues have shown him to be plagued with the self-aggrandizement of his banker friends: he feels that his current work is beneath him. He criticizes himself and Marullo for their respective roles, and he uses disparaging names for Italians. Hawley's language is racist, though he seems not to comprehend its character. He also looks down on divorced women who have casual sex—a prejudice of which he seems equally unaware. Considering that the first fifty pages of *The Winter of Our Discontent* have presented the small New England town, and its inhabitants, as proud, coasting on their family's lineage, even as they derogate newcomers (and particularly immigrants) for their lack of those roots, Steinbeck may have benefited from using more transitional scenes before beginning the long soliloquies that chart much of Hawley's thinking. As disproportionate as the opening dialogues, these set pieces of the protagonist's thought are difficult to both read and comprehend. For instance, Hawley speaks to himself about his friendship with Danny Taylor, whose career as a Naval officer seemed assured. He was accepted to the Naval Academy, but then he was expelled. Now returning to New Baytown, Danny "came back a drunk." Then, in a scene that marks Hawley's own indecision as he tries not to feel superior to his former friend, he gives Danny a dollar (*Winter* 589).

The segue from scene and dialogue to soliloquy appears instantaneous. Hawley fills in history as he muses, but much of what he thinks seems extraneous:

> The structure of my change was feeling, pressures from without, Mary's wish, Allen's desires, Ellen's anger, Mr. Baker's help. Only at last when the move is mounted and prepared does thought place a roof on the building and bring in words to explain and to justify. Suppose my humble and interminable clerkship was not virtue at all but a moral laziness? For any success, boldness is required.
> Perhaps I was simply timid, fearful of consequences—in a word, lazy. Successful business in our town is not complicated or obscure and it is not

widely successful either, because its practicers have set artificial limits for their activities. Their crimes are little crimes and so their success is small success. If the town government and the business complex of New Baytown were ever deeply investigated it would be found that a hundred legal and a thousand moral rules were broken, but they were small violations—petty larceny. (*Winter* 589)

In contrast to this pettiness, Hawley thinks for one of the first times in the novel about his own ruthless behavior during wartime:

> I don't feel guilt for the German lives I took. Suppose for a limited time I abolished all the rules, not just some of them. Once the objective was reached, could they not all be reassumed? There is no doubt that business is a kind of war. Why not, then, make it all-out war in pursuit of peace? Mr. Baker and his friends did not shoot my father, but they advised him and when his structure collapsed they inherited. (*Winter* 590)

Mired in the memories and the guilt common to veterans of war, Hawley does not use his earlier experiences to excuse his present lack of boldness. He does give readers totems that have helped him make decisions—his beloved aunt being one of those totems. Another is the family's mound of stone. And in the unexpected scene on Easter morning, when Marullo brings candy to the Hawley house, Ethan again reverts to memories of war. The dialogue between Mary and Hawley begins with the enigmatic comments Marullo has made: Hawley deduces that he is returning to Italy. He points out to Mary that being left in charge of the grocery could be the start of the predicted change. She cannot follow his reasoning. He brings her down to his life as a soldier—his medals were "awarded for wildness—for wilderness. No man on earth ever had less murder in his heart than I. But they made another box and crammed me in it. The times, the moment, it demanded that I slaughter human beings and I did.... I was a goddam good soldier... clever and quick and merciless, an effective unit for wartime" (*Winter* 598).

Napping before he and Mary leave for a party at the Bakers' house, Hawley experiences a "daymare," connected with his memories of being a soldier. Here, his boyhood friend Danny seems to be mortally affected by Hawley's powers, and he changes shape, melts, runs down over his tall frame. Hawley is helpless in his involvement: "With my palms I tried to smooth him [Danny] upward, back in place, the way you try to smooth wet cement when it runs out of the form, but I couldn't. His essence ran between my fingers. They say a dream is a moment. This one went on and on and the more I tried, the more he melted" (*Winter* 600). Hayley's terrible complicity in Danny's outcome moves his guilt about his own under-performance into a wider world. For the first time in the novel the reader cares about Hawley, even though his relationship to Danny seems inexplicable.

Throughout *The Winter of Our Discontent*, knowledge is pictured as trauma. Linked with one of Shakespeare's darkest tragedies, Steinbeck's last novel delivers an insight that contradicts the writer's career-long positivistic theme: self-knowledge is the most difficult for a person to acquire, but the most essential. It accrues not from collaboration (as Hawley's paternalistic relationship with his wife proves repeatedly) but from standing alone, separate from others, and taking the brunt of what the act of meeting conflict delivers. Steinbeck was right when he told Covici that *The Winter of Our Discontent* was a new kind of writing. In that July 1960 letter to his publisher he explained,

> You say it isn't a novel. Maybe you're right. It's not a novel like any I have seen or read or heard of, but as far as I know a novel is a long piece of fiction having form, direction and rhythm as well as content. At worst it should amuse, at half-staff move to emotion and at best illuminate.... its intention is the third. (*SLL* 677)

Explaining as he had to Elizabeth Otis, Steinbeck chooses the word that seems exceptionally apt for *The Winter of Our Discontent*: illuminate, illumination, the light that stems from true revelation.

Steinbeck plants Hawley's memories of war carefully. True illumination comes from trauma, from near-death experiences that sear the soul. In this novel, these experiences are connected with Danny even though they were not soldiers together, though Danny was spared (presumably) the same battlefield experience that had so marked Hawley (battlefield experience that no one among his present-day colleagues and friends ever mentions). Hawley has placed himself in society as the "Good Man," one above bad behavior and certainly above crime; he looks with longing on the kind of experiences his children have as they attempt to enter the "I Love America" essay contest: he has been taught that life is ennobling. Yet he knows within his own consciousness that he has had to be the killer, the avenger, and that he has performed acts no one will acknowledge.

Steinbeck's presentation of Hawley's true understanding comes in scenes prompted by his thoughts of Danny and Danny's never-expressed trauma—not only his daymare of Dannny's melting away, but all current conversations with Danny. The metaphor of Hawley's seeking knowledge is his half-remembered conversation with his brave sergeant, Mike Pulaski, "a polack from Chicago," quietly decorated, bravely enduring. It is Pulaski who tells him that his traumatic after-effects are legitimate, and that his trying to repress them is useless. Hawley has been burying his anguished memories, counting off the hours of the attack, learning stoicism. Instead, says the sergeant who has lived through so much,

> What you got to do is kind of welcome it.... Take it's something kind of long—you start at the beginning and remember everything you can, right to the end. Every time it comes back you do that, from the first right through the finish. Pretty soon it'll get tired and pieces of it will go, and before long the whole thing will go. (*Winter* 587–88)[1]

Like Marullo, Pulaski represents immigrant populations. Like Hawley, he does not duck his own profound knowledge. Fittingly, this memory of Pulaski's advice comes after Hawley has worked through the false pride of position that Baker expresses, and the subterfuge of sexual intimacy that Margie Young-Hunt seems to offer. An unspoken threat exists in both those seemingly polite language encounters, and, unfortunately for Danny, he accepts that Hawley—by virtue of his family's role in settling New Baytown—has become an acceptable spokesman for the privilege of blood. Hawley understands that he is as much the outsider as Danny has become, but in the skirmish to acquire Taylor Meadow, the only possible site for a landing strip, even the socially conscious Baker plays by his own set of rules.

Steinbeck had made clear that *The Winter of Our Discontent* was in no way a conventional novel. Accordingly, he at times reverts to the same kind of postmodern collage narrative that he had used in *East of Eden*. One of these compelling pieces is the story of the death of Mary's brother—not on any battlefield, but rather in the Hawley home. By including this story, Steinbeck brings the reader into a complicity with the narration: what does the account of the brother's death have to do with the montage of war-related experiences? This is the episode:

> Only a year ago Mary's brother Dennis died in our house, died dreadfully of an infection of the thyroid that forced the juices of fear through him so that

he was violent and terrified and fierce. His kindly Irish horse-face grew bestial. I helped to hold him down, to pacify and reassure him in his death-dreaming, and it went on for a week before his lungs began to fail. I didn't want Mary to see him die. She had never seen death, and this one, I knew, might wipe out her sweet memory of a kindly man who was her brother. Then, as I sat waiting by his bed, a monster swam up out of my dark water. I hated him. I wanted to kill him, to bite out his throat. My jaw muscles tightened and I think my lips fleered back like a wolf's at kill. (*Winter* 584, 588)

The progression within Hawley's conscious musing takes all readers into the darkening cycles of the mind: there is no explanation for this segue. The word "him" in the latter sentences is ambiguous—does Hawley want to kill the monster of his own mind, or Mary's brother? Is his reader supposed to understand what Hawley truly feels? Or is the question larger than narrative fact? Who can comprehend what "feelings" themselves are? The anxiety over the loved one's illness turns to impatience over the excruciating process of dying—elsewhere in the novel Hawley thinks with the same kind of impatience of how long Jesus took to die on his cross, an aside that feeds into this querulous commentary.

Meditating on his own thinking, Hawley reminds himself that his dark mood unleashed "a sea serpent or a kraken emerg[ing] from the great depths" (*Winter* 584). In a further progression, Steinbeck tells his reader,

>Sometimes a man seems to reverse himself so that you would say, "He can't do that. It's out of character." Maybe it's not. It could be just another angle, or it might be that the pressures above or below have changed his shape. You see it in war a lot—a coward turning hero and a brave man crashing in flames. Or you read in the morning paper about a nice, kind family man who cuts down wife and children with an ax. I think I believe that a man is changing all the time. (*Winter* 585)

A few pages on, Hawley/Steinbeck adds to this somewhat prosaic meditation the deeper confession: can the person whose thoughts these are ever decipher them for himself? "Sometimes I wish I knew the nature of night thoughts. They're close kin to dreams. Sometimes I can direct them, and other times they take their head and come rushing over me like strong, unmanaged horses" (*Winter* 587). Steinbeck here draws from apparently subterranean knowledge. Is he skewing Ethan Hawley's character before the reader's eyes? Or is he criticizing the aesthetic belief that characters *can* be known? Or is he taking the reader back into the imbroglio, beloved to him, that took place in a remembered conversation with Ed Ricketts and perhaps even Joseph Campbell?

Centering these concerns—ones that pertain to human psychology as well as to narrative structures—as Steinbeck does here in one segment of *The Winter of Our Discontent* makes the reader question what literally happens to Hawley as his journey of discovery continues.

What the narrative of Hawley's discovery unearths is that Baker will use whatever hold he can find to coerce Hawley to help him get Danny's land away from him. Hawley thinks he can outsmart all the Bakers of his world, but Mary is suitably impressed by their invitation to tea. Unfortunately, as Steinbeck makes clear, Hawley does not use his abilities to see what social interaction means.

Both Baker and Danny are more adept at reading Hawley than he is at dodging the uses Baker puts him to. (One of the narrative difficulties with readers as they read *The Winter of Our Discontent* was their tendency to identify Hawley as Steinbeck, even though Steinbeck had no war experience; his family was not rooted in New England; and none of Hawley's experiences reflected the author's life. Readers tended to be trapped by their own expectations—Steinbeck and Hawley were of an age; Steinbeck was known to enjoy philosophical discussions; he was himself a "good man.")

As both Benson and DeMott analyze *The Winter of Our Discontent*, Steinbeck was once again mired in his ambition to write a major novel that would also be an instructive text for his sons. More and more frequently, Steinbeck's writing was motivated by his concern for Thom and John IV: Benson comments that the manuscript of *East of Eden*, for example, at one time included the author's letters to the boys, though by the time of Steinbeck's death the letters had disappeared (Benson 672, 678).

In the years between *East of Eden* and *The Winter of Our Discontent*, hypothesizes Benson, Steinbeck had decided to use the Sag Harbor context. Not only would the small village create a more intimate community, it would enable him to show the present as "a time of confusion... marked by a climate of fear and suspicion." For all his untiring ambition, Steinbeck felt himself "caught between the compulsion to write and the impossibility of writing constantly at the level he insisted on for himself" (Benson 759, 766).

In these last two novels more than in earlier fiction, Benson points to the pastiche effect of Steinbeck's using bits and pieces of knowledge from random places. Such a practice was meant to bring Hawley to life, but perhaps it only kept readers from full identification with the character. Even as *The Winter of Our Discontent* was supposedly the internal consciousness of a small-town shopkeeper, Steinbeck could not help but create the wide-ranging and very literate mind of a great novelist. His aim as he wrote the novel was to draw on himself, using the way he thought and spoke—to himself in his own mind, as well as the way he appeared to his family and friends. Benson describes these aims as representing "the specific texture of consciousness and relationship" (Benson 872).

The ambivalence with which Ethan Allen Hawley leads his life is also difficult for readers to process. Even as he considers himself a prototypical "good" man, he subconsciously plots a bank robbery; he calls the Immigration Service to report Marullo's standing; and he gives Danny the thousand dollars he has requested. None of those acts is "good" in any sense of the word. Yet even after he discovers that his son has plagiarized his essay for the contest, using books that Hawley had himself found for him in the family attic, he cannot disown the boy: he justifies the youngster's corruption by recognizing that everyone who surrounds him is corrupt.

As the novel continues, Hawley does take the jobber's bribe, but asks for 6 % instead of 5; he accepts Danny's signed will rather than trying to find him and save him; and he negotiates with Baker so that he owns 51 % of the airport land. Even at the novel's end, when he sets off from home with razor blades in his pocket, heading for a likely place to commit suicide, his resolve crumbles and he returns home, taking the family talisman to Ellen and comforting her. To most readers, it could be said that the Tarot cards had brought Hawley and his family good luck. The dimensions of evil within Hawley's decisions might go unnoticed. Or those same dimensions might be attributed to the 1960s culture, which forgives when it might well prosecute. Making Hawley an "Everyman" for the current age does a great deal to absolve him from many of his decisions, whether or not he has acted on them.

Robert DeMott adds key information about the novel's ending. He points out, taking materials from the Pierpont Morgan Library copy of a manuscript of *The Winter of Our Discontent*, that the last thirteen sentences of the novel were not included in the first finished version. Seemingly at Covici's insistence, Steinbeck added this section, making clear that Hawley had changed his mind about taking his own life. Although he had left his house with razor blades, his intention changed:

he returned home, taking the family talisman with him so that Ellen might have access to that. (There is a notation to Covici on this manuscript, and DeMott quotes it: "And I hope this time it's clear. I really do hope so." [DeMott *Typewriter* 54, note 24]).[2]

In general agreement with Benson's reading of the novel, DeMott correctly asserts that both *East of Eden* and *The Winter of Our Discontent* are "intensely personal experimental novels." True to Steinbeck's belief that all writing had the obligation to be innovative, in keeping with the author's continually evolving aims and themes, his last two novels expressed that sentiment in a variety of strategies and themes. Jackson Benson had made that knowledge his mantra—that Steinbeck "did have a conscious desire not to repeat himself, to make each work different" (Benson 484).

NOTES

1. As insightful as information from today's best trauma theorists—Cathy Caruth, Kali Tal, Judith Herman, and others—Steinbeck's information about post-traumatic stress disorder and other kinds of delayed trauma reaction rings true. The nightmares that occur constantly, sometimes continuously, become the daymares that Hawley describes. He is the victim of his war experiences—and other death experiences—just as Danny Taylor is the victim of his experiences of repeated failure.
2. Drawing further from the Pierpont manuscript, DeMott mentions that an entire chapter about the human sexual warfare and gender differences between Ellen and Allen Hawley were later excised from the manuscript. He describes these pages as "disturbing material." (Manuscript 276–81. DeMott ibid.)

CHAPTER 11

Travels with Charley

Meandering in and out of Steinbeck's consciousness was his long-term desire to write about the Arthurian legend in modern-day English. Correctly, he had found that people who seemed to him ripe for the lessons of the Grail saw Sir Thomas Malory's *Morte d'Arthur* as erudite, learned, and—to be blunt about it—nothing they wanted to spend time on. Elaine accepted his fascination with her usual good grace, and soon after their marriage found herself working alongside Steinbeck on the precious Caxton manuscript at the Morgan Library in New York. Their lives for the next several years revolved around reading and microfilming this manuscript and the earlier Winchester manuscript at Winchester College, England. Steinbeck met the leading Malory scholar Eugene Vinaver, who helped him with all stages of his work. For a period of eight months in 1959, the Steinbecks rented a small English cottage, known as Discove Cottage, near Bruton, Somerset, where Steinbeck immersed himself in his translation and revisioning process.

In seeing Steinbeck delve so deeply into *Morte d'Arthur*, one begins to comprehend the kinds of attention, of true erudition, that he brought to most of his writing projects. Steinbeck was an unusually thorough writer. He unselfconsciously combined rigorous scholarly research with imaginative writerly genius. The gruff façade that marked Steinbeck's manner when he was working hard stemmed from his intentionally wide-ranging preparations.

His practice had grown more and more complex since the relatively simple immersion in the Okies' lives as they traveled to California in search of work. There in the mid-1930s, Steinbeck learned to saturate his consciousness with descriptive details, with personalities as different as those germane to the actual Tom Collins and Cicil McKiddy, described in language so idiomatic his friends wondered at its sources. As Steinbeck used these elements within his careful re-creations, in both *In Dubious Battle* and *The Grapes of Wrath*, he checked again and again for accuracy. And he also checked that the magical fusion of fact and fiction rose to— and sometimes soared above—the factual base.

Steinbeck's writing between *The Grapes of Wrath* in 1938 and his diligent work on Malory's text had maintained a profile reminiscent of that 1930s pattern. During those years, when he wrote journalism, the proportion of factual research was higher; when he had built a factual foundation, as he had in researching the Hamilton family for *East of Eden*, the elements of good fiction were dominant.

Were a critic to do a thorough re-tracing of Steinbeck's procedures as he wrote *The Sea of Cortez* in 1940, that person would find an even more intricate multi-leveled process. Steinbeck began serious reading and studying several years before he and Ricketts made the collecting expedition. And while Steinbeck planned to work from his own journal of the daily activities of the journey, he instead worked from Ricketts' and another journal available to him; the narrative of what happened on the expedition, however, came from Steinbeck's re-creation of those five weeks.

The problems Steinbeck faced in translating Thomas Malory's *Morte d'Arthur* were similarly complicated. There was, first of all, the actual translation from Middle English. Then there was the modernizing of the speech of the narration and its appropriate dialogue. As Steinbeck wrote on July 7, 1958, in one of his many letters to Elizabeth Otis (his letters to her and to Chase Horton are included, helpfully, as the "appendix" to the posthumously published *The Acts of King Arthur and His Noble Knights, from the Winchester Mss. of Thomas Malory and Other Sources*):

> I think this is a kind of milestone letter.... As nearly as I can see, the long and arduous and expensive research toward my new work on the *Morte d'Arthur* is just about complete.... I know you are aware of the hundreds of books bought, rented and consulted, of the microfilms of manuscripts unavailable for study, of the endless correspondence with scholars in the field, and finally the two trips to England and one to Italy

to turn up new sources of information and to become familiar with the actual scenes which must have influenced Malory. Some of the places are unchanged since he knew them in the fifteenth century and of the others it was necessary to know the soil and the atmosphere, the quality of the grass and the kind of light both day and night. A writer is deeply influenced by his surroundings and I did not feel that I could know the man Malory until and unless I knew the places he had seen and the scenes which must have influenced his life and his writing. (Steinbeck *Acts* 317–18)

He tells Elizabeth that the only complete manuscript is "the Caxton first edition which is at the Morgan Library." It differs "in certain things" from the "earlier manuscript at Winchester College in England."

Steinbeck has both manuscripts on microfilm; together they will form the basis for his translations. He then moves to explain his methodology:

> I intend to translate into a modern English, keeping, or rather trying to re-create, a rhythm and tone which to the modern ear will have the same effect as the Middle English did on the fifteenth-century ear. I shall do a specified number of pages of this translation every working day, that is, five days a week, and six to eight pages of translation a day. In addition, I shall every day set down in the form of a working diary, the interpretations, observations and background material drawn from our great body of reading. By doing these two things simultaneously I hope to keep the interpretive notes an integral part of the stories being translated. When the translation is finished I should then have a great body of interpretation which is an integral part of the spirit of the stories and their meanings. The introduction, which should be a very important part of the work, I shall leave for the last since it must be an overall picture of the complete work, both translation and interpretation. (ibid. 318–19)

After a few days of work as he described it here, Steinbeck wrote again to Elizabeth that the process is "absolutely fascinating." But he confessed that he had been wrong about the prose rhythms, so he must re-design his notes.

Congruent with his work on the Arthurian narratives, Steinbeck began writing a fiction/play (in his earlier manner of *Of Mice and Men*) based loosely on Cervantes' *Don Quixote*. "Don Keenan" as it was provisionally titled was set in the American West, and might have worked on the New York stage—but it was not a novel.

Cervantes' creation of the man so distant from his socially stratified Spanish culture that community members thought him mad appealed to Steinbeck for many of these same reasons. With each project, Steinbeck was clearly interested in all manifestations of the codes of chivalry and the characters' moral purpose, or their fabrication of what they assumed a moral purpose might be. In 1957, Steinbeck wrote enthusiastically to Elizabeth Otis that his work on these earlier texts was "like hearing remembered music." He had found what he called "remarkable things in the books" (Steinbeck *Acts* 299).

Using Steinbeck's thorough explanation about the importance of *process* shows his characteristic manner of working. Even though his health concerns eventually kept him from proceeding further with the Malory project, what he attempted in writing both *The Winter of Our Discontent* and the important writing about America that was to follow that novel, his travels throughout the United States with his and Elaine's blue French poodle Charley, the application of his studious methodology holds firm. Steinbeck saw the writing that went into both the late novel and *Travels with Charley* as some of his best: he had realized in the illness that struck him late in 1959 a keen warning that his working days were numbered. He was determined to make the most of what time remained to him.

Steinbeck critics have long pointed out that some of the author's excitement about his work on the Malory text was a means of his evading—or at least disguising—his anger at the political and cultural scene in America. As his essay about playwright Arthur Miller's testimony in Joseph McCarthy's House Un-American Activities Committee investigations showed, Steinbeck found little to approve in that senator's political machinations. He admitted that Miller might be considered guilty under the law, but he contextualized that remark in this earlier commentary:

> a man who is disloyal to his friends could not be expected to be loyal to his country. You can't slice up morals.
> Our virtues begin at home. They do not change in a court room unless the pressure of fear is put upon us. (Steinbeck *Nonfiction* 102)

No wonder that the Arthurian legends of harmony among men, brotherhood repeatedly achieved, and honor as a dominating principle appealed to the often-disgruntled Steinbeck. As critic John Seelye commented in a late essay, "The importance of the Arthurian material in Steinbeck's fiction is integral to his interest in eternal patterns of human relationships, an archetypal anchor in reality" (Seelye *Stage* 61).

Steinbeck quickly grew aware that he could not write about America in the voices and tropes of either the Arthurian cycle or Cervantes' quixotic tale. Becoming more and more realistic with each day he invested in his multiple translation processes, he decided that the best way to present America to readers who were themselves American was to write stories of people within the country's borders, and to use a journalistic façade so that readers would feel the truth of the characters' convictions.

It was as if Steinbeck were realizing that any audience of his fellow Americans would not be privy to research-based scholarship. The arcane appeal of a king and his knights, even metaphorically, was seriously limited. What the world of the United States at the turn into the 1960s would be interested in reading about was more likely to be the open road—a set of travel narratives that encompassed present-day America. In Steinbeck's mental imaging of his country circa 1960, he saw camping trailers, motels, maps, sunsets over both the Atlantic and the Pacific, Michigan pines, Nevada mountains, and Arizona deserts. To himself, he named this prospective odyssey through the United States "Operation Windmills." At times he referred to the project as "Operation America." When he wrote to Elizabeth Otis about the possibility of his writing a book as he traveled the country, he let her understand that his ambition was real—and that his *need* was equally real. In his June 1960 letter, he spoke about his feeling that time is evanescent:

> Frequently, of late, I have felt that my time is over and that I should bow out. And one of the main reasons for this feeling is that—being convinced in myself of a direction, a method or a cause, I am easily talked out of it and fall into an ensuing weariness very close to resignation. Once I was sure I was right in certain directions and that very surety made it more likely to be right.... concerning my projected trip, I am pretty sure I am right. (*SLL* 668)

After Steinbeck explained his choice of the truck/camper, and his choice of travel plan, he emphasized to Elizabeth, "I am trying to say clearly that if I don't stoke my fires and soon, they will go out from leaving the damper closed and the air cut off" (*SLL* 669). He had earlier written, "I just want to look and listen. What I'll get I need badly—a re-knowledge of my own country, of its speeches, its views, its attitudes and its changes.

It's long overdue—very long. New York is not America. I am very excited about doing this. It will be a kind of rebirth.... I'm not worried about being recognized. I have a great gift for anonymity" (*SLL* 667).

Once Elizabeth understood Steinbeck's urgency, she joined with him in convincing Elaine that he could, and should, make the journey.[1] At the conclusion of this correspondence, Steinbeck made clear that his naming his truck *Rocinante* was not simply a whim.

Long before Elaine had given her permission for Steinbeck's journey, he had spelled out his plans to his friends Frank and Fatima Loesser. Amid the specific details about his equipment and his directions, the writer concentrated lovingly on the physical planning that he was so good at incorporating:

> In the fall—right after Labor Day—I'm going to learn about my own country. I've lost the flavor and taste and sound of it. It's been years since I've seen it. Sooo! I'm buying a pickup truck with a small apartment above it, kind of like the cabin for a small boat, bed, stove, desk, ice-box, toilet—not a trailer—what's called a coach. I'm going alone, out toward the West by the northern way but zigzagging through the Middle West and the mountain states. I'll avoid cities, hit small towns and farms and ranches, sit in bars and hamburger stands, and on Sunday go to church. I'll go down the coast from Washington and Oregon and then back through the Southwest and South and up the east coast. Elaine will join me occasionally but mostly I have to go alone and I shall go unknown. (*SLL* 667)

Steinbeck's emphasis seemed to be on the travel itself. Undoubtedly, he was planning to do what he had done with *The Sea of Cortez* writing—accomplish the work of writing once the trip itself was completed. Whether he thought of his journey as a quest (with or without the connotations of a religious search), or as an intimate gathering of real Americana (performed by the unknown writer in his truck), Steinbeck was intent on making a substantial journey through the United States. (As it turned out, he visited parts of forty states; had he been allowed to enter Canada—he had not brought Charley's vaccination certificate so he was not allowed to cross the border from New York—the number might have been smaller.)

True to his basic interest in people, Steinbeck planned to put himself in contact with real Americans: in an early letter to Elizabeth Otis, he had explained that he had decided against traveling by bus and staying in motels because he wanted to see Americans at home. (If he was traveling in this way, he would be among other travelers, and "while they are traveling they are not what I am looking for. They are not *home* and they are not themselves"; *SLL* 668, italics Steinbeck's.) He also wanted to escape from the main highways at least some of the time. And he explained his choice of a truck in this way: "First, a truck is a respectable and respected working instrument as apart from a station wagon or an automobile or a trailer. Second—in a truck I can get into a countryside not crossed by buses. I can see people not in movement but at home in their own places. This is very important to me" (ibid.).

It did not take Steinbeck's reading the criticism of his fiction to understand that he was already known as a writer who cared about real people, and people who were often considered poor or *other* to mainstream culture. Steinbeck knew where to find insight into the true manifestations of any culture. He had written repeatedly about the good and decent human beings that he could talk with, observe, and offer coffee to. Rocinante was equipped for the frequent ritual of making, and drinking, coffee.

Another element of his insistence here to Elizabeth Otis was his belief in the capacity of those common people at home to represent an American mythos. Recently described by critic Miles Orvell as the tendency of Americans to deify both home and the small town—witnessed in Henry Ford's creation of the Ford Museum and Greenfield Village, artificial structures where the children of Ford workers were educated—Orvell points as well to the creation of the village at Williamsburg, Virginia, to the popularity of Norman Rockwell's illustrations, and to Garrison Keillor's *A Prairie Home Companion*, to maintain the popularity—and the authenticity—of the American small town. Steinbeck emphasizes this theme throughout *Travels with Charley*, but as he pauses to spend time in Sauk Center, Minnesota—home of early Nobel Prize winner Sinclair Lewis, the novelist best known for his fiction about small-town America in *Main Street* and *Babbitt*—he doubles down on this thematic emphasis. Ironically, even though Sauk Center has become a tourist destination because of Lewis, the people employed in its prosperity have no idea why Lewis is so honored.

Steinbeck's travels were meant to be ennobling. He was to learn how his country lived and made sense of twentieth-century change; he was to savor his coming to knowledge through what he saw as an isolated immersion experience, an experience that was, admittedly, somewhat selfish. As he meditated near the end of *Travels* (and a reader can find the longing in this comment): "There was a time not too long ago when a man put out to sea and ceased to exist for two or three years or forever. And when the covered wagons set out to cross the continent, friends and relations remaining at home might never hear from the wanderers again. Life went on, problems were settled, decisions were taken" (*Travels* 88).

Steinbeck's *Travels with Charley* tapped into the ages-old male experience narrative, the leaving-home story that was particular to men as they separated from family—especially from mothers—and home, a form of *bildungsroman* that had warped into the American "road" novel (Jack Kerouac's *On the Road*, as well as Erskine Caldwell's *Around About America* and Richard Reeve's *American Journey*).

It also fit Steinbeck's insistence that each piece of writing be innovative and different—different to his own canon and perhaps different to what was being read and reviewed in a time contemporary with it. Seemingly downplaying any attempt to write an innovative book, *Travels with Charley* mocked its author's craft-oriented pursuits. No reader would consider the book anything but a straight and honest narrative; few readers would notice how much of the story is told by the blue French poodle Charley rather than by the man driving the truck.

The rhythms of the narrative were another quietly contrived focus as Steinbeck wrote the story. *Travels* begins slowly—in fact, the onset of Hurricane Donna delays Steinbeck's leaving. Explicit as he has been about his departure date, knowing that when he heads north at the start snow and cold might soon be arriving, he necessarily delays the journey so that he can work to keep his Sag Harbor house and his boat, the *Fayre Eleyne*, safe. Admitting that his departure date, as well as the trip itself, grew out of his frustration that—because of his failing health—people were treating him as if his active life were over, Steinbeck ingratiates himself with his reader from the start. Paced for readability as the story is, *Travels* convinces the reader that it is intended to be "the solo journey of a person in search of himself."

The title argues a bit against that simple explanation. The full title of the book became *Travels with Charley* **in Search of America**. Scattered through descriptive paragraphs were such lines as "I come with the wish to learn what America is like," and "I had been keen to hear what people thought politically. Those whom I met did not talk about the subject, didn't seem to want to talk about it... (*Travels* 108–09). Emphasizing that his country is living in "a frightened time," Steinbeck never directly explains his most enigmatic comments. What he does is create a matter-of-fact progression of places, actions, and events, keeping the narrative in a tone that is both informative and reassuring. Even as the purported narrator disappears from sight, *Travels* creates a tone of facticity, humanized by experiences any reader would comprehend. In some ways *Travels with Charley* blends the ancient quest saga (whether or not the quest was for an object of belief, or even of religion)[2] with the informality of a personal journal. Soon after *Travels* begins, for example, Steinbeck writes,

> I discovered that I did not know my own country. I, an American writer, writing about America, was working from memory, and memory is at best a faulty, warpy reservoir. I had not heard the speech of Americans.... I had not felt the country for twenty-five years. In short, I was writing of something I did not know about, and it seems to me that in a so-called writer this is criminal. (*Travels* 5)

As part of his approachable demeanor, Steinbeck takes the time to describe his choice of clothing for his travels. Although he has more formal clothing hidden away in the truck, for the intervals when Elaine will be visiting, his daily garb will consist of khaki trousers, bought in an army-surplus store; a hunting coat with corduroy cuffs and collar and a game pocket in the rear; and Half-Wellington rubber boots with cork inner soles. His cap was his old "blue serge British naval cap with a short visor and on its peak the royal lion and unicorn, as always fighting for the crown of England" (*Travels* 32). Although Steinbeck admits that the cap is "ratty," the reader comprehends that his planning for the trip is, as usual, meticulous.

As Steinbeck begins his descriptions of the journey, heading north to Bangor, Maine as a starting point, he shies away from talk of mileage, speed limits, and even weather. His interest lies in the weather of the traveler's mind—along with the punctuation that Charley's routine helps to supply. Charley has a characteristic speech of his own, which Steinbeck describes as "Ftt. He is the only dog I ever knew who could pronounce the consonant F. This is because his front teeth are crooked.... The word 'Ftt' usually means he would like to salute a bush or a tree" (*Travels* 20–21). As if he were writing a play, Steinbeck next includes an animated scene—he entertains the Canucks who cross the Canadian border to dig potatoes—but he quickly returns to the melding of his thoughts with the terrain. Here in Maine, winter is approaching:

> I never knew or had forgotten how much of Maine sticks up like a thumb into Canada with New Brunswick on the east. We know so little of our

geography. Why, Maine extends northward almost to the mouth of the St. Lawrence, and its upper border is perhaps a hundred miles north of Quebec. And another thing I had conveniently forgotten was how incredibly huge America is. As I drove north through the little towns and the increasing forest rolling away to the horizon, the season changed quickly and out of all proportion. Perhaps it was my getting away from the steadying hand of the sea, and also perhaps I was getting very far north. The houses had a snow-beaten look, and many were crushed and deserted, driven to earth by the winters. (*Travels* 44)

Seemingly integral to the speaker's voice, the metaphoric description of the snow-beaten houses does not strike the reader as contrived. It is through the naturalness of this traveler's voice that Steinbeck avoids being didactic.

One of his most effective sections is his driving through the Middle West, recognizing what he called "the great hives of production—Youngstown, Cleveland, Akron, Toledo, Pontiac, Flint, and later South Bend and Gary." Steinbeck admits that "my eyes and mind were battered by the fantastic hugeness and energy of production, a complication that resembles chaos and cannot be." He continues, however, reminding his readers of his preference for the quiet farms and the lives nourished on them:

What was so wonderful was that I could come again to a quiet country road, tree-bordered, with fenced fields and cows, could pull up Rocinante beside a lake of clear, clean water and see high overhead the arrows of southing ducks and geese. There Charley could with his delicate exploring nose read his own particular literature on bushes and tree trunks and leave his message there, perhaps as important in endless time as these pen scratches I put down on perishable paper. There in the quiet, with the wind flicking tree branches and distorting the water's mirror... I could finally come to think about what I had seen and try to arrange some pattern of thought to accommodate the teeming crowds of my seeing and hearing. (*Travels* 84)

Steinbeck the narrative voice is never aiming for a lesson. He plants superb natural descriptions in the midst of what seem to be his strenuous efforts to create the story of the travel. There are comic sections when the good citizens of this town or that try to give clear directions (Steinbeck fancies himself the traveler who is always lost); there is often some comedy in the narrator's thoughts. There is this description, for example, of Steinbeck's finally reaching California, his home for the first half of his life:

> The Pacific is my home ocean. I knew it first, grew upon its shore, collected marine animals along the coast. I know its moods, its color, its nature.... I believe I smelled the sea rocks and the kelp and the excitement of churning sea water, the sharpness of iodine and the under odor of washed and ground calcareous shells. Such a far-off and remembered odor comes subtly so that one does not consciously smell it, but rather an electric excitement is released—a kind of boisterous joy. I found myself plunging over the roads of Washington, as dedicated to the sea as any migrating lemming. (*Travels* 137)

Steinbeck then balanced his aesthetic appreciation for his home state and the ocean that bordered it with a heavily idiomatic conversation among the patrons of one of his favorite paisano bars, the bar's owner, and himself. The abrupt change in tenor and tempo gave a vitality to the bar scene that it might not otherwise have had.

Perhaps mirroring Steinbeck's growing impatience with his planned trajectory, the writing within *Travels with Charley* begins to move more quickly. Married as Steinbeck is to Elaine Anderson of Texas, a graduate of the University of Texas at Austin, he knows he must do homage to the unusual traits of the largest state in the nation. He says of Texas, tongue in cheek, "Texas is a state of mind. Texas is an obsession." Later he adds, "Texas is a mystique closely approximating a religion" (*Travels* 173–74). Elaine meets him in that state as she did in Chicago and again, he omits those days from his chronicle. Steinbeck's odyssey belongs to Steinbeck and Charley, without interference from the world of reality.

To signal the slowing progress of the narrator once *Travels* leaves California, Steinbeck notes, "This journey had been like a full dinner of many courses set before a starving man. At first he tries to eat all of everything, but as the meal progresses he finds he must forgo some things to keep his appetites and his taste buds functioning" (*Travels* 160). He skirts parts of California; he spends more time than he has anticipated in the desert—where he does not kill the two unsuspecting coyotes caught so easily within his rifle sights. But by the time he comes to New Mexico, Steinbeck admits, "I was driving myself, pounding out the miles because I was no longer hearing or seeing. I had passed my limit of taking in..." (*Travels* 167).

Here the candidly observant Charley takes Steinbeck for a walk. Then his owner makes the dog a stack of pancakes, topping them with syrup and a stubby candle—a pretend birthday cake. At the end of New Mexico, on the walk he would not have taken but for Charley, he finds the Hawley talisman mentioned so prominently in *The Winter of Our Discontent*: "a good little new-split stone with a piece of mica in it—not a fortune but a good thing to have" (*Travels* 169).[3]

Steinbeck's consummate craft takes him up to the horrible early 1960s events that marked the start of America's visible and troubling racial unrest. Before he drives into New Orleans, before he makes it part of his plan to see the white women who are called "the cheerleaders" as they protest vehemently the fact that two small African-American children are allowed to attend white public schools, the fabric of *Travels with Charley* has been steady and comfortable. Reading the book has been an experience that would turn the United States into a remarkable place, one of forbearance, one of welcome. As Steinbeck said carefully toward the end of his account about the travel possible in the United States:

> From start to finish, I found no strangers. If I had, I might be able to report them more objectively. But these are my people and this my country.... For all of our enormous geographical range, for all of our sectionalism, for all of our interwoven breeds drawn from every part of the ethnic world, we are a nation, a new breed. Americans are much more American than they are Northerners, Southerners, Westerners, or Easterners. And descendants of English, Irish, Italian, Jewish, German, Polish are essentially American. This is not patriotic whoop-de-do; it is carefully observed fact. (*Travels* 159)

Yet what Steinbeck devotes his last segment of *Travels with Charley* to proving is that he is, in this conclusion and perhaps in others, dead wrong.

Nothing about Steinbeck's last thirty pages screams *hatred* or *racism*. But the writer conveys those emotions without question. The experience that Steinbeck is going to remember with sheer nausea begins casually. He has parked Rocinante and found a cab; in the cab he will go to the site where the "cheerleaders" are expected to perform. They are there every school day. The cab, however, will go only within a few blocks of the school's entrance. He comically reproduces the language of the driver:

"Is it that bad?" [Steinbeck asks.]

"It ain't is it. It's can it get. And it can get that bad." (*Travels* 192)

As the reader follows the narrator's description of the hate-filled language that white women in little hats are shouting, he endures the scene as long as he can, but then—trying to rid his mind of the "weary, hopeless nausea"—he goes back to his truck. En route, away from the location, he picks up hitch-hikers. Several say nothing. Another makes no pretense of favoring integration. Insulting as he is, he echoes the sentiments Steinbeck had heard laughingly expressed throughout this part of his drive—that the dark-faced figure in his passenger seat might be a nigger. The relief when the face is seen to be that of the black-furred Charley does not obviate the initial abuse should the darkness have represented skin color.

The last hitch-hiker is an African-American college student, who does not fear the kind of danger he finds himself in, living as he does in the South. In his conversation with Steinbeck, the issues of race hatred and the need for legal protections, with mention of Martin Luther King, Jr., and John F. Kennedy, take the reader back into the "civilization" that Steinbeck has been experiencing everywhere else along his route. The dark hate-filled spot that has marred his journey, the episode that has sent him flying back to Sag Harbor, has occurred only in the South. There is no excuse for it, or for its existence. As Steinbeck reminds himself, the South "is a troubled place and a people caught in a jam.... the solution when it arrives will not be easy or simple" (*Travels* 207).

The abrupt ending to the book was not read as emphasis, but rather as a petering out of the narrative itself. In a later publication, Steinbeck added a separate essay, a fairly restorative and comic account of his and Elaine's being invited to the Inauguration of John F. Kennedy. Flattered as they were, the unusually grim snowstorm on that day meant they decided to watch the ceremony on television, even though they had traveled to the nation's capital in order to attend it. As Steinbeck self-consciously remarked,

> I think I was the only man there who heard the inauguration while holding his wife's feet in his lap, rubbing vigorously. With every sentence of the interminable prayers, I rubbed. And the prayers were interesting, if long. One sounded like general orders to the deity issued in a parade-ground voice. One prayer brought God up to date on current events with a view to their revision. In the midst of one prayer, smoke issued from the lectern and I thought we had gone too far but it turned out to be a short circuit.
>
> How startling then to hear the simple stark oath of office offered and accepted. How moving. How deeply moving. I had never seen the ceremony before and it was good and I was glad. (*Travels* 213)

By returning to the pervasive tone of casual and careful observation, this last section enabled readers and reviewers to emphasize the positive experience—learning about a country diverse but capable, recognizing its faults but enveloping them in a heartiness that was only enhanced by the vision of the aging author and his dog, traveling in his road-worthy chariot for the express purpose of graphing and charting his beloved country. Reviewers raved about Steinbeck's "dog" book. The same reviewers who had not found much to praise in *The Winter of Our Discontent* turned up their enthusiasm gauges, and gave *Travels with Charley in Search of America* nothing but positive receptions.

Steinbeck's *Travels with Charley* was one of his best-selling books. Selected for the Book-of-the-Month Club, it sold more than 250,000 copies in a short time. It remained on the *New York Times* Best Seller list for over a year after *Holiday* magazine had serialized it. It was listed among the Top-10 Non-Fiction Best Sellers for months. And it may have led to Steinbeck's finally receiving the Nobel Prize for Literature.

Notes

1. He wrote a few days later to thank Elizabeth for helping with Elaine, who worried about Steinbeck's health in connection with the journey. He told Elizabeth then that "The thing isn't really Quixotic. It undoubtedly is selfish but there are times for that too" (*SLL* 670).
2. Speaking of the quest journey suggests the more religiously oriented pilgrimage. Many of Steinbeck's phrases link *Travels* with a sort of pilgrimage: the "spirituality" of travel in the context of traditional pilgrimage long held sacred by centuries of pilgrims. Knowledge is a kind of quest fulfillment, especially within the social-gospel Protestantism of Steinbeck's youth, when he was baptized and confirmed in the Episcopalian Church (where he also sang in the choir). See Stoneback 457–59.
3. Because Steinbeck's novel was already in print, the author's use of this talisman creates the circularity that unites all his writing into a meaningful continuum.

CHAPTER 12

The Nobel Prize for Literature

The Nobel Prize for Literature is seldom given on the basis of quantity of sales. In fact, many Nobel laureates are comparatively unknown outside their own country—and the selection committee has as one of its goals a distribution pattern that grants many small countries at least one recipient (as with the awarding of the prize in 1955 to Icelandic poet and dramatist Halldór Laxness). The community of judges for this annual award respects the diligent world of critical opinion, and an unvarying criterion is the writer's importance on a global scale. It is also difficult for fiction writers to win the prize: more than half the Nobel accolades have gone to poets.

In the case of John Steinbeck, what had happened to his world-wide prominence based on his 1938 novel *The Grapes of Wrath* was the diminishment of his global standing during World War II. The Swedish Academy gave *no* Nobel prizes during the war—there were no prizes from 1940 through 1944. In 1945 Gabriela Mistral, Chilean poet, was the awardee, followed by Hermann Hesse (German), André Gide (French), and T. S. Eliot (designated as British). In 1949 William Faulkner was the recipient, to no little criticism. In 1950 the prize went to British philosopher Bertrand Russell, followed by Pär Lagerqvist (Sweden) and François Mauriac (French), and in 1953 by Sir Winston Churchill (a global political figure who also wrote). In 1954 the Nobel was awarded to Ernest Hemingway, largely on the impetus of his remarkably wide-selling novella *The Old Man and the Sea*, which appeared in 1952 as a separate issue of *Life* magazine—and sold out its millions of copies within 48 hours.

© The Author(s) 2017
L. Wagner-Martin, *John Steinbeck*, Literary Lives,
DOI 10.1057/978-1-137-55382-9_12

155

To American observers, the positioning of Faulkner and Hemingway so close together within the listing of Nobel winners made good sense: because American writing (along with British) had been the mainstay of the modernist movement, to honor these two men seemed appropriate.[1] In readers' minds, John Steinbeck represented a later version of American prominence. Just as his award was deferred because of the hiatus of World War II, so his award would logically follow these tributes to American literary leadership on a global basis. (Although both Faulkner and Hemingway were comparatively young when they received their Nobel prizes, both were dead by the time of Steinbeck's receiving the award in 1962.)

This study began with an assessment of Steinbeck's hurt response to the grudging reaction of mainstream media when his winning the Nobel Prize was announced: the *New York Times*, for instance, added a comment that since Steinbeck's best writing was in the past, the selection committee might well have considered "perhaps a poet or critic or historian" instead of this novelist (Benson 916). With shallow disregard for the fact that most of the Nobel prizes were given for the writing of literature, the *Times* critic imposed a different standard on the selection committee—asking that some *critic* or some *historian* receive the accolade. The history of the prize made clear the long privileging of writers who were *poets*.

Viking Press had summoned Steinbeck, Elaine, and his agents and editors to a press reception the day of the award's announcement— October 25, 1962—and the mood was truly joyful. While the existence of Steinbeck's most recent book, the low-key *Travels with Charley in Search of America*, was most likely *not* the reason Steinbeck had been so honored, there is no reason to be disdainful of the publicity, and the universally good reviews, that book had received. Steinbeck's "dog book," as it was sometimes called, brought the weight of public opinion onto the side of the adventurous, appreciative, and undeniably macho Steinbeck—an aging man, determined to lead a life of some inconvenience in order to discover what his country was truly like during these self-consciously visible postwar decades. In the *Travels with Charley* publication, Steinbeck had adopted the cover of a genial observer. As he relinquished his dogmatic and, to some readers, his politically strident attitudes which people had found so evident in *The Grapes of Wrath*, *In Dubious Battle*, and his 1930s journalism, Steinbeck took on a character more like the professed, and usually beloved, sanguine American poets Carl Sandburg and Robert Frost. For all the academy's privileging of poetry in its ranking of awards, neither Sandburg nor Frost had ever won the highest global honor.

12 THE NOBEL PRIZE FOR LITERATURE 157

Even if the Nobel Prize for Literature in 1962 might have been seen as unearned, Steinbeck was delighted to have it. He nervously wrote his acceptance speech many times over; he disregarded the criticism that came with his winning the award; and even though he would have politely ducked going to Sweden (at one time asking his good friend Adlai Stevenson if he would go in his place and read the acceptance speech), he did the work required to perform admirably during the week of festivities. His shyness was universally known among his California friends; in the words of Ursula Le Guin, after she had spent some time with him through her acquaintance with his niece, "I have remembered it all my life ... the man's shyness, his willfulness, and his deep warmth" (Le Guin *Centennial* 55–56).

Read the night before Steinbeck's acceptance speech was scheduled, the award citation ran in part,

> Dear Mr. Steinbeck—You are not a stranger to the Swedish public any more than to that of your own country and of the whole world. With your most distinctive works you have become a teacher of goodwill and charity, a defender of human values, which can well be said to correspond to the proper idea of the Nobel Prize. In expressing the congratulations of the Swedish Academy, I now ask you to receive this year's Nobel Prize for Literature from the hands of His Majesty the King. (Benson 919)

In Steinbeck's acceptance speech, radical in that he included his wife in the opening listing of dignitaries the remarks addressed, he said a number of conventional things (conventional for this kind of speech; he had studied the printed copies of earlier remarks). After thanking the Academy for "finding [his] work worthy of this highest honor," he said,

> In my heart there may be doubt that I deserve the Nobel award over other men of letters for whom I hold respect and reverence—but there is no question of my pleasure and pride in having it for myself.
>
> It is customary for the recipient of this award to offer personal or scholarly comment on the nature and the direction of literature. At this particular time, however, I think it would be well to consider the high duties and the responsibilities of the makers of literature.
>
> Such is the prestige of the Nobel award and this place where I stand that I am impelled, not to squeak like a grateful and apologetic mouse, but to roar like a lion out of pride in my profession and in the great and good men who have practiced it through the ages.

Literature was not promulgated by a pale and emasculated critical priesthood singing their litanies in empty churches—nor is it a game for the cloistered elect, the tinhorn mendicants of low calorie despair.
Literature is as old as speech. It grew out of human need for it, and it has not changed except to become more needed.
The skalds, the bards, the writers are not separate and exclusive. From the beginning, their functions, their duties, their responsibilities have been decreed by our species.

More direct in his caustic comments about "establishment" figures, Steinbeck eventually moved to the kinds of remarks listeners expected. He spoke of what he called the "high duties and the responsibilities of the makers of literature," those who are "charged with exposing our many grievances, and especially charged to declare and celebrate man's proven capacity for greatness of heart and spirit." As he concluded, he emphasized that writers must "passionately believe in the perfectability of man..." (Benson 919–20).

What Steinbeck did not say in these remarks but did say several years later, when he was able to take advantage of the new global prominence that winning the Nobel had conferred, were two essential comments about himself as writer. The first of these appeared in his 1966 book *America and Americans*, where he meditated on the fluidity of real time in relation to the writer's work: "It is strange to me that I have lived so many lives. Thinking back, it seems an endless time and yet only a moment" (Steinbeck *Nonfiction* 160).

The second of Steinbeck's comments, seldom ever quoted, refers to the deep importance of writing to the writer. He said, "What some people may find in religion, a writer may find in his craft.... a kind of breaking through to glory" (Steinbeck *Conversations* 95).

The glory of which Steinbeck spoke here was the subliminal, personal, often unremarked satisfaction that the artist achieves in his work, his private joy rather than public accolades. Yet as a result of Steinbeck's receiving the Nobel Prize in Literature, he became something of a public figure. He was asked to represent the United States and PEN in overseas journeys. After winning only one Pulitzer Prize for Fiction—the 1940 award for *The Grapes of Wrath*—he received several impressive national awards soon after his 1962 Nobel: being named Honorary Consultant in American Literature to the Library of Congress in 1963; being given the United States Medal of Freedom in 1964; being awarded the Press Medal of Freedom that same year; being invited to membership in the National Arts Council in 1966.[2] The fact that he had earned good royalties and made impressive sales to film concerns in Hollywood seldom enters into such considerations; indeed, financial gain and commonplace popularity often work against more literary recognition.

The remaining years of Steinbeck's life until his death on December 20, 1968 were filled with travels—either as reporter on world situations or as private citizen asked to report to government representatives—and with honorary appearances, which he and Elaine both enjoyed. His only writing late in his life was the series of substantial essays which Viking published in 1966, *America and Americans*, Steinbeck's essays grouped around specially taken photographs of American people and places in an attempt to represent the 1960s American culture.

It was as if the presentation of the Nobel Prize in Literature late in 1962 was a kind of dividing line—not only for Steinbeck but for America itself. Whereas he had closed a later edition of *Travels with Charley in Search of America* with the last section—his and Elaine's watching the Kennedy Inauguration on their hotel television screen while the snow obscured the vision of people who attended the ceremony—American life that followed that Inauguration seemed to be turned upside down with the rapid changes both in this country and in its role as a global power.

On November 22, 1963, Lee Harvey Oswald assassinated President John F. Kennedy.

On November 27, 1963, President Lyndon B. Johnson, speaking before a Joint Session of Congress, asked that the Civil Rights Bill be passed in commemoration of President Kennedy's deep-rooted allegiance to its principles. The Bill passed the House on February 10, 1964; after much deliberation, on June 19, 1964, the Senate passed an amended version. On July 2, 1964, the House passed this amended version of the bill 289–126 and President Johnson signed the bill into law.

The American 1960s was a period of race riots and police oppression. Despite the conflicts throughout the United States, the Voting Rights Act of 1965 and the Fair Housing Act of 1968 were passed. In the midst of these stormy legislative battles, the country experienced an age of civilian deaths: Medgar Evers was assassinated in 1963; Mississippi Freedom workers Chaney, Schwerner, and Goodman in 1964; and Malcolm X (Little) in 1965, a year after *The Autobiography of Malcolm X* had been published. Robert Kennedy and Martin Luther King, Jr., were assassinated in 1968.

The struggles over racial power were symptomatic of the unrest over globalization: the Vietnam conflict (never termed a "war," though its unfair draft practices and its inability to decide whether allegiances should belong to the North Koreans or the South) was as divisive as racial politics. In Steinbeck's case, with his two sons both fighting in Vietnam—one drafted, the other enlisted—he struggled through his mounting health issues and traveled as a war correspondent to Hanoi and other parts of the Vietnamese operation. Elaine accompanied him, though she stayed in the cities while he flew over terrain. As she noted upon their return, Steinbeck's health was failing rapidly. Once they returned in 1967, he could not do much. In her words, "he spent his time dying" (Shillinglaw and Benson *Nonfiction* 281).

Part of Steinbeck's unrest about his dispatches from Vietnam accrued from his belief that the United States should *not* be involved in the war. When he had accepted the correspondent's job, he believed the country was right to pursue the conflict. At that time, unfortunately, he differed with his son Thom and, according to Thom's later book *The Other Side of Eden*, they broke completely over this matter. But as Steinbeck's articles made clear, the war itself was hauntingly despairing. In an early dispatch from Hanoi, he called it "a feeling war with no fronts and no rear. It is everywhere like a thin ever-present gas."

To help orient his readers, Steinbeck draws the distinction between the war dispatches he had written in World War II and the kind of writing he thinks Vietnam action will mandate: "It was easy to report wars of movement, places taken and held or lost, lines established and clear, troops confronting each other in force and fighting until one side or the other lost. But battles are conceivable.... Vietnam is not like that at all and I wonder whether it can be described...."

One of Steinbeck's points is that Elaine, staying in city hotels, is in as much danger as he is:

> This city is heavily fortified, but the bridge you cross to go to a small restaurant may be blown up before you return. The smiling man in the street selling colored etchings from a bulging briefcase may have a gummy lump of high explosive under the pictures—and he may not. There is the problem—he may be simply a smiling man selling pictures. That is the feeling all over the city. Any person, any place may suddenly erupt into violence and destruction; you have it with you every minute. (Steinbeck *Nonfiction*, 296–97)

There is the writer's former power in many of the Vietnam dispatches. When Steinbeck writes about the carnage after two men have thrown grenades into a family restaurant, two "low exploding" grenades so that the children playing on the floor are the primary targets, he downplays the dead. Instead, his focus is on the salvage that might be possible:

> Ambulances carried the broken bodies to the long building, once a French hospital and now ours. Then the amputations and the probing for pieces of jagged metal began.... Some of the tattered people were dead on arrival and some died soon after but those who survived were treated, splinted and bandaged. They lay on the wooden beds with a glazed questioning in their eyes. Plasma needles were taped to the backs of their hands, if they had hands, to their ankles if they had none. (Steinbeck *Nonfiction* 304)

Steinbeck the champion of the actual people comes through in this and many of his dispatches. Occasionally, as in this essay purporting to be an account of his last night of duty, his last trip by plane, he reminisces about the deaths of both Ernie Pyle and Robert Capa, retracing his memories back to World War II.

He admits to being scared, and to recalling how quickly any of us human beings can die: I had a drink with Ernie Pyle in San Francisco. Ernie ordinarily dressed like a tossed salad, but now he was wearing a new Eisenhower jacket. I said,

"Just because you're going to the Pacific do you have to be a fashion plate?"

Ernie said, "It's new. I shouldn't have bought it. I'm not going to need it." And his first time on the line he got a bullet between his eyes.

And [Robert] Capa leaving Paris for the war in East Asia. We made a date for dinner in Paris a week away. And Capa said, "I hate to go on this one. If I didn't need the money, I wouldn't go. I've had it. I tell you this is the last time." And it was.

And only last week lying in the bunker with a boy who said, "Five more days—no, four days and thirteen hours, and I'll be going home. I thought the time would never come." And it didn't. He was killed on the next patrol (Steinbeck *Nonfiction* 310).

The force of Steinbeck as a writer propelled all his work, even late in his life when observers seemed to think that, between the litany of strokes and heart episodes, back problems and other physical worries, there was little time for the inveterate concentration writing demanded. There was no falling away in quality. As he had written in the essays that were going to comprise *America and Americans*, if writing was there to be done, the writer had better do his best. Diligence, careful observation, word play— Steinbeck wrote at the top of his form until he could no longer write.

He recognized a general debility in one of his late letters (and Steinbeck's letters are among the strongest and most consistent of his writing),[3] but in another, as he was writing to Elizabeth Otis, the spirit of Steinbeck the writer admits only wanting to get to work:

> I look forward to Sag Harbor—after seeing you, of course. And, do you know, journalism, even my version of it, gives me the crazy desire to go out to my little house on the point, to sharpen fifty pencils, and put out a yellow pad. Early in the morning to hear what the birds are saying and to pass the time of day with Angel and then to hitch up my chair to my writing board and to set down the words—"Once upon a time." (*SLL* 860)

Notes

1. The Nobel awards between 1955 and John Steinbeck's prize in 1962 went to Laxness (Iceland), Juan Ramón Jiménez (Spain), Albert Camus (France), Boris Pasternak (Russia), Salvatore Quasimodo (Italy), Saint-John Perse (France), and Ivo Andria (Yugoslavia). Then came Steinbeck's award, which was followed by prizes to both Giorgos Seferis (Greece) and Jean-Paul Sartre (France). No other American would receive the Nobel until Saul Bellow, born in Canada, did so in 1974. One might note that in the twenty years between Hemingway's receiving the Nobel in 1954 and Bellow's in 1974, only Steinbeck was an American recipient.
2. Steinbeck's only other literary group membership had been his 1948 invitation to join the American Academy of Arts and Letters. He had been nominated for Academy Awards in 1944, 1945, and 1951 in the categories of "Best Story" and "Best Original Screenplay" for *Lifeboat*, *A Medal for Benny*, and *Viva Zapata!*, but movie awards do not equate to literary prominence.
3. To John Murphy he had written, "I would greatly prefer to die in the middle of a sentence in the middle of a book and so leave it as all life must be— unfinished. That's the law, the great law" (*SLL* 859).

BIBLIOGRAPHY

PRIMARY

Steinbeck, John. "About Ed Ricketts," *The Log from the Sea of Cortez* by John Steinbeck. New York: Viking, 1951:vii–lxvii. Print.
———. "Acceptance," *Nobel Lectures, Literature, 1901–1967.* Ed. Horst Frend. New York, 1969:575.
———. *America and Americans.* New York: Viking, 1966. Print.
———. "The Art of Fiction, XLV," Ed. Nathaniel Benchley. *Paris Review* (Fall 1969):161–88. Print.
———. *Bombs Away: The Story of a Bomber Team.* New York: Viking, 1942. Print.
———. *Burning Bright.* New York: Viking, 1950. Print.
———. *Cannery Row.* New York: Viking, 1945. Print.
———. *East of Eden.* New York: Viking, 1952. Print.
———. "Foreword," *Between Pacific Tides*, by Edward Ricketts and Jack Calvin, rev. ed. Stanford, CA: Stanford UP, 1948:v–vi. Print.
———. "Foreword," *Speeches of Adlai Stevenson.* New York: Random, 1952:5–8. Print.
———. *The Forgotten Village.* New York: Viking, 1941. Print.
———. *The Grapes of Wrath.* New York: Viking, 1939, 2006. Print.
———. *The Grapes of Wrath*, playscript. Ed. Frank Galati. New York: Penguin, 1991. Print.
———. *The Harvest Gypsies: On the Road to The Grapes of Wrath.* Ed. Charles Wollenberg. Berkeley, CA: Heyday, 1988. Print.
———. *In Dubious Battle.* New York: Covici-Friede, 1936. Print.
———. *Journal of a Novel: The 'East of Eden' Letters.* New York: Viking, 1969. Print.

———. *Letters to Elizabeth: A Selection of Letters from John Steinbeck to Elizabeth Otis*. Eds. Florian J. Shasky and Susan F. Riggs. San Francisco: Book Club of California, 1978. Print.

———. *The Log from the Sea of Cortez*. New York: Viking, 1951.

———. *The Long Valley*. New York: Viking, 1938. Print.

———. *Of Men and Their Making, The Selected Nonfiction of John Steinbeck*. Eds. Susan Shillinglaw and Jackson J. Benson. London: Allen Lane, Penguin, 2002.

———. *Of Mice and Men*. New York: Covici-Friede, 1937. Print.

———. *The Moon Is Down*. New York: Viking, 1942. Print.

———. "My Short Novels," *Wings* 26 (October 1953):4, 6–8. Print.

———. *Once There Was a War*. New York: Viking, 1958. Print.

———. *The Pearl*. New York: Penguin, 1947, 1994. Print.

———. "Preface," *Story Writing* by Edith Ronald Mirrielees. New York: Viking, 1962:vii–viii. Print.

———. *The Portable Steinbeck*. Ed. Pascal Covici, Jr. New York: Viking, 1946. Print.

———. *The Red Pony*. New York: Covici-Friede, 1937. Print.

———. "Reflections on a Lunar Eclipse," *New York Herald Tribune* (October 6, 1963), *Sunday Book Week*:3.

———. *A Russian Journal*. New York: Viking, 1948. Print.

———. *The Sea of Cortez: A Leisurely Journal of Travel and Research with a Scientific Appendix*, co-authored with Edward F. Ricketts. New York: Viking, 1941. Print.

———. *Selected Essays of John Steinbeck*. Eds. Hidekazu Hirose and Kiyoski Nakayama. Tokyo: Shinozaki Shorin P, 1983. Print.

———. *Steinbeck on Vietnam: Dispatches from the War*. Charlottesville: U of Virginia P, 2012. Print.

———. *Sweet Thursday*. New York: Viking, 1954. Print.

———. *Their Blood Is Strong*. San Francisco: Simon J. Lubin Society, 1938. Print.

———. *Tortilla Flat*. New York: Covici-Friede, 1935. Print.

———. *Travels with Charley in Search of America*. New York: Viking, 1962. Print.

———. *The Wayward Bus*. New York: Viking, 1947. Print.

———. *The Winter of Our Discontent*. New York: Viking, 1961. Print.

———. *Working Days: The Journals of The Grapes of Wrath, 1938–1941*. Ed. Robert DeMott. New York: Viking, 1988. Print.

SECONDARY

Aaron, Daniel. *Writers on the Left*. New York: Harcourt Brace, 1961. Print.

Abelson, Elaine S. "The Times That Tried Only Men's Souls: Women, Work, and Public Policy in the Great Depression," *Women on Their Own: Interdisciplinary*

Perspectives on Being Single. Eds. Rudolph M. Bell and Virginia Yans. New Brunswick, NJ: Rutgers UP, 2008:219–38. Print.
Adair, Vivyan C. "Of Home-Makers and Home-Breakers: The Deserving and the Undeserving Poor Mother in Depression Era Literature," *The Literary Mother: Essays on Representations of Maternity and Child Care*. Ed. Susan Staub. Jefferson, NC: McFarland, 2007:48–66. Print.
Astro, Richard. "Introduction," *The Log to the Sea of Cortez*. New York: Penguin, 1995:vii–xxiii. Print.
———. *John Steinbeck and Edward F. Ricketts: The Shaping of a Novelist*. Minneapolis: U of Minnesota P, 1973. Print.
Bailey, Kevin McLean. *The Western Flyer: Steinbeck's Boat, the Sea of Cortez, and the Saga of Pacific Fisheries*. Chicago: U of Chicago P, 2015. Print.
Barden, Thomas E., ed. *Steinbeck's Vietnam, Dispatches from the War*. Charlottesville: U of Virginia P, 2012. Print.
Barich, Bill. *Long Way Home: On the Trail of Steinbeck's America*. New York: Walker, 2010. Print.
Beatty, Sandra. "A Study of Female Characterization in Steinbeck's Fiction," *Steinbeck's Women: Essays in Criticism*. Ed. Tetsumaro Hayashi. Muncie, IN: Steinbeck Society of America, 1979:1–6. Print.
Benson, Jackson J. *The True Adventures of John Steinbeck, Writer*. New York: Viking, 1984. Print.
———. *Looking for Steinbeck's Ghost*. Norman: U of Oklahoma P, 1988. Print.
Blake, Fay M. *The Strike in the American Novel*. Metuchen, NJ: Scarecrow, 1972. Print.
Brinkley, Douglas. "The Other Vietnam Generation," *New York Times Book Review* (February 28, 1999):27. Print.
Brodwin, Stanley. "'The Poetry of Scientific Thinking': Steinbeck's *Log from the Sea of Cortez* and Scientific Travel Narrative," *Steinbeck and the Environment*. Eds. Susan F. Beegel, Susan Shillinglaw, and Wesley N. Tiffney, Jr. Tuscaloosa: U of Alabama P, 1997:142–60.
Browder, Laura. *Rousing the Nation: Radical Culture in Depression America*. Amherst: U of Massachusetts P, 1998. Print.
Campbell, Joseph. *The Hero's Journey: Joseph Campbell on His Life and Work*. Ed. Phil Cousineau. Shaftesbury: Element, 1999. Print.
———. *The Hero with a Thousand Faces*. Nofato, CA: New World Library, 2008. Print.
———. *An Open Mind. Joseph Campbell in Conversation with Michael Toms*. New York: Harper & Row, 1989.
Casey, Janet Galligani. "Agrarian Landscapes, the Depression, and Women's Progressive Fiction," *The Novel and the American Left: Critical Essays on Depression-Era Fiction*. Ed. Janet Galligani Casey. Iowa City: U of Iowa P, 2004:96–117.

Cederstrom, Lorelei. "The 'Great Mother' in *The Grapes of Wrath*," *Steinbeck and the Environment: Interdisciplinary Approaches*. Eds. Susan F. Beegel, Susan Shillinglaw, and Wesley N. Tiffany. Tuscaloosa: U of Alabama P, 1997:76–91. Print.

Chamberlain, John. "Books of the Times," *New York Times* (May 9, 1942):11. Print.

Coers, Donald V. *John Steinbeck Goes to War: The Moon Is Down as Propaganda*. Tuscaloosa: U of Alabama P, 1991. Print.

Conn, Peter. *The American 1930s: A Literary History*. Cambridge: Cambridge UP, 2009. Print.

Conversations with John Steinbeck. Ed. Thomas French. Jackson: UP of Mississippi, 1988. Print.

Cook, Sylvia J. *From Tobacco Road to Route 66: The Southern Poor White in Fiction*. Chapel Hill: U of North Carolina P, 1976. Print.

Cousins, Norman. *Present Tense: An American Editor's Odyssey*. New York: McGraw-Hill, 1967. Print.

Cowley, Malcolm. *The Dream of the Golden Mountains*. New York: Viking, 1980. Print.

Cox. Martha Heasley. "The Conclusion of *The Grapes of Wrath*: Steinbeck's Conception and Execution," *San Jose Studies* 1 (November 1975):73–81. Print.

Currell, Susan. *The March of Spare Time: The Problem and Promise of Leisure in the Great Depression*. Philadelphia: U of Pennsylvania P, 2005. Print.

Davis, Robert Con, ed. *Twentieth Century Interpretations of The Grapes of Wrath*. Englewood Cliffs, NJ: Prentice Hall, 1982. Print.

DeMott, Robert. "Introduction," *The Grapes of Wrath*. New York: Penguin, 2006: ix–xlv.

———. *Steinbeck's Reading: A Catalogue of Books Owned and Borrowed*. New York: Garland, 1984. Print.

———. *Steinbeck's Typewriter: Essays on His Art*. Troy, New York: Whitston, 1996. Print.

Deneer, Patrick J. et al, eds. *A Political Companion to John Steinbeck*. Lexington: UP of Kentucky, 2013. Print.

Denning, Michael. *The Cultural Front; The Laboring of American Culture in the Twentieth Century*. New York: Verso, 1996. Print.

Dimock, Wai Chee and Michael T. Gilmore. *Rethinking Class: Literary Studies and Social Formations*. New York: Columbia UP, 1994. Print.

Ditsky, John, ed. *Critical Essays on Steinbeck's The Grapes of Wrath*. Boston: Hall, 1989. Print.

Donohue, Agnes McNeill, ed. *A Casebook on The Grapes of Wrath*. New York: Crowell, 1968. Print.

Dow, William. *Narrating Class in American Fiction*. New York: Palgrave, 2009. Print.

Edmunds, Susan. *Grotesque Relations: Modernist Domestic Fiction and the U.S. Welfare State.* New York: Oxford UP, 2008. Print.
Ellwood, Robert. *The Politics of Myth: A Study of C. G. Jung, Mircea Eliade, and Joseph Campbell.* Albany: State U of New York P, 1999. Print.
Entin, Joseph. *Sensational Modernism: Experimental Fiction and Photography in Thirties America.* Chapel Hill: U of North Carolina P, 2007. Print.
Everson, William K. *Archetype West: The Pacific Coast as a Literary Region.* Berkeley, CA: Oyez, 1976. Print.
Feied, Frederick. *The Tidepool and the Stars: The Ecological Basis of Steinbeck's Depression Novels.* New York: Xlibris, 2001. Print.
Fender, Stephen. *Nature, Class, and New Deal Literature: The Country Poor in the Great Depression.* New York: Routledge, 2012. Print.
Fenech, Thomas. "Introduction," John Steinbeck's *Tortilla Flat.* New York: Penguin, 1997:vii–xxvi. Print.
———., ed. *Conversations with John Steinbeck.* Jackson: UP of Mississippi, 1988. Print.
———. *The FBI Files on John Steinbeck.* Woodlands, TX: New Century, 2002. Print.
Foley, Barbara. *Radical Representations.* Durham, NC: Duke UP, 1993. Print.
———. *Telling the Truth: The Theory and Practice of Documentary Fiction.* Ithaca, New York: Cornell UP, 1986. Print.
Fontenrose, Joseph. *John Steinbeck: An Introduction and Interpretation.* New York: Barnes and Noble, 1963. Print.
French, Thomas. *Steinbeck and Covici: The Story of a Friendship.* Middlebury, VT: Paul S. Eriksson, 1979. Print.
French, Warren. "Introduction," *In Dubious Battle.* New York: Viking, 1992:vii–xxix. Print.
———. *John Steinbeck.* New York: Twayne, 1961, 1974. Print.
———. ed. *A Companion to the Grapes of Wrath.* New York: Viking, 1963. Print.
Frohock, W. M. *The Novel of Violence in America,* 2nd ed. Boston: Beacon, 1964. Print.
Gage, Tom. "Steinbeck Knew Dad Better Than I Did," *East of Eden: New and Recent Essays.* Eds. Michael J. Meyer and Henry Veggian. Amsterdam: Rodopi, 2013:1–24. Print.
Galati, Frank. *John Steinbeck's The Grapes of Wrath.* New York: Penguin, 1991. Print.
Gannett, Lewis. *John Steinbeck: Personal and Bibliographical Notes.* New York: Viking, 1939. Print.
George, Stephen K. and Barbara A. Heavilin, eds. *John Steinbeck and His Contemporaries.* Lanham, MD: Scarecrow, 2007. Print.
Gibson-Graham, J. K., Stephen A. Resnick, and Richard D. Wolff, eds. *Class and Its Others.* Minneapolis: U of Minnesota P, 2000. Print.

Gladstein, Mimi R. "Deletions from the *Battle*; Gaps in the *Grapes*," *San Jose Studies* 18 (1992):43–51. Print.

———. "Friendly Fire: Steinbeck's *East of Eden*," *The Betrayal of Brotherhood in the Work of John Steinbeck: Cain Sign*. Ed. Michael J. Meyer. New York: Edwin Mellen, 2000:375–400. Print.

———. *The Indestructible Woman in Faulkner, Hemingway, and Steinbeck*. Ann Arbor, MI: UMI Research P, 1986. Print.

———. "Mr. Novelist Goes to War: Hemingway and Steinbeck as Front-Line Correspondents," *War, Literature, and the Arts* 15.1/2 (2003):258–66. Print.

———. "Steinbeck's Dysfunctional Families: A Coast-to-Coast Dilemma," *John Steinbeck's Global Dimensions*. Eds. Kyoko Ariki, Luchan Li and Scott Pugh. New York: Scarecrow, 2008:57–69. Print.

Gregory, James N. *American Exodus: The Dust Bowl Migration and the Okie Culture in California*. New York: Oxford UP, 1989. Print.

Hanley, Lawrence. "'Smashing Cantatas' and 'Looking Glass Pitchers,' The Impossible Location of Proletarian Literature," *The Novel and the American Left*. Ed. Janet Galligani Casey. Iowa City: U of Iowa P, 2004:132–50. Print.

Hapke, Laura. *Daughters of the Great Depression: Women, Work, and Fiction in the American 1930s*. Athens: U of Georgia P, 1995. Print.

Harmon, Robert B. and John Early. *The Grapes of Wrath: A Fifty Year Bibliographic Survey*. San Jose, CA: San Jose State University Steinbeck Research Center, 1990. Print.

Hartsock, John. *A History of American Literary Journalism: The Emergence of a Modern Narrative Form*. Amherst: U of Massachusetts P, 2000. Print.

Hayashi, Tetsumaro. "Steinbeck's *Winter* as Shakespearean Fiction," *Steinbeck Quarterly* 12 (Sumer-Fall 1979):107–15.

———. "Women and the Principle of Continuity in *The Grapes of Wrath*," *Kyusbu American Literature* 10 (1967):75–80. Print.

———., ed. *Steinbeck's The Grapes of Wrath: Essays in Criticism*. Muncie, IN: Ball State U Steinbeck Research Institute, 1990. Print.

Haytock, Jennifer. *The Middle Class in the Great Depression: Popular Women's Novels of the 1930s*. New York: Palgrave, 2013. Print.

Heavilin, Barbara A. "The Invisible Woman: Ma Joad as an Epic Heroine in John Steinbeck's *The Grapes of Wrath*," *Kyusbu American Literature* 32 (1991):51–61. Print.

Howarth, William. "The Mother of Literature: Journalism and *The Grapes of Wrath*," *Literary Journalism in the Twentieth Century*. Ed. Norman Sims. New York: Oxford UP, 1990:53–81. Print.

Hughes, R. S. *Beyond the Red Pony: A Reader's Companion to Steinbeck's Complete Short Stories*. Metuchen, NJ: Scarecrow P, 1987. Print.

Hutner, Gordon. *What America Read: Taste, Class, and the Novel, 1920–1960*. Chapel Hill: U of North Carolina P, 2009. Print.

Irr, Caren. *The Suburb of Dissent: Cultural Politics in the United States and Canada During the 1930s*. Durham, NC: Duke UP, 1998. Print.

Jones, Gavin. *American Hungers, The Problem of Poverty in U. S. Literature, 1840–1945*. Princeton, NJ: Princeton UP, 2008. Print.

Kazin, Alfred. "The Unhappy Man from Unhappy Valley," *New York Times Book Review* 1.29 (May 4, 1958). Print.

Kazin, Michael. *American Dreamers; How the Left Changed a Nation*. New York: Knopf, 2011. Print.

Kennedy, David M. *Freedom from Fear: The American People in Depression and War, 1929–1945*. New York: Oxford UP, 1999. Print.

Kennedy, William. "'My Work Is No Good,'" *New York Times Book Review* 1 (April 9, 1989): 44–5. Print.

Kiernan, Thomas. *The Intricate Music: A Biography of John Steinbeck*. Boston: Little, Brown, 1979. Print.

Klein, Marcus. *Foreigners: The Making of American Literature, 1900–1940*. Chicago: U of Chicago P, 1981. Print.

Kozol, Wendy. "Madonnas of the Fields: Photography, Gender, and 1930s Farm Relief," *Genders* 2 (Summer 1988):1–23. Print.

Lang, Amy Schrager. *The Syntax of Class*. Princeton, NJ: Princeton UP, 2003. Print.

Lange, Dorothea and Paul S. Taylor. *An American Exodus: A Record of Human Erosion*. New York: Reynal and Hitchcock, 1939. Print.

Larsen, Stephen and Robin Larsen. *A Fire in the Mind: The Life of Joseph Campbell*. New York: Doubleday, 1991. Print.

Levant, Howard. *The Novels of John Steinbeck: A Critical Study*. Columbia: U of Missouri P, 1974. Print.

Levine, Lawrence W. *Highbrow/Lowbrow: The Emergence of Cultural Hierarchy in America*. Cambridge, MA: Harvard UP, 1988. Print.

Lipsitz, George. *The Possessive Investment in Whiteness: How White People Profit from Identity Politics*. Philadelphia, PA: Temple UP, 2006. Print.

———. *Rainbow at Midnight: Labor and Culture in the 1940s*. Urbana: U of Illinois P, 1994. Print.

Lisca, Peter. *The Wide World of John Steinbeck*. New Brunswick, NJ: Rutgers UP, 1958. Print.

Lynch, Audry. *Steinbeck Remembered*. Santa Barbara, CA: Fifhian P, 2000. Print.

Magny, Claude-Edmonde. *The Age of the American Novel: The Film Aesthetic of Fiction between the Two Wars*, trans. Eleanor Hochman. New York: Ungar, 1972 (1948). Print.

Mak, Geert. *In America: Travels with John Steinbeck*. London: Harvill Secker, 2014. Print.

McElvaine, Robert S. *The Great Depression: America, 1929–1941*. New York: Times Books, 1984. Print.

McGovern, James R. *And a Time for Hope: Americans in the Great Depression.* Westport, CT: Praeger, 2000. Print.

McKay, Nellie. "'Happy[?]-Wife-and-Motherdom': The Portrayal of Ma Joad in John Steinbeck's *The Grapes of Wrath,*" *New Essays on the Grapes of Wrath.* Ed. David Wyatt. New York: Cambridge UP, 1990:47–69. Print.

McWilliams, Carey. *Factories in the Field: The Story of Migratory Farm Labor in California.* Boston: Little, Brown, 1939. Print.

Meyer, Michael J. and Henry Veggian, eds. *East of Eden: New and Recent Essays.* Amsterdam: Rodopi, 2013. Print.

Miller, Joshua L. *Accented America: The Cultural Politics of Multilingual Modernism.* New York: Oxford UP, 2011. Print.

Millichap, Joseph R. *Steinbeck and Film.* New York: Ungar, 1983. Print.

Mitman, Greg. *The State of Nature: Ecology, Community, and American Social Thought, 1900–1950.* Chicago: U of Chicago P, 1992. Print.

Motley, Warren. "From Patriarchy to Matriarchy: Ma Joad's Role in *The Grapes of Wrath,*" *American Literature* 54 (1982):397–412. Print.

Mullen, Bill and Sherry Linkton, eds. *Radical Revisions: Rereading 1930s Cultures.* Urbana: U of Illinois P, 1996. Print.

Murphy, James. *The Proletarian Moment: The Controversy over Leftism in Literature.* Chicago: U of Illinois P, 1991. Print.

Nericcio, William A., ed. *Homer from Salinas, John Steinbeck's Enduring Voice for California.* San Diego, CA: San Diego State UP, 2009. Print.

Noble, Donald R., ed. *John Steinbeck.* Pasadena, CA: Salem P, 2011. Print.

Orvell, Miles. *The Death and Life of Main Street.* Chapel Hill: The U of North Carolina P, 2012. Print.

Osborne, William R. "The Texts of Steinbeck's 'The Chrysanthemums,'" *Modern Fiction Studies* 12 (Winter 1966–1967): 479–84. Print.

Ouderkirk, Bruce. "The Unconventional Morality of *East of Eden,*" *East of Eden, New and Recent Essays.* Eds. Michael J. Meyer and Henry Veggian. Amsterdam: Rodopi, 2013:231–56. Print.

Owens, Louis. *John Steinbeck's Re-Vision of America.* Athens: U of Georgia P, 1985. Print.

———. *The Grapes of Wrath: Trouble in the Promised Land.* Boston: Twayne, 1989. Print.

———. and Hector Torres. "Dialogic Structure and Levels of Discourse in Steinbeck's *The Grapes of Wrath,*" *Arizona Quarterly* 45 (Winter 1989):75–94. Print.

Parini, Jay. *John Steinbeck, A Biography.* London: Heinemann, 1994. Print.

Parrish, Michael. *Anxious Decades: America in Prosperity and Depression, 1920–1941.* New York: Norton, 1992. Print.

Peeler, David P. *Hope Among Us Yet: Social Criticism and Social Solace in Depression America.* Athens: U of Georgia P, 1987. Print.

Pells, Richard H. *Radical Visions and American Dreams: Culture and Social Thought in the Depression Years.* Middletown, CT: Wesleyan UP, 1973. Print.

Pratt, Linda Ray. "Imagining Existence: Form and History in Steinbeck and Agee," *Southern Review* 11 (Winter 1975):84–98. Print.

Rabinowitz, Paula. *Labor and Desire: Women's Revolutionary Fiction in Depression America.* Chapel Hill: U of North Carolina P, 1991. Print.

———. *They Must Be Represented: The Politics of Documentary.* New York: Verso, 1994. Print.

Radway, Janice. *A Feeling for Books: The Book-of-the-Month Club, Literary Taste, and Middle-Class Desire.* Chapel Hill: U of North Carolina P, 1997. Print.

Raeburn, John. *A Staggering Revolution, A Cultural History of Thirties Photography.* Urbana: U of Illinois P, 2006. Print.

Railsback, Brian. "Searching for 'What Is': Charles Darwin and John Steinbeck," *Steinbeck and the Environment.* Eds. Susan F. Beegel, Susan Shillinglaw, Wesley N. Tiffney, Jr. Tuscaloosa: U of Alabama P, 1997:127–41. Print.

Railsback, Brian and Michael J. Meyer, eds. *A John Steinbeck Encyclopedia.* Westport, CT: Greenwood, 2006. Print.

Railton, Stephen. "John Steinbeck's Call to Conversion in *The Grapes of Wrath*," *Readings on John Steinbeck.* Ed. Clarice Swisher. San Diego, CA: Greenhaven P, 1996: 165–75. Print.

Ricketts, Edward F. *The Outer Shores.* 2 vols. Ed. Joel W. Hedgpeth. Eureka, CA: Mad River P, 1978. Print.

——— and Jack Calvin. *Between Pacific Tides.* 3rd ed. Foreword by John Steinbeck. Stanford, CA: Stanford UP, 1952.

——— and John Steinbeck. *Sea of Cortez.* New York: Viking, 1941. Print.

Rideout, Walter. *The Radical Novel in the United States, 1900–54.* Cambridge, MA: Harvard UP, 1956. Print.

Ritter, William Emerson. *The Unity of the Organism, or the Organismal Conception.* 2 vols. Boston: Gorham, 1919.

Roberts, David. "Travels with Steinbeck," *American Photographer* 22 (March 1989):44–51. Print.

Rodger, Katherine A., ed. *Renaissance Man of Cannery Row: The Life and Letters of Edward F. Ricketts.* Tuscaloosa: U of Alabama P, 2003. Print.

Rollins, William, Jr. "What Is a Proletarian Writer?" ("Review and Comment"). *New Masses* 14.5 (January 29, 1935). Print.

Schulberg, Budd. "John Steinbeck: A Lion in Winter," *The Four Seasons of Success.* Garden City, New York: Doubleday, 1972:187–97. Print.

Schultz, Jeffrey and Luchen Li. *John Steinbeck, A Literary Reference.* New York: Checkmark, 2005. Print.

Seed, David. *Cinematic Fictions.* Liverpool: U of Liverpool P, 2010. Print.

Seelye, John. "Come Back to the Boxcar, Leslie Honey; or, Don't Cry for me, Madonna, Just Pass the Milk: Steinbeck and Sentimentality," *Beyond*

Boundaries: Rereading John Steinbeck. Eds. Susan Shillinglaw and Kerin Hearle. Tuscaloosa: U of Alabama P, 2002:11–33. Print.

———. "Introduction," John Steinbeck's *The Red Pony.* New York: Penguin, 1994:vii–xxix. Print.

———. "Why Everybody/Nobody Reads John Steinbeck," *Steinbeck on Stage and Film.* Ed. Joel E. Smith. Louisville, Kentucky: Actors Theatre of Louisville, 1996:61–62.

Sexias, Antonia. "John Steinbeck and the Non-Teleological Bus," *What's Doing on the Monterey Peninsula I (March 1947).* Reprinted in *Steinbeck and His Critics.* Eds. E. W. Tedlock, Jr. and C. V. Wicker. Albuquerque: U of New Mexico P, 1957:275–80.

Sheffield, Carlton. *Steinbeck: The Good Companion.* Portola Valley, CA: American Lives Endowment, 1983. Print.

Shillinglaw, Susan. *Carol and John Steinbeck: Portrait of a Marriage.* Reno: U of Nevada P, 2013. Print.

———. "Introduction," *Steinbeck and the Environment.* Eds. Susan F. Beegel, Susan Shillinglaw, Wesley N. Tiffney, Jr. Tuscaloosa: U of Alabama P, 1997:8–13. Print.

———. *On Reading The Grapes of Wrath.* New York: Penguin, 2014. Print.

———. "The Wrath of a Nation: Reading *The Grapes of Wrath*, 1939–2007," *Homer from Salinas.* Ed. William Anthony Nericcio. San Diego. California: San Diego State UP, 2009:56–83. Print.

———., ed. *John Steinbeck: Centennial Reflections by American Writers.* San Jose, CA: San Jose State U, 2002. Print.

Shimomura, Noboru K. *A Study of John Steinbeck: Mysticism in His Novels.* Tokyo: Hokuseido P, 1982. Print.

Shulman, Robert. *The Power of Political Art: The 1930s Literary Left.* Chapel Hill: U of North Carolina P, 2000. Print.

Simmonds, Roy S. *John Steinbeck: The War Years, 1939–1945.* Lewisburg, PA: Bucknell UP, 1996. Print.

———. "The Original Manuscripts of 'The Chrysanthemums,'" *Steinbeck Quarterly* 7 (Summer-Fall 1974):102–11.

———. *Steinbeck's Literary Achievement.* Muncie, IN: Ball State U/Steinbeck Society, 1976. Print.

———. "Steinbeck's 'The Murder': A Critical and Bibliographical Study," *Steinbeck Quarterly* 9 (Spring 1976):45–53. Print.

Spilka, Mark. "Sweet Violence in Steinbeck's Eden," *Eight Lessons in Love.* Columbia: U of Missouri P, 1997:242–51. Print.

St. Pierre, Brian. *John Steinbeck, The California Years.* San Francisco, CA: San Francisco Chronicle, 1983. Print.

Staub, Michael E. *Voices of Persuasion: Politics of Representation in 1930s America.* Cambridge: Cambridge UP, 1994. Print.

Steigerwald, Bill. *Dogging Steinbeck: How I went looking for Steinbeck's America, found my own America, and exposed the truth about 'Travels with Charley.'* Pittsburgh, PA: Fourth River, 2012. Print.
Steinbeck, Elaine and Robert Wallsten, eds. *Steinbeck: A Life in Letters.* New York: Viking, 1975.
Steinbeck, John IV. *In Touch.* New York: Knopf, 1969. Print.
Steinbeck, John IV and Nancy Steinbeck. *The Other Side of Eden: Life with John Steinbeck.* Amherst, New York: Prometheus, 2001. Print.
Stoneback, H. R. "Pilgrimage Variations," *Hemingway: Eight Decades of Criticism.* Ed. Linda Wagner-Martin. East Lansing: Michigan State UP, 2009:457–76. Print.
Stott, William. *Documentary Expression and Thirties America.* New York: Oxford UP, 1973. Print.
Susman, Warren I. *Culture as History: The Transformation of American Society in the Twentieth Century.* Washington, DC: Smithsonian Institution P, 2003. Print.
Swensen, James R. *Picturing Migrants: The Grapes of Wrath and New Deal Documentary Photography.* Norman: U of Oklahoma P, 2015. Print.
Szalay, Michael. *New Deal Modernism: American Literature and the Invention of the Welfare State.* Durham, NC: Duke UP, 2010.
Terkel, Studs. *Hard Times, An Oral History of the Great Depression.* New York: Pantheon, 1970, 1978.
———. "Introduction: We Still See Their Faces," *Fiftieth Anniversary Edition of The Grapes of Wrath.* New York: Viking, 1989:v–xx. Print.
Terrill, Tom and Jerrold Hirsch, eds. *Such as Us: Southern Voices of the Thirties.* Chapel Hill: U of North Carolina P, 1978. Print.
Tetsumaro, Hayashi and John H. Timmerman. *John Steinbeck: The Years of Greatness, 1936–1939.* Tuscaloosa: U of Alabama P, 1993. Print.
Thurber, James. "What Price Conquest?" *New Republic* 106 (March 16, 1942):370. Print.
Timmerman, John H. "Introduction," *The Long Journey* by John Steinbeck. New York: Penguin, 1995:vii–xxxi. Print.
———. *John Steinbeck's Fiction: The Aesthetics of the Road Taken.* Norman: U of Oklahoma P, 1986. Print.
———. *Searching for Eden: John Steinbeck's Ethical Career.* Macon, GA: Mercer UP, 2014. Print.
Trask, Michael. *Cruising Modernism: Class and Sexuality in American Literature and Social Thought.* Ithaca, New York: Cornell UP, 2003. Print.
Underwood, Doug. *Chronicling Trauma: Journalism and Writers on Violence and Loss.* Urbana: U of Illinois P, 2011. Print.
Valenti, Peter. "Steinbeck's Ecological Polemic: Human Sympathy and Visual Documentary in the Intercalary Chapters of *The Grapes of Wrath*," *Steinbeck and the Environment.* Eds. Susan F. Beegel, Susan Shillinglaw, Wesley N. Tiffney, Jr. Tuscaloosa: U of Alabama P, 1997:92–112

Valjean, Nelson. *John Steinbeck, The Errant Knight*. San Francisco, CA: San Francisco Chronicle: 1975. Print.
Veggian, Henry. "Bio-Politics and the Institution of Literature: An Essay on *East of Eden*, its Critics and its Time," *East of Eden, New and Recent Essays*. Eds. Michael J. Meyer and Henry Veggian. Amsterdam: Rodopi, 2013:87–122. Print.
Wagner-Martin, Linda. *A History of American Literature from 1950 to the Present*. London: Wiley-Blackwell, 2013. Print.
———. "Introduction," *The Pearl* by John Steinbeck. New York: Penguin, 1994: vii–xxiv. Print.
———. *The Mid-Century American Novel, 1935–1965*. New York: Twayne, 1997. Print.
———. *The Modern American Novel, 1914–1945*. New York: Twayne, 1990. Print.
Wald, Alan M. *American Night: The Literary Left in the Era of the Cold War*. Chapel Hill: U of North Carolina P, 2012. Print.
Wartzman, Rich. *Obscene in the Extreme: The Burning and Banning of John Steinbeck's The Grapes of Wrath*. New York: Public Affairs, 2008. Print.
Watkins, T. H. *The Hungry Years: A Narrative History of the Great Depression in America*. New York: Henry Holt, 1999. Print.
Williamson, Jennifer A. *Twentieth-Century Sentimentalism, Narrative Appropriation in American Literature*. New Brunswick, NJ: Rutgers UP, 2014. Print.
Wilson, Edmund. *The Shores of Light (1920s and 1930s)*. New York: Farrar Straus, 1952. Print.
Wyatt, David. *The Fall into Eden*. Cambridge: Cambridge UP, 1986. Print.
———., ed. *New Essays on The Grapes of Wrath*. New York: Cambridge UP, 1990. Print.
Zirakzadah, Cyrus E. and Simon Stow. *A Political Companion to John Steinbeck*. Lexington: UP of Kentucky, 2013. Print.

Index

A
Abramson, Ben, 19
Academy Award, 44, 62, 123, 162
Adamson, Louis, 45
Agee, james (*Let Us Now Praise Famous Men*), 48
Albee, Edward, 124
Albee, George, 2–5, 17, 20, 25, 32–33, 37–38, 43, 49, 114
Alexander, Will, 50
Algren, Nelson, 48
Allee, W. C., 65–66
Alston, Shorty, 43
American Academy of Arts and Letters, 162
American dream, 52–54
American Federation of Labor, 57
American language, 2, 5–9, 19–20, 23, 37, 39–40, 59–60, 89, 149, 158
American writers, vii–viii, x
America as subject, 113, 144–150
Anderson, Sherwood (*Winesburg, Ohio*), 7
Andria, Ivo, 162
Arris, Bruce and Jean, 9
Arthurian legend, 19, 29, 125, 141–145
Arvin Migrant Camp, 45–46, 48, 57

Astro, Richard, 65, 73
Austen, Jane, ix

B
Bailey, Marge, 11
Ballou, Robert O., 7, 12
Balzac, Honore de, ix
Banks, Russell, 71
Bellow, Saul, 162
Benchley, Nathaniel, x, 100, 105
Benson, Jackson, viii–ix, 4–5, 7–9, 15, 17, 19, 22, 28–29, 31–32, 37, 39, 43–44, 60–63, 66, 69, 73, 88, 90, 92, 98, 100–101, 104–106, 111, 117, 120–121, 124, 138–140, 156, 158
Beskow, Bo, viii, 106
Bible, 11–12, 55, 117–120, 130–133
Bildungsroman, 148
Billings, Josh, 92
"Bloody Thursday", 37
Bly, Robert, 10–11
Book-of-the-Month Club, 42, 49, 76, 98, 103, 154
Boren, Lyle, 61

© The Author(s) 2017
L. Wagner-Martin, *John Steinbeck*, Literary Lives,
DOI 10.1057/978-1-137-55382-9

Bourke-White, Margaret (*You Have Seen Their Faces*), 48
Bristol, Horace, 47–48, 51
Brodwin, Stanley, 67, 70
Bruscia, Jimmy, 90
Buck, Pearl, vii

C
Cabell, James Branch, x, 4
Cage, John, 9
Caldwell, Erskine (*You Have Seen Their Faces*), 48, 124, 148
California, x–xi, 7, 24, 33, 36, 38, 46–47, 49–52, 55, 57–58, 61, 88–91, 111, 116, 151
  See also Salinas Valley; Stanford University
Camaraderie among men, 8–12, 88–89
Campbell, Alice, 111
Campbell, Joseph (*The Hero with a Thousand Faces*), 8–12, 17, 20, 62, 68–69, 93, 138
Camus, Albert, 162
C & AWIU Cannery and Agriculture Workers Industrial Union, 31–32, 43
Cantwell, Robert, 29
Capa, Robert, 81, 104, 161
Caruth, Cathy, 140
Casey, Janet Galligani, 58–59
Chalmers, Pat, 37
Chamberlain, John, 77
Chandler, S. J., 42
Chaney, James, 159
Chaplin, Charlie, 56–57, 124
Charley, *see Travels with Charley in Search of America*
Chaucer, Geoffrey (*Canterbury Tales*), ix, 1
Chicago Maternity Center, 61

Churchill, Sir Winston, 155
Civil Rights Bill, 1964, 159
Class, 54–55, 57
Cohn, Peter, 48–49, 53
Coleridge, Samuel Taylor, ix
Colletti, Tiny, 90
Collins, Tom, 48, 50–51, 57, 63, 142
Commonwealth Club of California, 24
Communism, 31, 38, 45
Communist writers, 29, 54
Conrad, Barnaby, 124
Conroy, Jack, 48
Covici, Pascal, 19, 33, 53, 59, 66, 69, 87–88, 98, 101–102, 122–123, 132, 135, 139–140

D
Dailey, Dan, 103
Darwin, Charles (*The Origin of Species, Voyage of the 'Beagle'*), 67, 120
Day, Grove, 4, 17
Dean, James, 123
Decameron, The (Boccaccio), 1, 5
Decker, Caroline, 37, 43
De Kruif, Paul (*The Fight for Life*), 61
Democratic Convention, 124, 127
DeMott, Robert, 4, 7, 117–120, 124–125, 138–140
Depression, x, 19–20, 28–29, 58–59, 68
Dickens, Charles, ix
Dickinson, Emily, ix
Discove Cottage, 141
Domestic novel, 56, 59
Donne, John, ix
Don Quixote (Cervantes), 111, 143
Dos Passos, John, 48, 63, 71, 124
Dostoyevsky, Fyodor (*Crime and Punishment*), ix
Dust Bowl, 52–53

E
Eliot, George, x
Eliot, T. S. (*Waste Land*), 155
Enea, Sparky, 90
Esquire, 4
Evans, Walker (*Let Us Now Praise Famous Men*), 48
Evers, Medgar, 159

F
Fairbanks, Douglas, Jr., 84
Fair Housing Act, 1968, 159
Farm Security Administration, 48, 50
Faulkner, William, vii–ix, 2, 124, 155–156
Feied, Frederick, 68, 71–73
Fenton, Frank, 15
Fernandez, Emilio, 94
Feuer, Cy, 124
Fitzgerald, F. Scott, viii–ix, 16, 54
Flaubert, Gustav, ix
Ford, Henry, 147
Frazer, James (*The Golden Bough*), 93
French, Thomas, 66
French, Warren, 36–37
Frohock, W. H., 79
Frost, Robert, 156

G
Galbraith, Catherine and John Kenneth, 124
Gannett, Lewis, 80
Gide, Andre, 155
Gingrich, Arnold, 4
Gladstein, Mimi Reisel, 56, 85
Goethe, Johann Wolfgang Von (*Conversations with Eckermann*), 8, 10–11
Golden Boy (Clifford Odets), 63

Goodman, Andrew, 159
Gragg, Hattie, 13
Grail narratives, ix, 4, 141–142
Gray, Richard, 58
Gregory, Susan, 13
Gridley Migrant Camp, 45, 50

H
Haakon VII Cross, 77
Halper, Albert, 29
Hardy, Thomas, ix
Harkins, James, 43
Harrison, Jim, 71
Hearst, William Randolph, 42
Hemingway, Ernest, vii–x, 20, 54, 71, 77, 85, 155–156, 162
Herbst, Josephine, 54
Herman, Judith, 140
Hersey, John, 124
Hesse, Hermann, 155
Hine, Lewis, 48
Hinrich, Herb, 61
Holiday, 154
Hollywood, 51, 57, 61, 75, 77, 103, 159
Holmes, John Maurice, 43
Hoover, Herbert, 42
Hope, Bob, 83
Horton, Chase, 142
Howard, Loren, 101, 106
Howarth, William, 48–49, 57–58
Hughes, Langston, 48
Hulme, Edward Maslin, 15
Humor, 1–2, 15, 16, 19–20, 22, 37–38, 70, 83, 88, 100, 111, 130–131, 153
Hurston, Zora Neale, 48
Hutner, Gordon, 59, 103

I
Ingels, Beth, 9

J
Jackson, Toni, 9, 111
James, William (*Principles of Psychology*), 116
Jeffers, Robinson, 9
Jimenez, Juan Ramon, 162
John Reed Clubs, 31
Johnson, Lyndon B., 159
Jung, Carl, 8–10, 93

K
Kafka, Franz ("Metamorphosis"), ix
Kaufman, George S., 50
Kazan, Elia, 113–114, 123
Keillor, Garrison (*A Prairie Home Companion*), 147
Kennedy, John F., 153–154, 159
Kennedy, Robert, 159
Kerouac, Jack (*On the Road*), 148
King, Martin Luther, Jr., 148, 159
Klein, Herb, 73
Klein, Marcus, 56
Kofoid, Charles, 65

L
Lange, Dorothea (*An American Exodus, A Record of Human Erosion*), 47–48
Largerqvist, Par, 155
Laxness, Halldor, 155, 162
Le Figaro, 124
Le Guin, Ursula, 157
Le Seuer, Meridel, 48, 54
Lewis, Sinclair (*Main Street*), vii, 147
Library of Congress, 158
Life, 47, 158
Lisca, Peter, 55, 63
Little, Malcolm (*The Autobiography of Malcolm X*), 159
Loesser, Frank and Fatima, 146
Longfellow, Henry Wadsworth, ix
Lorentz, Pare (*The Plow That Broke the Plains, The River*), 57–59, 61, 63, 75
Lorca, Federico Garcia, ix
Louisville Courier-Journal, 124, 127
Lovejoy, Ritchie and Tal, 9, 87, 105
Lynch, Audry, 69

M
Madison Square Garden, x
Magny, Claude-Edmonds, 56–57
Malory, Sir Thomas (*Morte d'Arthur*), 140–142
Mansfield, Jayne, 103
Marine biology, 9–11, 88–89
    See also Ed Ricketts
Marquez, Gabriel Garcia, 122
Martin, Ernest, 124
Marxism, 45
Mauriac, Francois, 155
McCarthy, Joseph, 144–145
McCarthy, Mary, 39, 42
McIntosh, Mavis, 1, 7, 19, 24, 29, 35, 38
McKay, Nellie, 56
McKiddy Cicil, 31–32, 36–37, 142
McNally, Terrence, 124
Melville, Herman (*Moby-Dick*), ix, 116–117, 125
Mexicans, 1–3, 13, 19–20, 38–39, 54, 74, 94, 96–97, 102
Mexico, 38–39, 73–75, 85, 94, 96–97, 102
Milestone, Lewis, 44, 76, 113

Miller, Arthur, 124, 144
Miller, Ted, 1, 5
Millichap, Joseph, 94–95
Milton, John (*Paradise Lost*), ix, 35, 116
Mirrielees, Edith, 3
Mistral, Gabriela, 155
Modernism, viii–ix, 3, 21–23, 56–57, 92, 122
Modern Library, 23, 29
Morrison, Toni, xi, 122
Murphy, John, 162
Myth, ix–x, 51–54

N
Nathan, George Jean, 63
Nation, The, 39, 42
National Arts Council, 159
National Book Award, 62
New York *American*, x–xi
New York Drama Critics' Circle Award, 50–51
New York *Herald Tribune*, viii, 62, 80–81, 93, 104
New York stage, 42
New York Times, 156
Nobel Prize for Literature, vii–viii, 154–159, 162
North American Review, 16, 26

O
Office of War Information, 75
O'Hara, John, 1, 3
O. Henry Prize, 16
Olsen, Tillie, 54
O'Neill, Eugene, vii
Orvell, Miles, 147
Osborne, Paul, 123
Osborne, William, 13

Oswald, Lee Harvey, 159
Otis, Elizabeth, 7, 24, 29, 38, 49–52, 59–61, 113–114, 128–130, 135, 142–143, 145–147, 162
Ott, Evelyn, 9
Oudenkirk, Bruce, 122
Our Town (Thornton Wilder), 63
Owens, Louis, 7, 40, 55, 84, 93, 111

P
Pacific Biological Laboratory, 12, 38, 87, 90
Pacific Grove, 8–12, 20–21, 24–25, 32–33, 38, 68, 113
Pacific Ocean, x, 1, 151
Page, Myra, 54
Paisano, 13, 19–24, 90, 96–97, 151
  See also Mexican
Panama Canal, x–xi, 50
Paramount, 38–39
Parini, Jay, 7, 37–38, 69, 90, 124
Paris, 104, 124, 161
Paris Review, x, 1, 3, 53–54, 129–130
Pasternak, Boris, 162
Paul, Louis, 84–85
Pearl, The, ix, 98
PEN, 124, 158
Perse, Saint-John, 162
"Phalanx", 43
"Philosophy of 'Breaking Through', The" (Ed Ricketts), 9, 74
Photography, 46–47, 57
Play-novel hybrid, 39, 76–77, 108, 143–144
Postmodernism, 122, 136–137
Post Walcott, Marion, 48
Pound, Ezra, 3
Press Medal of Freedom, 158–159
Prologue to Glory, 63

Pulitzer Prize for Fiction, viii, 62, 114, 158
Punch, 127
Pushkin, Aleksondr Sergeevich, ix
Pyle, Ernie, 93–94, 161
Pynchon, Thomas, 122

Q
Quasimodo, Salvatore, 162

R
Race, 54, 103, 114–120, 133, 152–153
Raeburn, John, 46
Railsback, Brian, 67
Ray, Eleanor and Martin ("Rusty"), 123–124
Reeve, Richard (*American Journey*), 148
Religion, ix, 53–54, 130–131, 146, 154, 158
Republican Convention, 124, 127
Ricketts, Edward (*Between Pacific Tides*), 8–12, 20, 31, 33, 43, 61–62, 65–69, 75–76, 81, 87–90, 93–94, 99–106, 108–110, 113, 117, 124, 129, 138, 142
Ritter, William Emerson, 65
Rivera, Diego, 33
Rocinante, 146–147, 150, 152
Rockwell, Norman, 147
Roosevelt, Franklin D., 61, 75–76
Rothstein, Arnold, 48
Russell, Bertrand, 155
Russia, 51, 104

S
Salinas Valley, 1, 5–7, 13, 31, 34, 40, 50, 80, 104, 114, 117–120
Sandburg, Carl, 156
San Francisco *News*, 45–49, 51, 58
Sartre, Jean-Paul, 162
Saturday Evening Post, 16
Saturday Review, 127
Scardigli, Remo and Virginia, 9
Schwerner, Michael ("Mickey"), 159
Seed, David, 46, 57–58, 63
Seelye, John, 59, 144–145
Seferis, Giorgos, 162
Shahn, Ben, 48
Shakespeare, William (*Richard the Third*), ix, 130, 135
Sheffield, Carlton A. ("Dook"), 84–85, 115
Sherwood, Robert, 76
Shillinglaw, Susan, 8–9, 11–12, 17, 28–29, 53, 59–60, 62–63, 100–101, 106, 108, 117
Short story, 1–19, 33–34, 41–44
Simmons, Roy, 13, 77–80, 83–85, 87, 91, 98
Spanish Civil War, 76
Spengler, Oswald (*Decline of the West*), 8
Spilka, Mark, 16
"Spiritual Morphology of Poetry, A" (Ed Ricketts), 74
Stanford University, viii–ix, 8, 17
Steffens, Lincoln, 31
Steinbeck, Carol Henning, xi, 8–12, 17, 20, 25–29, 32–33, 38–39, 49, 51, 57, 59, 61–62, 66–67, 76, 80–81, 90, 95, 100–101, 106, 123, 129

Steinbeck, Elaine Anderson Scott, viii, 107, 113–114, 121, 123–124, 145, 151, 153–154, 156, 159–160
Steinbeck, Gwyn Conger, 62, 76–81, 93–94, 99–103, 113–115
Steinbeck, John
  ambition as writer, 8, 11, 24–26, 37–38, 129
  blue-collar work, ix, 19, 32
  celebrity, 23, 42, 158–159
  competitiveness, x, 11
  craft of writing, ix–x, 2–3, 16, 21, 39–42, 51–55, 87–89, 92, 123, 129, 158
  family relationships, 2, 4, 7–8, 11, 20–21, 24–27, 31–37, 39, 93–98, 105–106
  film, 47, 57–58, 62, 75
  friendships, 8–11, 17, 21–23, 32, 39–42, 68–69, 101–105, 123–125
  illnesses/trauma (accidents, PTSD, wounding, depression), 60–62, 83–85, 87, 93–94, 105–107, 113–114, 127, 129–130, 139–140, 145–146, 160
  interest in war, 62, 75–85, 93–94, 133–135
  journalism, 34, 42, 45–49, 50–51, 81, 129, 142
  love of dogs, 19, 39–40, 144–150 (*see also Travels with Charley*)
  love of nature, 4, 10–11, 46–56, 117–119
  masculinity, 11, 14–16, 22, 35, 59, 101, 132–133
  as "minstrel", ix
  Nobel Prize for Literature, vii–viii, 154–159, 162

phalanx theory, 34
politics, viii, 31–32, 36, 52–58, 144–145
poverty, 7–8, 11–12, 16–17, 20–21, 24–25, 32–33, 49, 50, 130
Pulitzer Prize for Fiction, viii, 62, 114, 158
short story as form, 1–19, 33–34, 41–44
Un-American sentiments, viii, 20
WORKS-Books; *Acts of King Arthur and His Noble Knights, The*, 142–143; *America and Americans and Selected Nonfiction*, 158–159, 162; *Bombs Away, The Story of a Bomber Team*, 62, 80; *Burning Bright*, 106–108, 110, 113–114; *Cannery Row*, 9, 22, 85, 87–94, 97–98, 101, 107–108, 110–111, 129; *Cup of Gold*, xi, 2, 5, 19; *Dissonant Symphony* (unpublished), 2; *Don Keenan* (unpublished), 143–144; *East of Eden*, 3, 7, 96, 101, 113–128, 136, 138–139, 142; *Forgotten Village, The*, 62, 73–76, 100; *Grapes of Wrath, The*, viii, 48, 52–63, 66, 68, 75–76, 88, 95, 97, 99–101, 108, 114–115, 123, 125, 142, 155–156, 158; *In Dubious Battle*, viii, 33–39, 42–43, 45, 48, 53, 57, 61, 68, 76, 79, 101, 142, 156; *Journal of a Novel: The East of Eden Letters*, 119; *L'Affaire Lettuceberg* (never published), 49; *Log from the Sea of Cortez, The*, 69, 108–110;

Steinbeck, John (*cont.*)
  Long Valley, The, 7, 13–17, 33–34, 43–44, 61, 118; *Moon Is Down, The*, 62, 76–81, 100, 108; *Of Mice and Men*, 39–44, 45, 48–50, 52, 57, 63, 75–76, 90, 95, 100–101, 108, 143; *Once There Was a War*, 81; *Pastures of Heaven, The*, xi–2, 4–7, 13, 19–20, 24, 32, 118; *Pearl, The*, 85, 94–98, 100, 125; *Red Pony, The*, 26–28, 33, 38, 61, 75–76, 89–90, 98 (*see also* "The Red Pony"); *Sea of Cortez, The*, 55, 62, 65–73, 75–76, 88, 90–91, 94, 97–98, 108, 117, 142; *Short Reign of Pippin IV, The*, 125; *Sweet Thursday*, 110–111, 123; *Their Blood Is Strong*, 45–48, 58; *To a God Unknown*, xi, 7–9, 11–13, 15, 45; *Tortilla Flat*, 19–25, 29, 34–35, 38–39, 48, 57, 61, 87, 90, 100, 129; *Travels with Charley in Search of America*, 144–154, 156; *Wayward, Bus, The*, 100–103, 108; *Winter of Our Discontent, The*, 127–140, 152, 154
  WORKS—Short fiction, journalism, screenplays, other; "About Ed Ricketts", 67–68, 108–109; "Breakfast", 33–34; "Case History", 43; "Chrysanthemums, The", 13–16; "Dubious Battle in California", 42–43; "Flight", 38; "Gift, The", 26–28; "Great Mountains, The", 26–28; "Harness, The", 38; "Harvest Gypsies, The", 45; "Johnny Bear", 38; "Leader of the People, The", 38; "Lifeboat", 62, 162; "Lonesome Vigilante, The", 33–35; "Medal for Benny, A", 62, 162; "Murder, The", 2, 13, 15–16; "Pearl of the World, The", 94; "Positano", 124–125; "Promise, The", 27–28; "Raid, The", 33–34; "Red Pony, The", 25–28; "Saint Katy the Virgin", 15; "Snake, The", 38; "Starvation under the Orange Trees", 50–51; "Stories of the Blitz", 83; "Task Group 8014", 85; "Troopship", 82–83; "*Viva Zapata!*", 113–114, 162; "Waiting", 83; "White Quail, The", 38
Steinbeck, John Ernst (father), 32, 38, 89
Steinbeck, John IV, 103, 121, 138, 160
Steinbeck, Mary, 4, 100, 125
  See also Mary Dekker
Steinbeck, Olive, 8–9, 24–26, 31, 32, 98, 129
Steinbeck, Thom (*The Other Side of Eden*), 96, 121, 138, 160
Stevenson, Adlai, 124, 157
Stowe, Harriet Beecher (*Uncle Tom's Cabin*), 58
Street, Peggy, 9
Street, Toby, 1, 9, 11, 62, 114
  "The Green Lady", 11
Strikes, 31, 35–40, 42
Swope, John, 80

T

Tal, Kali, 140
Taylor, C. V., 65
Taylor, Paul S. (*An American Exodus*), 47–48
Terman, Louis, 8
Thomas, Bill, 7
Thomsen, Eric, 45–46, 48
Thurber, James, 77
Thurmond, Thomas Harold, 43
Tiffney, Wes, 70–71
Time viii, 9
Timmerman, John, 13, 25, 33, 43, 46–47, 114–116, 120–121, 125, 127–128, 130
Tolstoi, Leo, ix
Tom Jones, 111
Tortilla Flat, 13, 19–26
Tristram Shandy (Laurence Sterne), 111
Twain, Mark, 15

U

Underwood, Doug, 84–85
United States Medal of Freedom, 158
U.S.A. (John Dos Passos), 63

V

Van Fleet, Jo, 123
Vedic hymns, 2, 12
Veggian, Henry, 121–122
Vietnam, 48, 160, 162
Viking, 59, 61, 76, 156

Vinaver, Eugene, 141–143
Voting Rights Act, 1965, 159

W

Wartzman, Rich, 48, 57, 62
Weatherwax, Clara, 29
"Weedpatch", *see* Arvin Migrant Camp
Western Flyer, The, 67, 69–70
West, George, 45
Weston, Jessie L. (*From Ritual to Romance*), 93
Whitaker, Francis, 9, 31
White, Pearl, 114
Whitman, Walt, ix
Whittier, John Greenleaf, ix
Wilhelmson, Carl, 1, 10, 60
Williams, Carl, 31
Williamson, Jennifer, 56
Williams, Red, 90
Williams, Terry Tempest, 17
Winter, Ella, 31
Woman's Home Companion, 94
Wordsworth, William, ix
World War II, 75–85, 95, 110–111, 133–135, 155, 160–161

Y

Yerby, Frank (*The Vixen*), 103

Z

Zoot Suit Race Riots, 97